MODERN SOVIET ECONOMIC PERFORMANCE

MODERN SOVIET ECONOMIC PERFORMANCE

Trevor Buck and John Cole

Basil Blackwell

First published 1987

Basil Blackwell Ltd
108 Cowley Road, Oxford, OX4 1JF, UK

Basil Blackwell Inc.
432 Park Avenue South, Suite 1503
New York, NY 10016, USA

British Library Cataloguing in Publication Data
Buck, Trevor
Modern Soviet economic performance.
1. Soviet Union–Economic conditions—1976–
I. Title II. Cole, John. 1927–
330.947'0854 HC336.25
ISBN 0-631-14417-X

Library of Congress Cataloging in Publication Data
Buck, Trevor
Modern Soviet economic performance.
Bibliography: p.
Includes index.
1. Soviet Union—Economic conditions—1976–
I. Cole, J. P. (John Peter), 1928– . II. Title.
HC336.25.B826 1987 330.947'085 86-24457
ISBN 0-631-14417-X

Typeset in 10 on 12pt Sabon by
Opus, Oxford
Printed in Great Britain by
Billing & Sons Ltd, Worcester

CONTENTS

Acknowledgements		vi
Preface		vii
1	The Soviet Economic System	1
2	Fairness	33
3	Allocation and Production	51
4	Excess Demand and Inflation	79
5	Unemployment	95
6	Investment	106
7	Innovation	118
8	Economic Growth	138
9	Living Standards	151
10	Hard or Soft Budgets	168
References		180
Index		188

ACKNOWLEDGEMENTS

Grateful thanks are due to Sue Corbett at Blackwells for her gentle, firm direction of the project, and above all to an anonymous publisher's reviewer who provided excellent criticisms and suggestions for new directions that we might follow. Jill Wilson mastered our long-hand and her new word-processor with great calmness and skill : many thanks. Comments on odd chapters were gratefully received from Alistair Bruce, Sandra Buck, Dan Wilson, Júlia Dudás, Phil Hanson, Paul Hare, Mike Bleaney, Hans-Jürgen Wagener, Mike Wright and by Jeremy Russell at Shell UK Ltd. Zsuzsa Kapitány, Judit Szabó and János Kornai discussed soft budgets in general terms. Of course, all the usual disclaimers apply.

PREFACE

Many commentaries have been written on the performance of the Soviet economy. They are often either too journalistic for an academic audience or too academic for the layman, written by a community of specialists for their own consumption. This book tries to enjoy the best of both worlds. John Cole wrote substantial parts of chapters 3 and 9. He speaks Russian, has visited the Soviet Union several times, and provided all the primary statistics for this study. Trevor Buck is an economist who contributed the remaining material and retained overall control of the project. He has twice taken parties of British students on industrial study visits to the Soviet Union.

With this mixture of authors, the book is written in a style that should be digestible for the layman and for students of comparative economics and economic or regional geography. It tries to analyse rather than just describe and uses the conceptual framework suggested by the Hungarian economist, János Kornai. Kornai is concerned with the extent to which industrial enterprises are rewarded (or penalised) by market forces according to the success (or failure) of their financial performance. Where success is generously rewarded and failure is severely penalised, then Kornai would identify hard budget constraints, although in practice administration as well as market forces may determine the hardness of constraints.

It is suggested that the general hardness and softness of constraints in industry can provide a broad explanation of the comparative performance of different economic systems. Hard budget economies experience *excess supply* everywhere, and for example this can manifest itself in high unemployment (outside the firm), rapid technological advance and a particular kind of economic growth. Although central planning *can* operate with hard budgets, we will argue that the Soviet Union can generally be described as a relatively soft budget economy characterised by universal *excess demand*. We do not argue that either hard or soft budgets are 'bad', merely that they each give rise to a particular pattern of economic performance that can only be judged against particular values.

On an emotional level, the book tries to make a modest contribution to the reduction of international tensions. Both authors experienced an individualistic upbringing in the West and would not want to live for long in the Soviet Union. Despite this position, however, we do not see why the relative performance of Western and Soviet-type economies should contribute to inter-system rivalries. It seems clear that it does. For example, an experienced and influential British politician, Lord Carrington, now Secretary General of NATO, is reported as saying: 'OK, our economy is not all that good, but there's nothing wrong with the system. The Soviet system just doesn't work. You've only got to look at the failure of the Russian economy: they have to go to America in order to feed themselves' (*Guardian*, 31 December 1983, p. 8). Now, the USA imports sophisticated manufactured goods from Japan and oil from the Middle East, and Britain is a net food importer on a large scale. None of this trade is held to constitute failure, however.

We will propose that, despite many relative weaknesses (and strengths), the Soviet economy is not in a state of collapse. On the other hand, the economic managers of the Soviet Union and other economies of the Soviet bloc have obviously got their hands full already and we cannot believe that, whatever their political and other objectives, the Soviet Union is anxious to impose its *economic* system on the rest of the world.

Politics and economics are interdependent in Marxist theory, and the Soviet system of the public ownership of the means of production and central planning has been employed by Cuba and Viet Nam. We remain convinced, however, that the practitioners of Soviet-type planning do not, as such, generate pressures for international domination. Without value-judgements, neither capitalism nor central planning can be proved to be superior. In our opinion neither system can feel particularly proud of its performance in economic terms.

Trevor Buck
John Cole
University of Nottingham

CHAPTER ONE

THE SOVIET ECONOMIC SYSTEM

This chapter is divided into five sections: after some background in the first section, the second provides a description of the Soviet economic system for a Western reader with no previous experience of it; the third section is concerned with the crucial role that information plays in central planning; the fourth reviews Kornai's theory of suction and pressure that we feel comes closest to explaining the performance of the Soviet system; and the fifth introduces readers to the chapters that follow.

BACKGROUND

In this section we try to explain the Soviet system by contrasting it with the operations of a very large international corporation in the West (Shell UK Ltd) with which the reader may be familiar. It was Harry Schwartz (1965) who popularised the 'USSR Incorporated' analogy. Here, the Shell Company is used to emphasise the similarities and (mostly) the differences between the capitalist and Soviet systems.

We would argue that the process of central planning still dominates the allocation of industrial and agricultural resources in the Soviet Union, despite attempts at reform and the development of informal, and often illegal, unplanned transactions between enterprises and between individual citizens. Nobody knows how extensive these black and grey markets are. (The latter are unlawful market dealings that are rarely prosecuted.) In one sense, they may be viewed as an essential characteristic of central planning itself.

It was unfortunate for Lenin and later Stalin that Karl Marx provided them with only a critique of capitalism. This gave them *carte blanche* after the 1917 Revolution, but little guidance on the form an economic system should take in the post-revolutionary period. In the long run the aim was pure communism: a utopian world in which money and the state would wither away and basic needs would be satisfied within self-sufficient communes. Today, visitors to Moscow are proudly shown the practically free public transport network as an example of communism. In addition, factory managers point to sports centres, built on 'free' Saturdays by the workers who then use the facilities without charge, as a step in the direction of communism, many decades after the revolution.

Since 1917, a 'temporary', transitional state of socialism has prevailed. At first it took the form under Lenin of 'War Communism' (until 1921) and then the 'New Economic Policy', but by the early 1930s a system of the public ownership of the means of production and decisions by central directive had been completed under Stalin, a regime that shows every sign of surviving until the end of this century at least. It is this regime that, in our opinion, gives the Soviet economic system its unique character. It should, however, be emphasised that state socialism has been subjected to massive reforms in CMEA (Comecon) countries outside the Soviet Union and it may not be accurate to describe all CMEA members as 'Soviet-type' economies.

There are only two ways of allocating resources, if we ignore decisions within families, clans and similar collectives, although various mixtures of the two may evolve. The first is the *market* transaction. For example, if Shell Oil (UK) Ltd wishes to obtain supplies for an offshore oil installation in the North Sea, then the local manager is empowered to purchase on the open market. Helicopter transport, food, toilet rolls can all be procured by the manager or his purchasing office, by inviting tenders or simply by placing an order with a supplier. In these market transactions it is quite usual for communications to take place between company employees of equivalent status, e.g. between Shell's local purchasing officer and a supplier's (often local) sales office. In other words, communications are *horizontal* and do not need to pass up and down through the managerial hierarchies of the respective companies.

In such decentralised transactions a great deal of information is exchanged between buyers and sellers that need not concern head office. A local food supplier can advise when a particular fresh vegetable is abundant and cheap. The buyer can warn of the need for extra, unplanned helicopter flights in the near future. Even with transactions that are complex and long term, it is possible for sophisticated contracts to anticipate problems. For example, Shell would contract engineers to build their drilling platforms rather than make them 'in-house'. Payments would keep step with progress and penalty clauses could be invoked for unplanned delays or other contingencies.

Without denying the potential drawbacks with market transactions in the form of monopolies, bankruptcies and the unpredictability of prices, for example, it seems clear that market transactions offer *flexibility*. Replacements for unexpected breakdowns or unsatisfactory supplies may be only a telephone call away and head office need never be concerned with operating details. Information on scarcities and demands is conveyed by market prices, and Adam Smith's 'invisible hand' lives.

Ignoring the allocation of resources within small, self-sufficient communities, the only alternative to markets is allocation through the 'visible hand' of administration, hierarchy or *planning*. Information is now collected and transmitted *vertically* up through a managerial hierarchy until it reaches the decision-makers. They transmit their decisions in the form of directives to lower-level employees, who are supposed to carry out their instructions. Western readers will have encountered this kind of resource allocation throughout their education, in their tax affairs, in the armed forces, if they have served, and certainly at work if they are employed by a large corporation. Although markets are used extensively under capitalism, it is not feasible to contract for everything. For example, the economies of large-scale production may determine that iron and steel should be made as part of the same process rather than cold iron being bought in by a separate steel producer. 'In-house' production in a large, hierarchical corporation will also be preferred to external contracting between separate companies, if Oliver Williamson's ideas on transaction cost economies are valid.

Williamson (1981) feels that the visible hand of administration (or in-house production) offers substantially lower transaction costs compared with market transactions between companies, especially if products are technically complex and/or are unique (i.e. are produced and sold on a 'one-off' basis). With such transactions, not all contingencies can be anticipated, and Williamson predicts that buyers and sellers may behave opportunistically to exploit the 'bounded rationality' of the other party, which is economic jargon for the fact that dealers cannot obtain all the information relevant to a transaction and could not handle it all even if it were obtainable.

So, for example, Shell takes on board oil-drilling in the North Sea as well as processing at its refineries, rather than risk the high prices and unreliable deliveries of an autonomous supplier, although it would still contract with outsiders for the repair of broken office windows. Planning enables the corporation to *co-ordinate* its main activities: oil prospecting, drilling, refining and sales to the final consumer, although in practice these activities may reside in subsidiaries or divisions of Shell. Planning, as opposed to market transactions with other companies, thus enables Shell to organise the sequencing of its operations properly. If planning goes well, there should be none of the serious bottlenecks in production that markets sometimes bring. If it goes badly, at least Shell should have plenty of notice, which should give the management a chance to modify its plans accordingly. Planned integrated activities are appropriate wherever scale economies or the interdependence of operations rules out separate market transactions. The difficulties of operating a city's underground railway network with each station as a separate commercial entity are obvious and would be explained by Williamson in terms of transactional costs.

The problems with administrative co-ordination are well known in the Soviet Union, and apply there to the whole economy rather than to just one part of one industry, as with Shell. Of course, information necessary for the sequencing of activities may be easier to obtain from suppliers who are now on the same payroll and do not have the same incentive for opportunistic behaviour as separate corporations. Fine, but there is a large literature in economics on the self-interested behaviour of corporate managers who may seek objectives, such as an easy life, which are not always consistent with the maximum profitability of the company. In any case, even the most devoted company manager cannot know everything.

For these reasons, rules-of-thumb (or intelligent guesses influenced by decisions in the past) evolve within the company, enabling decisions to be made in very complex, uncertain circumstances, while at the same time representing 'political' truces or compromises between different interest-groups within the organisation. Naturally, corporations rarely admit publicly to the use of such rules-of-thumb, and often insist that their activities are administered 'rationally' after all available information has been collected. Readers who have worked in a Western company will know differently, however, and will have noticed that the process of allocating resources between competing departments of a firm (or 'budgeting') resembles a subjective art and not an objective science. A department's budget will often be last year's authorisation plus (or minus) a percentage, and such 'incrementalism' is extremely prevalent in the head offices of large corporations and in the budget decisions of central government (see Jackson, 1982, pp. 146–72). It is just not feasible to conduct a 'rational' review of a company's entire operations for each planning period, or 'zero-base budgeting' (ZBB) as it is called by accountants. Here is an extract from a modern management accounting text (Macariello, 1984, p. 336) on the subject:

> Much has been written about zero-base budgeting since it was first implemented by Peter Pyhrr at Texas Instruments during the 1960s. The discussion about ZBB appears to have been useful. However, the really new part of ZBB – having DEC [Discretionary Expense Centre] managers justify their entire operation on an annual basis – is not workable. . .
>
> ZBB is a misnomer. Budgeting is inherently an incremental process. This is due to the limits of human information processing that make it extremely difficult, if

not impossible, to evaluate all activities from scratch each period. Moreover, there is the pressure of time; the budget process normally takes place within a three or four-month period of time. Whenever ZBB has been used, a large portion of activities has been exempted from zero-base review. So rather than zero-base review, it has more often been 80 per cent-base review, with only 20 per cent of the budget subject to complete review on an annual basis. This is merely another example of incremental budgeting.

We would need a tape-recorder inside every corporate manager's office to prove that incrementalism is prevalent. Incrementalism is easier to demonstrate from official inquiries into public bureaucracies however, and there is no reason to expect private bureaucracies to behave differently. For example the Jarratt Inquiry into the efficiency of British universities (Committee of Vice-Chancellors and Principals, 1985) found that (pp. 21–2) 'in some of the universities there is still a strong emphasis on maintaining the historical distribution of resources. Planning and resource allocation tend to be incremental rather than dynamic.' In the sub-report on the authors' own University of Nottingham (Committee of Vice-Chancellors and Principals, 1985) it was concluded that (p. 5) 'its reaction to the recent funding constraints has, on the whole, been to maintain the status quo at the expense both of diluting its existing strength and of new developments'. It is not intended to pillory university bureaucracies, which are little different from any other, and cut-backs in 1986 have been more discriminating. Inertia and incrementalism are a feature of all bureaucracies. They certainly are a dominant characteristic of Soviet planning.

So, capitalism is a mixture of markets and hierarchies (planning). Shell, like many other large companies, now prefers to buy in from other companies goods and services that are beyond its immediate competence to provide, although strategic decisions are still reserved for the Group Holding Company and separate service companies. Operating companies (who actually make things) are largely left to their own devices, to sink or swim in their markets without central interference, although expenditures (market transactions) beyond certain authorisation levels must be approved at higher levels of the planning pyramid. The Group Holding Companies need not concern themselves with operational details and can spot operating companies with poor performance by comparing similar activities in different countries. In this sense Shell resembles the multidivisional (or 'M'-) form advocated by Williamson (1981), and Shell has effectively created markets within the overall hierarchy of the firm.

There can be no question of a universally 'optimal' combination of markets, hierarchies and multiple divisions. Tinbergen (1967) considered an optimal regime that could evolve as governments realised the appropriateness of markets and plans in particular circumstances. For such a regime we must assume, however, that governments are 'rational actors' and that individual sectors of the economy can be organised piecemeal. (In practice, economic systems come as a 'package deal' and cannot be assembled like purchases chosen from supermarket shelves.) In the West, it seems clear that economies of scale require the planned supply of water, and the interdependence of routes suggests a planned railway system. Agriculture is an industry exposed to major uncertainties and these would seem to demand on-the-spot decisions by farmers motivated by a stake in the value of total production less costs. Technology does have an influence on the suitability of market and plan for particular circumstances but it is rarely a conclusive one. At the end of this chapter, in figure 1.2, eight different kinds of economic efficiency are shown, and the 'best' economic system must depend on the weights given to these, and to non-economic, objectives.

It will be shown below that like capitalist firms, the 'USSR Inc' also uses a mixture of markets and plans, though in different proportions. Apart from this difference, there are three others that seem important. First, an operating company in Shell is answerable to the Group Holding Company in a similar fashion to the Soviet enterprise and its ministry, but in the case of Shell, the operating company must also compete to some extent with other oil companies, and the Group Holding Company must publish financial information on all its activities which is perused by the Stock Market and its analysts. The verdict of the Stock Market will act as an external check on Shell's growth or decline, and shareholders can dispose of Shell shares dispassionately if they consider long term prospects, or even quarterly earnings, poor. The Soviet enterprise is responsible to *its* ministry, but the ministry is partly responsible *for* the enterprise and may not draw attention to poor enterprise performance. Stock Markets contribute to relatively 'hard' budget constraints for capitalist firms, which are discussed later in this chapter.

In contrast with the Soviet enterprise, profits ('net income') in the Royal Dutch/Shell Group of companies fell by about 16 per cent in 1981 and stayed at that level during 1982 despite inflation. Largely as a result, capital expenditure did not grow in real terms between 1979 and 1982 and in 1983 it was cut by 10 per cent through the postponement of development programmes. Total employees fell by 10,000 between 1981 and 1983, from 166,000. Although certain cycles can be discerned in Soviet industries, redundancies without the offer of alternative employment are rare. Of course 'USSR Inc' as a whole cannot shed labour like a capitalist firm, even if it wanted to.

The second difference is concerned with the fact that companies like Shell may diversify to spread risks. Shell seems rather unusual in this respect. It has a Non-traditional Businesses Division, which in the past has diversified into forestry, metals and even duck-breeding, but these ventures have not always been successful and the company has now decided that its expertise lies in the oil and gas industries. Expansion beyond these industries is no longer contemplated. Diversification enables companies to avoid putting all their eggs in one basket and reduces the riskiness of the overall venture. In the Soviet Union, on the other hand, product diversification by the enterprise involves complex supervision of the enterprise by a number of ministries, and is therefore discouraged.

Third, even a massive corporation like Shell is obviously not the whole of the British oil and gas industry. Just like the individual corporation above, the whole of the capitalist system or nation does not have all its eggs in one basket either. Each corporation has its own view of the future. In Shell's case, a number of scenarios of the future are constantly being produced and revised (see Jefferson, 1983). Corporations make mistakes, but others have made different judgements on the future and can take advantage of these errors. The resources of a capitalist industry are rarely all committed to a single strategy, which may of course prove to have been mistaken with the benefit of hindsight.

At this stage, readers patiently waiting for some background to the Soviet economic system may reasonably ask: 'What on earth has all this to do with the Soviet Union?' We would claim that a review of the familiar characteristics of the Western system can be used to throw light on that of the Soviet Union, using the analogy of 'USSR Inc'. If capitalism consists of markets plus the superimposition of hierarchies in corporations and government, then the Soviet economic system can be seen as its converse, since some horizontal market transactions are added to the basic vertical hierarchies of central planning.

It was Lenin who first predicted that in the Soviet Union 'The whole of society will have become a single office and a single factory' (Lenin, 1968 edn, p. 337). Under Soviet planning, the central hierarchy controlling 'USSR Inc', like the capitalist firm's board of directors, determines economic strategy.

This view of 'USSR Inc' implies a planned economy quite different from the 'indicative' planning of Western capitalism, where central agencies provide information for firms and perhaps point out the outcomes they would desire, but then leave firms to make their own investment, employment and output decisions. Within the hierarchy of 'USSR Inc' the central administration tries to allocate all resources by directive. Enterprises are able to comment on plans in advance, but otherwise are only required to carry out central plan directives.

The institutions of 'USSR Inc' are more difficult to describe than the organisational chart of a Western corporation, however, since there are representatives of *two* hierarchies at most levels of the Soviet economic system (see the next section). It should be remembered that, despite complex institutional detail, the core of the Soviet economy is a central authority that issues directives down through an administrative hierarchy to enterprises. The reader must be reminded at this stage that the economy of the whole of the USSR is many times larger than that of the largest capitalist transnational companies. Also the territorial extent on which 'USSR Inc' operates is about a hundred times as large as the UK and has about five times as many citizens. The great size of the USSR almost inevitably assures that virtually all natural resources for complete economic development are available, which largely frees central planners from dependence on foreign economies. At the same time natural resources, population and productive enterprises are widely dispersed over an enormous area, many goods are moved over hundreds and sometimes thousands of kilometres, and communications are greatly stretched. In this respect one could not have chosen a more difficult country to plan centrally. Many geography texts on the Soviet Union describe this situation in detail. The next section of this chapter concentrates on a short description of the Soviet economic system and an analysis of economic information in relation to it.

THE SOVIET ECONOMIC SYSTEM

Readers requiring more detail and rigour than this section provides are recommended to see Nove (1982). Figure 1.1 shows a highly simplified chart of the formal institutions of Soviet planning. The Council of Ministers has direct charge of 31 'All-Union' ministries administered at the federal level, and indirect control of another 22 Union-Republican ministries, which administer products of lower priority through planning hierarchies within the Soviet Union's 15 Socialist Republics (SSRs).

Formally, the Council (or rather its Presidium, since the whole Council only meets four times a year) receives its general instructions from the Supreme Soviet, which also operates a powerful Presidium, as the Supreme Soviet only meets twice annually. This Supreme Soviet, or its Republican equivalent, is in turn elected from the soviets themselves, which are local authorities at regional, city and village levels.

On the face of it, the Soviet Union operates a system of 'democratic centralism'. There is a public discussion of economic reforms, which is in practice restricted to means rather than ends. Legislative proposals are made at the centre in the light of these discussions and are approved from the level of the soviets upwards. Economic plans for the various ministries are produced with the help of the State Committee for Planning (Gosplan) and the central statistical administration, and are enthusiastically

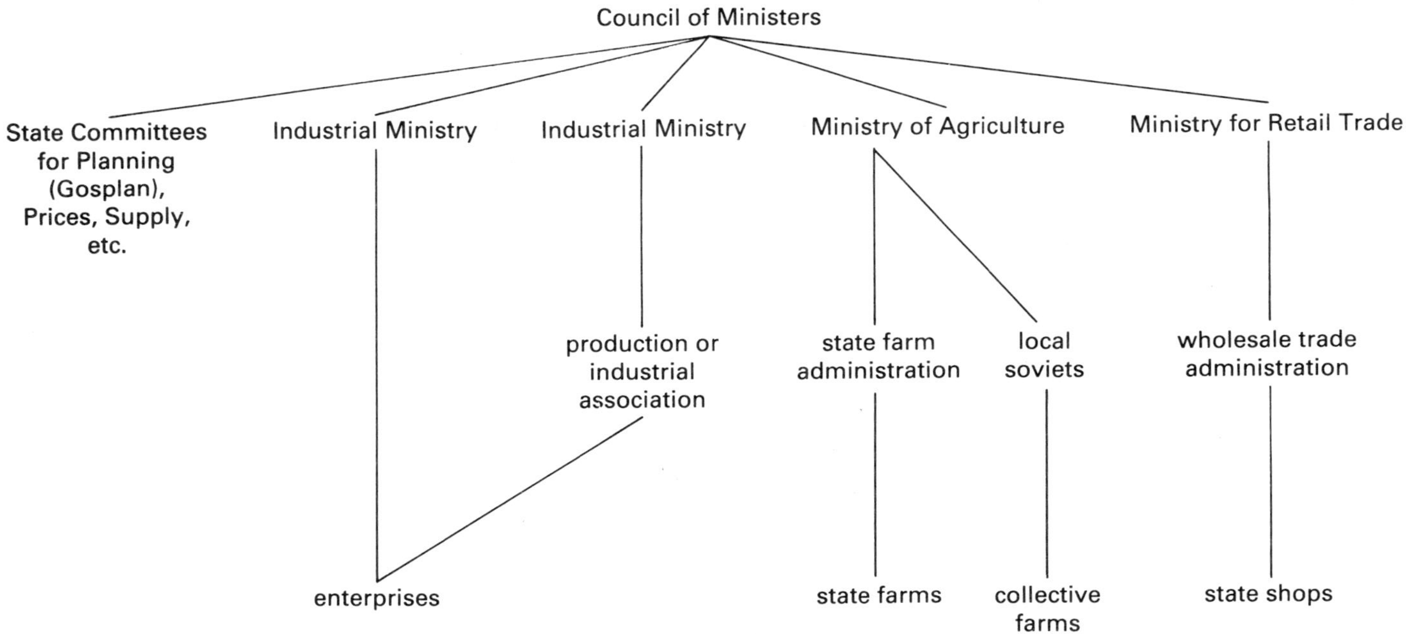

Figure 1.1 Soviet economic institutions. In 1984, there were 62 ministries and 22 State Committees. Only a few are shown here, and important omissions include Finance, Defence and Foreign Trade. In practice, industrial enterprises can be controlled directly by the ministry ('All Union' industries'), at the level of the republic or by local authorities.

endorsed by unanimous votes on a show of hands at all levels. Output plans eventually become law.

Behind all this formal activity, however, lies the second, 'shadow' hierarchy of the Communist Party of the Soviet Union (CPSU). The Party is even more centralised than the economic institutions and recourse has to be made much more frequently to Moscow than is the case through the formal economic channels.

At the centre, the Congress of the CPSU meets every five years, but is represented meanwhile by the Central Committee of the Party which is served by a full-time secretariat. The Central Committee in turn has its own Presidium, or Politburo, which effectively makes all strategic decisions. The Central Committee of the CPSU has a department to supervise the activities of each ministry, and all important appointments down to the directorships of individual industrial enterprises are made from the *nomenklatura*, or list of candidates approved by the Party. It is suggested below that this system contributes to relatively 'soft' budget constraints in Soviet industry, since the ministry and the Party see enterprise performance as being to some extent their responsibility, following the appointments and other decisions made from the centre. This weakens the resolve at the centre to identify and penalise poor enterprise performance compared with capitalist enterprises exposed (to some extent) to the disciplines of the capital market and to competition in product markets.

The ministries and the Party simultaneously control most economic activity in the Soviet Union, either directly from Moscow or through their republican equivalents. It is not suggested, however, that Party control is explicit, with the exception of important decisions of a strategic nature. Plan formulation takes place between enterprise employees and their superiors in the associations, ministries or ministerial branches. Most of the participants are likely to be communists, but the Party itself only becomes important in the supervision of plan performance, in canvassing support for the plan within enterprises and, crucially, by providing a network of contacts for enterprise employees when supply uncertainties threaten plan fulfilment. The state's ownership of the means of production gives control over all industrial enterprises. Enterprises are governed by a single director, who is responsible to the appropriate Ministerial branch, although in practice the director is subject to additional influences from the state Bank, the Ministry of Finance, the Committees for People's Control and State Security, and the Party, both within the enterprise and locally.

The director is required to use the state's assets, for which the enterprise has had to pay a capital charge of 6 per cent since 1967 (these assets were 'free' before then). The enterprise is instructed in its *Tekhpromfinplan* what to produce and when to deliver, and purchases of capital, labour and materials must be authorised by the ministry. Wages and prices are fixed centrally, although the grading of jobs may be locally 'flexible' and enterprises may set their own prices for 'special' orders. Within all this central control, the enterprise is required to recoup all expenditures and generate a profit, which is held for incentive funds or taxed away by the state. Losses, however, are not uncommon.

Some economic activity is not subject to this central control, however. Co-operative enterprises exist in retailing and agriculture, although in practice their operation does not differ greatly from State enterprises. The collective farms are administered by elected managers, although the Party dominates these appointments and effectively controls the collective's activities. These farms have been on average only about one-third the size of the state farm (analagous to the industrial enterprise), although the amalgamation of collective farms recently has increased them to state-farm dimensions, but members are still entitled to larger private plots. Otherwise, minimum wage rules, sales at state prices and planned investment levels render collectives broadly equivalent to state enterprises.

Above-plan production by collective farms can, however, be sold on markets outside state control. In addition, workers on state farms and collectives earn on average about half their real incomes from the produce of private plots. Other economic activity outside State control includes the distribution of 'local' materials, such as sand and gravel, the services of private craftsmen and individual professionals, and of course 'black-market' activity, which is discussed later.

Outside the production sphere, households are free from central control in their expenditure decisions and individuals can choose their own jobs from the occupations on offer. Residence in some large cities is centrally controlled, however, and graduates from higher education are often directed to jobs for the first two or three years after graduation. (As an encouragement to greater effort, graduates with the best examination results are sometimes given the privilege of the employment location of their choice.)

Returning to activities under central control, plans are made for a variety of time perspectives. 'Comprehensive' or 'perspective' plans are constructed for periods of one to two decades ahead. These deal with broad developments in population, resources and international affairs, which may be expected to influence strategic decisions in the long term. The Politburo of the CPSU, advised by Gosplan, the Central Statistical Administration and other specialists, will have noted, for example, the mismatch between the relatively high rate of growth of the Soviet Union's Moslem population in the south and the labour shortages in the west and east. It will be considering in the long term whether to attract population to the west and east, to move jobs to the south, or both.

Five-year plans are concerned with more immediate issues, but are still not operational in the sense that they are the subject of directives to enterprises. Gosplan is handed down strategic instructions from the Politburo and the Council of Ministers, and advice from the ministries and state committees concerning medium-term priorities. For example, in the 1971–5 plan, a higher priority was assigned to consumer as opposed to producer goods although poor harvests subsequently frustrated this aim. In the 1976–80 plan, investment resources were again supposed to be switched from industry to farming and agriculture-support industries, while in the eleventh five-year plan (1981–5) energy was a major preoccupation. In his address to the Supreme Soviet in November 1981, the Chairman of Gosplan (also Vice-Chairman of the Council of Ministers) announced in general terms an energy conservation programme. The five-year plan also included fairly general targets for broad sectors of industry. For example, 'atomic and hydroelectric power generation' were together planned to increase their output by 70 per cent in the 1981–5 plan. For 1986–90, consumer goods are emphasised yet again, but also investment in machinery, rather than a new plant, in the old manufacturing regions.

Although five-year targets are formed after taking into account advice from the ministries (on power stations under construction and commission, for example), and are disaggregated for each year, they are not fully operational in the sense that individual enterprises are given detailed instructions to achieve them. They are only used operationally for the calculation of bonus payments to enterprise staff when actual output is known.

Five-year targets do, however, become reference-points for the operational one-year enterprise plans, usually disaggregated further into quarters and months. (With energy generation, of course, monthly output variations will be crucial.) For the most important 'funded' commodities, of which there are about 2,000, output targets are 'negotiated' for each enterprise through their ministries, in a process described below when the problem of information is discussed. (The most important industrial products like steel, cement and building materials are 'funded' in the sense that they are controlled, distributed and financed by Gosplan directly.) Gosplan's task is to achieve plan consistency, calculating financial, labour and materials balances for each funded commodity.

Of these, the materials balance is the most important, and a simplified version is shown as table 1.1. Imbalances can be accommodated through imports and exports or by changing sales plans. In practice, this may often involve lower deliveries to state shops in the low-priority retail sector. It can be seen that although 'paper' consistency can be achieved for one commodity, the technique does not ensure overall consistency, even just

Table 1.1 Materials balance for a 'funded' commodity

Sources	*Uses*
Opening stocks	Production for:
Imports	other state enterprises
Production	construction
	export
	Closing Stocks

Materials balances are also drawn up for around 300 commodities in the five-year plan.

for 'funded' commodities. For example, the production of motor cars may match the demand for them in a materials balance that hides, however, the fact that tyre supplies will not permit planned production at the level considered, since the balance only deals with one product at a time. The production targets from the materials balance are disaggregated by the ministries and issued to associations and enterprises as 'control' figures for the purpose of planning input requirements.

After the negotiation of input needs (discussed below), Gosplan can try to match the supply of and demand for different 'funded' commodities. These will only be equal by coincidence and revised output targets must be issued. In practice it seems that only one round of adjustments is feasible and only 'first-order' relationships can be considered. For example, a shortage of steel pipes necessary for the generation of electricity from natural gas may lead to an increase in the output target of the steel industry, but the plan revision would probably not take into account the additional energy required for steel production. Given the complexity of the task, it is no surprise that plans often arrive late and that enterprises survive by continuing with earlier plans.

For 'funded' commodities, Gosplan itself issues detailed output instructions, and enterprises must obtain authorisations and certificates to present to the state Bank for the payment of materials, machinery inputs and wages. About a further 18,000 commodities are centrally co-ordinated by Gosplan and Gossnab (the Central Supply Agency), but without the full materials-balancing exercise. A further 50,000 or so goods are planned on a decentralised basis by Gossnab and the ministries without involving Gosplan, and about another 25,000 commodities are internally planned by the ministries without considering the needs of other industries (see Bornstein, 1985, p. 7).

INFORMATION AND SOVIET PLANNING

The previous section has described the basic institutions of Soviet planning, although it must be emphasised that much significant detail has had to be omitted. Under capitalism it was noted that *markets* are used to allocate resources, and prices convey information for parties to a transaction. For example, if Shell's activities in the North Sea generate an additional demand for onshore housing, the values of existing houses and shares in house-building companies should rise. Higher prices and profits provide information to the industry and new resources should be attracted to house-building in the area. Supply can thus respond to an increase in demand without the Shell management having to draw up materials balances, although in practice this process of market adjustment will not be smooth or without some undesirable implications. Prices will not always reflect relative scarcity and demand. For example, monopolists can restrict output and entry to an industry in order to drive up price, and multinational companies may choose 'transfer' prices for intermediate goods transferred between subsidiaries in different countries in order to influence host governments, or to minimise their tax liabilities.

Deliberate administrative decisions must largely replace prices and markets in resource allocation under Soviet central planning. This choice is ideological, but also owes something to the reluctance of members from top to bottom of the planning hierarchy seriously to consider relinquishing control through market reform, and also to Soviet prices, which are not designed for the purpose of efficient resource allocation.

Soviet prices serve two purposes. Primarily, they permit the aggregation of outputs. Electric power generation can be measured in kilowatt hours, but if different sources of electricity must be aggregated, recourse must be made to 'tons-of-oil-equivalent' or some similar measure. Rouble prices offer a convenient means of aggregation and the results can be used in the calculation of bonus payments, discussed below. Secondly, prices can be designed to achieve social goals. For example, low prices for housing (when available!), public transport and fuel are intended to raise the real incomes of workers, but subsidies must be paid for out of other sources of revenue, especially the taxation of enterprise profits.

Despite recent price reforms and the use of turnover taxes to clear retail markets, Soviet prices do not usually reflect demand and scarcity. Marxist theory sees value as being created by labour time in production, and before 1956 Soviet prices were calculated as a 'mark-up' on average labour costs, which were inflated to include the 'crystallised' labour in materials and the depreciation of buildings and machines. In theory, prices were calculated using a 3.5 per cent profit 'mark-up', but in practice many goods were sold at a loss. Interest charges were gradually introduced, and profit coefficients and average-cost norms increased in an attempt to eliminate enterprise losses, but the 'mark-up' mentality in Soviet prices remains. This of course disregards the margin and encourages cross-subsidisation, but more importantly and quite deliberately, it ignores use-values and prevents the communication of information in prices necessary for efficient resource allocation by markets.

If directives are to replace markets, however, severe informational needs are generated. About 24 million commodities must be planned (Bornstein, 1985, p. 7) and the authorities require detailed information on production possibilities. A mischievous article in *Pravda*, predicted in 1967 that the formulation of the 1981–5 plan would employ 100 million people for five years! Clearly, information must be gleaned from a variety of sources and short cuts adopted.

Soviet planners obtain information by collecting it in advance and by studying past performance. In addition they reduce the need for information at the centre through various forms of decentralisation.

Advance Information

The formal process of Soviet planning involves the acquisition of advance (or what the economist calls ex-ante) information from industry. Research institutes and pilot plants within the ministries provide some information on the production potential and requirements of different branches of industry. More generally, however, Gosplan must simply *request* information from the ministries and, through them, the enterprises themselves.

There is clearly a danger now that the enterprises will write their own plans. It is likely that during the negotiations between planners, ministries and enterprises described above, enterprise directors will behave like departmental heads in capitalist corporations during budget reviews, claiming that output targets are impossibly high and input authorisations low. Spare capacity may be hidden from the planners by self-interested directors favouring an 'easy life' or large bonus payments.

In this respect, the internal political bargaining within a corporation like Shell at budget review time must resemble the competition for scarce resources within Soviet ministries and enterprises. Of course, 'USSR Inc' is a far more complex operation than Shell UK, but this is merely a question of degree; for example one North Sea operation can involve Shell in health care, transport, housing, catering, entertainment and many other functions. There is another vital difference of degree in terms of the size and complexity of the Soviet economy compared with other smaller centrally planned economies. This leads to quite different outcomes, and will be referred to in Chapter 10 below.

There is, however, one important difference between Shell's and Soviet planning that we see as crucial. Within Shell, budgets tend to favour *profitable* activities, divisions and subsidiaries, and if the North Sea operation is to be expanded, Shell need not concern itself too much with the provision of onshore shops or housing. The market mechanism should take care of these. In the Soviet Union, however, the *gross outputs* of all funded commodities must be centrally co-ordinated. It is the gross output of one industry that constitutes the input of another, and the planners will not be delighted if a highly profitable industry does not supply inputs to another as planned. Co-ordinated plans will be disrupted, and the effect of the bottleneck will spread. High profitability will be no consolation, and we shall argue below that this important difference between central planning and capitalism contributes to 'soft' budgets in the former.

After the collection of all feasible advance information, it is still necessary for Soviet planners to take 'short cuts' in the calculation of plans. Materials balances are themselves fairly crude procedures, but even with the help of computers, the planners cannot hope to conduct a full input–output analysis which could involve up to 250 billion inter-sectoral flows. The perfect plan is just as unattainable as perfectly competitive capitalism.

Past Performance

Neither Shell nor Gosplan can acquire perfect information in advance. Shell refuses to forecast and relies instead on broad alternative 'scenarios' of the future (see Jefferson, 1983, p. 193). Gosplan must co-ordinate outputs centrally, however. If advance information is not available, it must resort to other devices.

It was noted above that 'incrementalism', or the tendency for firms to base this year's departmental budget on last year's, is widely adopted as a rule-of-thumb under capitalism. It is simply not possible to collect each year all the information needed for the review of the entire operation of a department, division or subsidiary, despite the dream of 'zero-base' budgeting.

Incrementalism in the Soviet Union is referred to as 'from the achieved level' (FTAL) planning. It involves the calculation of target outputs (and inputs) for the next plan period by applying fixed coefficients (percentages) to actual achieved output in the previous period. Thus, output targets will be last year's plus a mark-up, and input authorisations will be marked down, in an attempt to force enterprises to increase productivity.

Besides raising the productive efficiency of enterprises, however, FTAL may offer two other benefits. First, we noted above that it is not easy to achieve consistency in central plans. For example, increasing gas output may displace coal or oil and generate additional demands for steel pipes and other equipment. FTAL planning tends to reinforce the status quo and discourages such changes, although in practice the mark-ups can reflect actual output in relation to targets in the past and the priority given to a particular product by the politicians. Since only marginal changes from the status quo are envisaged under FTAL planning, planners can be reasonably sure that if last year's plan avoided any major inconsistencies, so will next year's, since they resemble each other so closely. Of course, unforeseen difficulties may still occur.

Second, all rules-of-thumb in any organisational hierarchy represent *truces* between different interest groups. For example, when universities are required to cut staff or students, this is often achieved on the basis of a proportionate cut, across all departments. FTAL plans imply rough justice: mark-ups (and mark-downs) involve pain, but at least everybody else is seen to be suffering too. 'Zero-base' budgeting or planning, which broadly corresponds to the ex-ante 'rational' decisions (see the section on 'advance information' above), is itself hard and painful work for planners, who must discriminate among their colleagues.

So FTAL planning is prevalent under Soviet central planning and with capitalist bureaucracies. One cynical writer concluded in relation to Soviet FTAL planning: 'This is the foundation of all the technique, all the methodology of Soviet planning. The rest is secondary' (Birman, 1978, p. 161). This static technique of using past performance as a basis for enterprise plans should not imply that production itself turns out to be static and uneventful. Despite the efforts of enterprises to 'pad' the plans to hoard labour and other inputs, the planners usually succeed through a series of mark-ups in making the plans 'taut', or difficult to achieve in practice. With all enterprises being subjected to 'taut' plans, one uncertain event can disrupt the production of one good, but this can have wider implications.

In many ways Soviet industry is exposed to less uncertainty than its capitalist equivalent. Enterprises do not face domestic competition and the economy is virtually insulated from foreign trade. There is a general level of excess demand for producer and consumer goods and few unexpected fluctuations, so producers can be confident of disposing of any output. The process of materials balancing should provide some co-ordination of outputs, whereas under capitalism co-ordination is achieved 'ex-post' (or retrospectively), often involving plant closures. New technologies are supposed to be planned and introduced gradually in the Soviet system.

Most of these factors work both ways, however. Under capitalism, there is a diversity of decentralised decisions concerning output and technology. Given that no state can boast perfect foresight, it may be prudent not to have 'all eggs in one basket'. With Soviet enterprises being subjected to 'taut' plans with excess demand for inputs and output, one unforeseen event can deny crucial inputs for many other enterprises, and imports are not generally favoured as a substitute source. Wilczynski (1973, p. 60) reports that in one year, in the Lvov district, enterprises experienced sixteen changes in their plans imposed from above! The refusal of energy planners to consider the development of electric alternatives to the turbo-drill (unusable beyond depths of 3 kilometres) obstructed the development of new, deep oil deposits in Siberia (Stein, 1981).

Supply uncertainties remain a chronic feature of Soviet industry and it is paradoxical that enterprises usually blame those planners who are supposed to co-ordinate supplies. To remedy these matters, the Soviet authorities have experimented with at least three forms of decentralisation to reduce the need for information and central co-ordination.

Decentralisation

Decentralisation and economic reform may be viewed as refinements to central planning or, by critics, as the substitution of market processes without which, in their view, the economy would grind to a halt. Three forms of decentralisation are considered here: bonus schemes, horizontal links and associations in industry.

Bonus schemes

Bonus schemes are a device borrowed from market economies that nevertheless can strengthen central plans by encouraging enterprises to produce the quantities of output that the ministries seek for their plans, and by persuading enterprises to reveal their output potential. It was explained in the last section that central planners are concerned above all that enterprises do not disrupt their co-ordinated plans by falling short of targets for gross output. During the 'classical' period of Soviet central planning (to about 1965), bonus payments to managers and workers were calculated broadly according to the degree of overfulfilment of *gross-output* targets, and were paid out of the wages fund as a production cost and not a distribution of profit. (In fact, bonuses were also paid for cost reductions and for producing the proper mixture of goods, but over-taut plans led enterprises to concentrate on the dominant bonus indicator, gross output.) Bonuses tied to gross-output targets made central planning easier by discouraging underfulfilment. (Overfulfilment is less of a problem in an economy with universal excess demands and overproduction can in any case be stored or disposed of. Holding stocks is virtually a costless exercise as far as enterprises are concerned.) By 1965, bonuses paid were about 7 per cent of average wages for administrators, 8 per cent for manual workers, and 14 per cent for engineers (Adam, 1980, p. 360).

Gross-output bonuses created five major problems, however. First,

Soviet prices made the value of gross output a fairly arbitrary measure. Second, enterprises often overfulfilled their targets by diverting inputs (officially or otherwise, see below) from others, thus disrupting their plans. Third, the planners could not afford to authorise the payment of bonuses year after year for stable outputs, so only output in excess of FTAL targets qualified for bonus. Unfortunately this gave rise to a 'ratchet' effect whereby enterprises held back current effort in fear of raising next year's target and making life difficult for themselves in the future. Fourth, an emphasis on gross output tended to reduce productivity, since enterprises were not penalised for the extravagant use of inputs already in excess demand. Indeed gross output bonuses encourage such profligacy. Fifth, gross output did not have to be sold to qualify for the bonus.

For these and other reasons, capital and labour productivity (dependent upon the *quality* of inputs) slowed and Soviet economic growth came to rely on massive increases in the *quantity* of labour and capital rather than its quality. Therefore in 1965 economic reforms were introduced to reduce the emphasis on gross output. In these Liberman (or Kosygin) reforms, bonuses were to be based on the profit rate and delivered sales (or occasionally absolute profit) in order to discourage undemanded production. Profits were now revered as a 'synthetic indicator' that would simultaneously encourage enterprises to increase sales *and* reduce costs. Of course, the reformers were at pains to emphasise that 'socialist profit' was very different from its capitalist namesake. Socialist profit could not be increased by monopolists holding back output to drive up price, since prices were administered from the centre, and low rates of investment and bonuses paid out of profits could not cause major variations in the personal ownership of property. Similarly, it was not suggested that profit should be the only criterion for investment appraisal where the activities of different enterprises are interdependent, since here only profit-related bonus payments are being considered.

One big problem with profit-related bonus payments in the Soviet Union was again the fairly arbitrary level of wages and producer prices. For example, coal-miners receive very high wages for work that is seen as vital, hard and dangerous, but the price of a basic commodity like coal is deliberately set very low by the politicians. High costs and low prices produce financial losses, and so bonuses related to profits are inappropriate for such industries. Massive price 'reforms' (a universal euphemism for 'increases') were therefore implemented in 1967 and 1982 to bring prices closer to market-clearing levels. (The 1967 revised price lists ran to 38,000 pages, which gives the reader some idea of the complexity of Soviet planning.) The problem persists, however.

The other problem with Soviet profit-related bonuses after 1965 was that, as a hangover from the old system, the achievement of profits and sales targets determined the amount of the *wages bill* that was to be transferred to the bonus funds. Hence the bonus system continued to stimulate overmanning and high wages, and the encouragement of higher productivity was thwarted to some extent: the bigger the wages bill, the better the bonus.

Throughout the 1970s the bonus system gradually became more complicated, but if anything closer to the pre-reform payments based on gross output. In 1979, a few more steps on the 'treadmill of reform' (Schroeder, 1982a) replaced a diversity of bonuses with four bonus indicators: (1) *delivered sales* became a threshold indicator whereby, for example, no bonus would be paid at all if sales fell below 98 per cent of target; (2) the *quality mix*, or the value of sales weighted according to the proportions falling into standard categories of qualities; (3) '*normative net output*' (see below); and (4) *labour productivity*, which seems to correspond to net normative output per worker (see Hanson, 1983).

Of these new indicators, sales and the quality of sales are largely estimated by the enterprises themselves, and so seem to involve a degree of self-assessment. Buyers are in any case unlikely to complain about deliveries and quality, where there is overall excess demand (see the section entitled 'The economics of shortage' below). It seems therefore that any effective reform must depend upon 'normative net output' (NNO). This new variable approximates to 'value added' in the West, or wages plus profit, alternatively defined as revenues minus non-wage costs (materials and depreciation). NNO involves norms, however: to every unit of gross output (q) is applied a standard wage coefficient or allowance (w) and profit rate (p). In other words,

$$\text{NNO} = q(w + p)$$

and enterprises enjoy a transfer of profit to the bonus fund for every percentage point that NNO targets are overfulfilled. This new indicator discourages overmanning and high wages to the extent that credit is only given for the *standard* wage content of output (w), and the only way that an enterprise can raise NNO is to raise gross output (q) or switch inputs to the production of goods with a high value-added content. Since non-wage costs are deducted from revenues to calculate NNO, there is now every incentive to economise on capital and materials. Although profits are now a prerequisite for bonus payments, the amount paid would seem, once again, to depend largely upon *gross output*, thus invoking all the problems identified above and giving rise to 'soft budgets' (see the section on the economics of shortage below). In addition, the use of NNO may create other distortions. A Soviet economist (Selyunin, 1983) recently showed that, in a chemical machinery plant, NNO could be raised by switching scarce labour from products with a high wage (low profit) component in

NNO to others with a low wage content. The outcome in 1983 was that while NNO increased by 11 per cent, the value of output fell by 1.2 million roubles. (This may, of course, have been the planners' intention.) One cry from a manager's heart came from a discussion at the 'Pravda Business Club' (*Pravda*, 1983). He complained (p. 9) that 'We are simply tangled in indices . . . We don't know what "god" to pray to.' Another manager claimed however that in practice enterprises still emphasised gross output:

> 'There have gotten to be too many plan indices. The resolution states that their number is supposed to be reduced, but just the opposite has happened. Ten years ago we at our plant had 18 basic indices; today we have 59. No matter how hard we try, we can never fulfill them all. So we start evaluating them: Which is the most important? If we use too much metal, we'll catch some flak. If we build up large stocks, we won't lose our jobs. But if we fail to fulfill the plan, no matter what the cost of doing so might be, we could lose them. So the very means of evaluating enterprises' performance is itself faulty. Even if I fulfill the plan by 98% but save 10% of (allocated) metal or, say, eliminate 200 jobs, I still may get fired. So is it worth working on such things? In general, the drive for gross output continues'. (*Pravda*, 1983, p. 9)

The Soviet planners have really become quite sophisticated in the design of bonus systems and have gone beyond the mere encouragement of target achievement. Bonus payments now try to elicit information concerning the feasible outputs of enterprises – information vital to the co-ordination of central plans. The economics literature on the subject of optimal incentives is vast and complex, but the gist of it is that, if enterprises are suitably rewarded, they can be persuaded to part with information sooner rather than later. This process can go as far as enterprises effectively setting their *own* targets and even rates of bonus payments, since their choices will reveal their judgements about output likely to prove attainable.

These considerations are reflected to some extent as 'counter-planning' in Soviet industry whereby enterprises are encouraged to counter (or revise) the ministry's targets in either direction, secure in the knowledge that the planners will not penalise above-target performance with higher (FTAL) targets in the next period. In practice, however, although great stress since 1980 has been laid on stable, five-year targets, enterprises have been reluctant to reveal their capacities and overfulfil their plans because of uncertain input supplies (see Hanson, 1983, p. 8).

Despite these shortcomings, bonuses are paid on a large scale in the Soviet Union, up to 30 per cent of total pay for managers (Schroeder, 1982b, p. 14). Paradoxically, Western managers enjoy much lower levels of bonus payments, although basic wages and salaries may be higher and promotions are used to motivate performance. Companies like Shell offer stock options to directors, but otherwise would argue that the annual performance of subsidiary companies and divisions is dominated by external effects like movements in exchange rates and the price of oil, and not by managerial efforts and skill. Large bonuses on a Soviet scale are therefore rare.

Horizontal links

Horizontal links are an alternative to bonus payments as a source of decentralised decisions. They occur in various forms: for example, goods and services that are not centrally co-ordinated, 'self-production' by enterprises, and grey and black markets. In effect nobody knows their significance with any accuracy.

We do know that in 1970 26,000 products were 'non-planned', or in other words were produced within ministries for their own consumption, and did not enter the central planning exercise proper. Within enterprises as well as ministries, however, there must be a great deal of undisclosed self-production, since the only alternative source of inputs is the central plan. 'In-house' repair facilities seem more prevalent in Soviet factories than in the West, where a telephone call can bring a specialist repairer from outside. It is undeniably true also that much above-target output is concealed and retained within the enterprise to enable industrial 'expediters' (or 'pushers') to barter for desperately needed materials on 'grey' markets; this is strictly unlawful, but tolerated by the authorities. In addition, the Soviet state is prepared to allow the legal market provision by individuals of 'non-essential services' such as appliance repairs and various professional services that attract discouragingly high rates of income tax, and there are 'free' markets in all towns selling above-quota agricultural goods from collective farms and the produce of private plots.

Finally, there are black markets. Visitors to the Soviet Union are always impressed by the great disparity between the clothes that citizens (especially children) wear and the stocks on display in the shops. Undoubtedly many clothes are home-made (this is just another form of horizontal link, between producer and consumer), but it also seems inevitable that many garments are sold unlawfully without appearing on the shelves. Clothes are probably the visible tip of an iceberg of black-market activity. It seems that agriculture and transport, in particular, are subject to black market activities. Gregory and Stuart (1981, p. 171) report that a quarter of all alcohol is obtained on black markets, that 500 million litres of petrol were stolen in 1972, and that about 10 per cent of total earnings come from activities outside the main place of employment. Apart from such isolated guesses, however, we cannot estimate with accuracy the prevalence of black markets in the Soviet, or any other, economy.

Black-market activities can be interpreted in two conflicting ways. They can be seen as a necessary characteristic of central planning, rescuing the system from uncertainties that cannot be handled at the centre. In this sense, black markets aid central planning. Alternatively, they may distract from official, planned activities, diverting resources from the central plans, thus weakening them rather than strengthening. Both interpretations are probably correct simultaneously, and Feldbrugge (1984) shows that the first kind of activity is effectively tolerated by the authorities and the second kind often severely punished as economic crime.

Associations in industry

Finally, decentralisation can be achieved by internalising previously separate enterprises, forming 'associations'. Capitalism has employed the 'multidivisional form' since the 1920s in large corporations threatening to become too bureaucratic. Strategic decisions are retained at head office, and divisions (or profit centres) are otherwise left as quasi-firms to run their own operations. Head office now needs very little specialist knowledge to compare the performance of, say, identical oil refineries in Britain and the Netherlands.

The Soviet Union has taken advantage of this organisational innovation since 1961, forming associations which vary from small groupings of similar enterprises in 'production' associations to 'industrial' associations effectively replacing whole branches of ministries and even 'research–industrial' associations that embrace all enterprises in an industry plus related research institutes. These associations, and also the Territorial Production Complex, which merges enterprises in adjacent linked industries, are potentially fruitful for the Soviet planners. Many transactions are internalised within associations, need not concern the planners and furthermore are monitored by the enterprises for quality and delivery. (This helps to dispose of the famous 'big nail' problem of product mix in Soviet central plans, where a nail factory produces *large* nails to fulfil its target, which has been expressed in terms of weight–see Miller, 1984.) Associations may also bring planners closer to the enterprises, however, enabling them to spot divergences from plans more quickly and interfere more with day-to-day operations. In practice it has been concluded (Buck, 1985) that associations have reinforced central hierarchies rather than decentralised decisions in Soviet industry.

THE ECONOMICS OF SHORTAGE

The foregoing background was intended to give readers the flavour of Soviet planning without detail unnecessary for our purposes. Of course important details have had to be overlooked, but this has been deliberate. Institutional detail is difficult to pin down in the Soviet economy, since it varies so much from industry to industry and from time to time.

We would argue that it is the allocation of resources through an administrative hierarchy that is responsible for the achievements and shortcomings of the Soviet economy that will be catalogued in the following chapters. It is dangerous to describe such a system as 'central planning', since this detracts from the power that resides away from the central authorities through the provision of information. Central decision-makers cannot rely much on prices for information on production possibilities, and they are forced to concentrate on targets for gross output, if plans are to be co-ordinated, with predictable consequences. Unlike 'USSR Inc', Shell UK is exposed to some product market competition and to the discipline of the capital market. There is no equivalent Soviet institution that can judge the performance of ministries and enterprises dispassionately. The central planners find it relatively easy to direct the *quantity* of labour and capital to be used in enterprises but lack the information to determine their *quality*, or productivity.

In our opinion, the relative performance of the Soviet economy described in the chapters that follow has changed little in the last few decades and can be explained with only a fairly rudimentary knowledge of the planning institutions and an understanding of the 'economics of shortage'. This opinion is extremely controversial. In contrast, Drewnowski (1982) explains the recent performance of the Soviet economy in terms of its moral fabric, involving suppression of the truth, eradication of dissent and the repudiation of fairness. A paper in the same volume as Drewnowski's, by Wiles (1982a), considers many contributory factors, including military expenditure and the depletion of natural resources, but places particular emphasis on social impatience and indiscipline, involving alcoholism and queuing, for example. (Some of these phenomena could be symptoms of shortage.)

The Soviet economy does not appear to us to be in a state of unusual crisis, although the burden of new defence technologies will be much harder to bear than in the USA. It is our contention that just *one* characteristic of the Soviet economy provides a reasonably accurate explanation of economic performance over many decades, and that little is new in the problems now facing the Soviet central authorities. That single feature is the existence of a *relatively soft budget (and administrative) constraint* in Soviet industry, a concept developed by the Hungarian economist, János Kornai. It must be emphasised at the outset, however, that none of Kornai's work is concerned directly with the Soviet economy, only with Hungary or with economic systems in the abstract. For the purposes of this book, Kornai's ideas are 'extended' into areas for which they were not originally intended. He considers the 'classical capitalist firm', the 'traditional socialist firm' (see Kornai, 1980, vol. A, p. 27), and the actual Hungarian firm (Kornai, 1983), but has never analysed Soviet industry explicitly.

Besides adapting and extending Kornai's ideas to the Soviet context, another modification to Kornai's theory is proposed. Kornai is concerned with the extent to which good (or bad) *financial* performance by the firm is rewarded (or penalised) by *market forces*. Soft and hard budgets will be considered in more depth in the next two subsections, but Kornai is basically concerned with the extent to which firms with a large excess of revenues over costs (i.e. profits) are rewarded and allowed to grow, and the extent to which unprofitable firms are penalised and threatened by liquidation. Where market rewards and penalties are strong/weak, the budget constraint is described as hard/soft. Soft budgets render producers insensitive to consumers' demands and encourage producers to demand excessive supplies of all inputs like labour, capital and materials. They lead inevitably to excess demand and sellers' markets for virtually all inputs and outputs, or what Kornai calls a 'shortage' or 'suction' economy. This contrasts with the relatively hard budgets that Kornai associates with capitalism, where excess supply, buyers' markets and 'pressure' economies are the rule.

Kornai insists that only competitive market forces can produce hard constraints and that one cannot 'simulate live competition with extremely complicated legal rules devised on a desk' (1983, p. 229). It seems clear, however, that administrative, as opposed to market, discipline *can* impose hard effective constraints on industry, at least in particular sectors. High-priority branches of the Soviet economy such as defence, space research, high-voltage electricity transmission, and the production of welding equipment, of cooling technologies for blast-furnace linings, of electronic copper castings and of surgical instruments experience 'hard' administrative supervision, and similar examples can be cited from Western bureaucracies. For instance, hard administrative constraints usually apply in the armed forces, in the treatment of acute medical emergencies and in the administration of admissions procedures for most educational establishments. The maintenance of high standards of performance in these areas is vitally important, and poor performance attracts press criticism and a deterioration in the career prospects of miscreant bureaucrats, if not dismissal.

Kornai's hard budget constraints can therefore be seen as a subset of hard constraints generally, which can be enforced by administrative methods as well as markets. *The general hardness and softness of constraints in industry refers therefore to the extent to which good and bad performance is rewarded and penalised by markets and/or by administrative supervision.*

The limits to administration are recognised. Although it may be possible to apply hard administrative constraints in East German industry across all sectors, the Soviet economy is far more complex and operates in a different cultural environment (see chapter 10 below). It is not without significance that Western health services are far less successful in dealing with chronic complaints, which are less obvious and newsworthy than acute disorders. From personal experience, the administrative performance of university academics is far less satisfactory outside the high-priority area of admissions procedures.

In the context of the Soviet economy, it is particularly important to recognise that hard constraints in industry can be achieved by markets or administration, if one is to understand Soviet economic achievements, problems and attempted reforms. It is easy to argue that the complexity of the Soviet economy and the limits on administrative capacity make it impossible to impose 'hard' administration on more than a minority of high-priority sectors (see, for example, Nove, 1982).

At the same time, it is impossible to demonstrate that the hardness of markets or administration is a good or a bad thing. Hard and soft constraints produce all kinds of advantages and disadvantages that can only be appraised subjectively by the application of particular value-judgements. Since constraints can, in theory, be hardened by tighter administration or by stronger market forces, the concept of hardness in itself implies no preference for central planning or capitalism. In practice, however, it is suggested that conditions in the average capitalist firm have produced an economic system with the characteristics of a relatively 'hard budget' economy, and that the actual Soviet economic system conforms to expectations for a 'soft budget' economy, with only a few exceptions.

The next three sections describe these characteristics and explain the structure of the chapters that follow. Readers wishing to see critical interpretations of Kornai's work, which forms the basis for these sections, should consult reviews by Wagener (1982), Hall (1983), Marrese and Mitchell (1984), and Britton and Gay (1984). The perspective that Kornai's ideas offer on the Soviet economy may be considered a mono-causal or one-dimensional view of that system, but in our judgement they capture much of its essence.

Hard Constraints

It is pointless to pretend that actual capitalism comes close to attaining Kornai's five characteristics of a *perfectly* hard budget constraint, where less than perfect performance is penalised instantly by liquidation. Kornai's five characteristics of perfectly hard budgets are as follows (see Kornai, 1980, vol. B, pp. 302–3):

1 Firms are price-takers, and survival depends upon sufficient sales of output.

2 The tax system is applied uniformly with no exceptions for individual enterprises.
3 No state subsidies are available to finance any financial deficits.
4 All inputs must be paid for in cash out of revenues, there being no credit or external finance.
5 Capital inputs (investment) must be financed out of profits. Dividends cannot be invested internally, once they have been distributed.

Actual capitalism can never come near to satisfying these five conditions for *perfectly* hard budgets, except in the perfect competitive model of the neoclassical textbooks, and even perfect competition embraces external finance from a capital market. Firms can influence prices through advertising, and monopolists can restrict output. Tax authorities often have the discretion to delay tax collections from companies approaching bankruptcy, but with some prospects for revival and subsequent tax payments. Within just one industry, Rolls-Royce was rescued and nationalised by a Conservative government in Britain, Chrysler was given subsidised federal loans in similar circumstances in the United States, and De Lorean was able to sustain unprofitable production for a number of years, thanks to state aids from both countries.

Nevertheless we, and Kornai, would assert that the budget constraint under capitalism is relatively hard: potential new entrants to an industry, competition from imports, take-over or technological change may threaten the tightest monopoly and keep its prices down, if only in the long run; electorates may become tired of loss-making, state-owned enterprises and long-term subsidies in the end. (We do not want to argue that this is an inherently desirable state of affairs, just that relatively hard budgets are a fact and give rise to certain phenomena to be discussed in the remainder of this book.) It was explained above that low profits for Shell in 1981 and 1982 caused cuts in employment and planned investment in 1983. Markets provide a relatively dispassionate and harsh discipline.

If constraints under capitalist markets in the West are generally quite hard, then Kornai would suggest that a number of implications follow for economic performance (see pp. 29–31). Meanwhile it is interesting to note that both Marx's theory of underconsumption and Keynes's theory of effective demand would support this view of capitalism as an 'excess supply' or 'pressure' system (see Kornai, 1980, vol. A, p. 29):

> 'Marx's analysis of the deep contradiction which exists in capitalism between the tendency for unlimited enlargement of production and the limited absorption capacity of the market is well known.
>
> Keynes's attention was centered on this sphere of problems. He studied how effective demand for goods could be increased, in order that resource utilization, primarily the employment of manpower, should improve'.

Soft Constraints

We would not want to pretend, either, that Soviet planning approaches Kornai's polar case of the perfectly soft budget constraint:

1 enterprises can pass on cost increases to the buyer as higher prices. Deficits do not threaten survival.
2 enterprises influence the tax rules and are granted exemptions.
3 free state grants cover financial deficits.
4 credit is available and without a serious analysis of prospects. Defaults on the repayment of credits are permissible.
5 risks are shared with outsiders, especially the state.

The Soviet system does, however, exhibit the characteristics of *relatively* soft budget constraints. Despite an accounting system called *khozraschet*, which requires each enterprise to retain revenues to cover costs, planned losses are not unusual. The ministries and Party officials often act in support of enterprises in financial difficulties and place burdens on the successful. Where, despite state support, administrative targets are underfulfilled, plans and norms can be relaxed. Buyers are in a weak position to reject goods of low quality. In general, the planning hierarchy does not impose a harsh discipline on the activities of enterprises in the way that markets do. Enterprises, ministries and the Party may often be viewed as partners, covering up errors and misjudgements. In addition, and despite recent economic reforms (see above), the Soviet central plans are more concerned with the fulfilment of gross-output targets than financial deficits. (If the authorities reward some aspect of performance other than gross output, then the outcome in terms of gross output is indeterminate, even in advance, and plans cannot be co-ordinated.) Input authorisations therefore are relatively unconstrained, although in practice authorised inputs do not always materialise and shortage is exacerbated, thus encouraging enterprises to hoard labour and other inputs, adding to excess demands. It is paradoxical, but understandable, that excess supply within enterprises co-exists with excess demands outside them. Indeed they feed on each other.

We must emphasise that relatively soft constraints in the Soviet economy are an untestable assertion on our part, though one that corresponds to the explicit intentions of Stalin (or an approved economist who wrote in his name). Kornai (1980, vol. B, p. 214) reports that suction (or excess demand) was deliberately sought in the Soviet Union. He quotes from Stalin's speech to the 16th Party Congress in 1949: 'here in the Soviet Union consumption of the masses grows continually, advancing ahead of the rise of production . . . the growth of the domestic market will advance beyond the growth of industry, serving as a spur to industry to continually expand production'. Stalin's view represents a classical defence of the excess-demand suction (shortage) economy, and emphasises that it has been consciously chosen, for many good reasons. It follows, for example, that enterprises will demand extra labour inputs if they contribute to gross revenues, despite the fact that they contribute even more to enterprise costs. Material inputs will be demanded and hoarded when not needed immediately. In relation to capital inputs, non-rigorous investment appraisal and the absence of any desperate need to repay credit on time will generate an 'investment hunger' among enterprises. For the enterprise it is important to initiate investment projects, perhaps by understating costs, since, once started, they are unlikely to be stopped.

None of the foregoing should imply that central planning is incapable of applying hard budgets or simulating them administratively. In the Soviet Union, for example, the Defence Ministry does not generate excess demand for military equipment and is unwilling to accept output of low quality. Some 27 years after Stalin's speech to the 16th CPSU Congress quoted above, Gorbachev addressed the 23rd Congress in 1986 and declared that factories that make regular losses under the new cost accounting guidelines are to be allowed to go bankrupt, and that managers and workers will lose their bonuses if they produce goods that consumers do not want. Time will tell.

In the chapters that follow, however, it will be argued that central planning for an economy the size of the Soviet Union means that relatively hard constraints applied administratively impose a massive burden on the vertical hierarchies of Soviet industry and can only be sustained for a minority of sectors, like defence. Otherwise, budgets can only be hardened by horizontal market-type devices.

PLAN OF BOOK

The notion of relatively soft budget constraints in the Soviet economy cannot explain in detail every aspect of Soviet economic performance compared with that in the West, but it will be argued that it captures the essence of perhaps the most important mechanism at work. The remaining chapters are built around a logical structure of the components of economic efficiency, developed in figure 1.2. This structure distinguishes between efficiency at the (micro) level of the industrial enterprise and at the (macro) level of the economy as a whole, and between efficiency at a fixed point in time (static) and over time (dynamic).

The concepts in figure 1.2 are viewed in a Kornai perspective in figure 1.3, which in turn becomes the basis for the rest of this book. It has already been explained that although Kornai has commented at length on the

Figure 1.2 Components of economic efficiency.

	Micro	*Macro*
Static	Distributive efficiency, or fairness Productive efficiency, or the extent to which the *absolute* output of each good approaches the maximum, with given inputs Allocative efficiency, or the extent to which *relative* output proportions reflect demand and supply conditions	Level of unemployment Inflation
Dynamic	Allocative efficiency over time, or the extent to which the ratio of investment to current consumption reflects time preference Adaptive efficiency, or the responsiveness of supply to *new* demands, and vice versa	Extensive growth of income through increases in the *quantity* of capital and labour Intensive growth of income through increases in the *quality* of inputs

Together, these components of efficiency determine overall living standards.

characteristics of a 'traditional socialist firm' and of Hungarian firms, he has never been explicit about the Soviet firm. In addition, his analysis has certainly been concerned with under-investment and over-full employment, but he has never applied his perspective systematically to all the components of efficiency in figure 1.2.

It cannot be emphasised strongly enough therefore that, in the chapters that follow, the Kornai 'view' or 'perspective' only implies Kornai's stated opinion, if it is accompanied by a full acknowledgement or quotation. In each chapter, Kornai's ideas are extended in a context that was often not considered by him. For example, Kornai had little to say about income

Figure 1.3 Economic efficiency with soft constraints.

	Micro	*Macro*
Static	*Chapter 2* Fairness modified by excess demand (perks and private incomes) *Chapter 3* Low productive and allocative efficiency	*Chapter 4* Excess demand and inflation perhaps hidden *Chapter 5* Low external unemployment, but perhaps unemployment hidden within enterprises
Dynamic	*Chapter 6* Investment 'Hunger' at the expense of current consumption *Chapter 7* Low levels of adaptiveness, innovation, etc.	*Chapter 8* High rates of extensive growth through over-employment and over-investment Low rates of intensive growth through low productive efficiency and adaptiveness

Together, these components of efficiency determine overall living standards.

distribution, apart from the fact that other efficiency components had to be traded off against justice or equity (see Kornai, 1985, p. 31). In chapter 2, however, the Kornai 'perspective' is extrapolated into the area of income distribution and the inverted commas around 'Kornai view' or 'perspective' are no longer used.

The same reservation must be entered regarding the 'official Soviet' view that is presented beside the Kornai perspective on each component of efficiency in the eight chapters that follow. Unless there is a direct quotation, it should be assumed that this represents the authors' imaginative *guess* at what the 'official Soviet' view would be, if it existed. It is suggested that with these two views in mind, a more structured approach to the empirical evidence on each component may be analysed.

In general, the official Soviet statistics will be treated with respect, although Western estimates will also be presented where available. Our judgement is that where statistics do not suit the Soviet politicians, they are simply not published, are discontinued when they become embarrassing, or are reduced to index numbers with shifting bases. We know that poor statistical sampling techniques render certain estimates unreliable, but generally there is no conscious falsification.

CHAPTER TWO

FAIRNESS

In this book we deal with each component of Soviet economic efficiency in turn, although in no case can a particular component be defined unambiguously. For example, unemployment and inflation can be measured in a variety of ways: the British government redefined official unemployment four times between 1982 and 1986. Leaving measurement problems aside, however, one can safely assume that attributes like lower inflation or faster economic growth are 'good', other things being equal.

With 'fairness' the problems of definition and measurement are no less acute but there is an additional complication: there is no unanimity on what constitutes a 'good' distribution of utility, income or wealth, even if measurement were not controversial. At the extreme 'right' of the spectrum of views on equity or fairness in the West, many would like to see a distribution of income sufficiently unequal to reflect what they consider to be an extremely uneven distribution of talent and motivation among individuals, and Utilitarians would wish to maximise aggregate utility by concentrating income and wealth in the hands of those with the greatest capacities to enjoy them. At the centre, there stand those who would reward individuals according to their productivity on condition that everybody had equal opportunities in the pursuit of education and employment. To the left, egalitarians emphasise the satisfaction of basic human needs, assumed to be evenly distributed.

In this chapter, we are interested in income (not utility) and propose the value-judgement that a more equal distribution of incomes is *per se* better than a less equal one. A skewed income distribution produces jealousies and unrest that may disrupt the achievement of other economic (and non-economic) objectives, and therefore a more even distribution of income seems desirable in itself.

Of course economic objectives conflict. For example, more unemployment (chapter 5) is often the result of attempts to reduce inflation (chapter 4). Income differentials may have to *widen* to secure productive efficiency (chapter 3) or economic growth (chapter 8) but these wider differentials are seen as a cost, grudgingly conceded by the Soviet state in the pursuit of more pressing objectives. Other things being equal, this chapter will view narrower income differentials as being desirable in their own right. Readers with opposing values will have to reverse the conclusions that emerge from this chapter.

As with other chapters, this one will first present the official Soviet view on equity; second, show how Kornai's work suggests a very different perspective; and third review empirical evidence on the actual Soviet distribution of incomes in the light of these competing sets of predictions. Actual measurements will be left until the third section, but it will be convenient to refer to different components of household or personal income in each section.

In particular, the distinctions between primary, secondary and tertiary income should be understood. For the purpose of illustrating these distinctions only, table 2.1 shows some of the basic components of Soviet household income for 1980, although it must be emphasised that these CIA estimates are very close to the original Soviet official statistics, which are in turn incomplete and flawed. In table 2.1, row 1(b) appears to be understated compared with row 1(a), although casual observation suggests that soldiers are used extensively on civilian construction projects. If our assertion in chapter 1 is correct and collective farmers are now practically indistinguishable from state employees, then row 1(c) could reasonably be merged with row 1(a). Rows 1(d) and 1(e) deal with agricultural produce. State and collective farm workers are allocated private plots of land which yield produce for sale (row 1(d)) and self-consumption, which is not included, along with the agricultural output from land allotted to urban workers. In addition to private plots, state and collective farm workers receive payment in kind (row 1(e)) as well as cash. It seems likely that the agricultural prices applied in the calculation of rows 1(d) and 1(e) have been too low and these components of Soviet primary income are understated.

Rows 1(f) and 1(g) in table 2.1 are the most controversial items. Row 1(f) refers to the perquisites and fringe benefits attached to various forms of employment, and no estimate of their value is shown here. 'Private incomes' in row 1(g) comprise only those activities that are registered with the state and attract income tax. According to the 1977 decree, this includes the private activities of service workers such as hairdressers or repairers of motor cars or electrical appliances. It will be shown later in this chapter that the estimate of 'private incomes' in row 1(g) of table 2.1 is grossly understated. Row 1(h) refers to the nominal interest paid on savings deposits and row 1(i) is strictly a statistical rounding device.

Table 2.1 Soviet household income, 1980

Description	*Income (billion roubles)*
1. *Primary ('gross') income*	
(a) Wages and salaries, state civilian employment	229.3
(b) Wages and salaries, state military employment	8.9
(c) Money payments from collective farms to members	16.5
(d) Sale of farm produce by farm households	14.3
(e) Farm income in kind	19.2
(f) Other non-monetary income	n.a.
(g) Private incomes (artisans, etc.)	4.8
(h) Interest received	3.6
(i) Balancing item – other income	12.6
Total primary income	309.2
2. *Secondary ('net') income*	
Total primary income (above) plus:	
(a) Net transfer payments (pensions, holiday pay, etc., less income tax)	17.5
Total secondary income	326.7
3. *Tertiary ('total') income*	
Total secondary income (above) plus:	
(a) State expenditures on child care, health care, education, etc.	33.8
Total household income	360.5

Figures include rounding errors.
Source: Figures adapted from Bergson, 1984, p. 1062, using definitions proposed by Ellman, 1984, p. 110. Imputed housing rents are omitted on the recommendation of Matthews, 1978, p. 11.

After primary (gross) income, table 2.1 shows the net effect of income tax and transfer payments such as pensions, stipends and holiday pay. In practice it will be argued that most of these items are fairly proportional to gross income and make little difference to the Soviet income distribution. This does not apply to row 3(a), however, and the calculation of tertiary income. The enjoyment of child care, education and medical facilities is a major constituent of 'real income'. Housing is omitted from rows 3(a) and 1(f) because the CIA estimate of imputed net rent is quite unrealistic, and because the value of modifications to the housing priority status of employees has not been estimated.

The concepts of primary ('gross'), secondary ('net') and tertiary ('total') income should now be understood broadly, and in this chapter we can proceed to consider first the official and then the Kornai views on Soviet income distribution.

SOVIET EQUITY – THE OFFICIAL VIEW

Official Soviet attitudes on income distribution have undergone a series of drastic revisions, and as usual Karl Marx's writings became the focus of official deliberations, this time on income distribution. Marx's dream was of a communist utopia in which all the last vestiges of capitalism had been swept away. According to the 1891 English translation of his 'Critique of the Gotha Programme' quoted in Nove and Nuti (1972, p. 24), 'only then can the narrow horizon of bourgeois right be crossed in its entirety and society inscribe on its banners: From each according to his abilities, to each according to his needs!' Since human needs are assumed to be evenly distributed among individuals, full communism implies an egalitarian distribution of income.

During the 'transitional' stage of 'actually existing socialism', which has continued to separate capitalism from full communism in the Soviet Union since 1917, Marx conceded in 1875 that 'the individual producer receives back from society – after deductions have been made – exactly what he gives to it' (Nove and Nuti, 1972, p. 22). Lenin seized on this intermediate Marxist maxim of 'to each according to his contribution' and it was spelled out in the 1920 'The ABC of Communism' by Bukharin and Preobrazhensky, quoted in Nove and Nuti (1972, p. 35): 'Our meaning is that at the outset, in the first days of communist society, products will probably be distributed in accordance with the amount of work done by the applicant; at a later stage, however, they will simply be supplied according to the needs of the comrades'. Later, equal pay was totally denounced by Stalin in 1931 as 'petty-bourgeois egalitarianism' and differentials widened, with an emphasis on 'equal pay for equal work'. Since Stalin's death in 1953 there has been a shift back towards equality with large increases in the minimum wage, but by the time of the economic reforms of July 1979 there was a call to end the process of 'excessive wage levelling'.

Despite these shifts in fashionable thinking towards income distribution however, it is easy to understand why Soviet officials can claim that their system is relatively equitable. First, central planning includes central wages, pensions and prices policies, which allow the central authorities to choose at will any desired distribution of incomes, within limits. Such a situation contrasts with the West, where public pay and pensions are centrally determined together with income tax-rates, but otherwise income distribution is left largely to the market mechanism. Thus the Soviet authorities can modify the income distribution to reflect current industrial priorities and the current philosophy with regard to equity. In relation to wages, Pryor (1985, p. 240) shows that Soviet industrial priorities produce a pattern of wages by industry broadly similar to that prevailing in the West, where productivity largely determines wages in the labour market. Pryor, does however, note (1985, p. 241) that centrally determined group and individual bonus schemes distinguish Soviet wages, whereas straight 'time' payments are usual in the West. Paradoxically, Soviet wages may be more closely tied to labour productivity than in the West.

Second, central planning is intended to prevent capitalist 'exploitation of man by man'. Although savings deposits, bonds, consumer durables and half the housing stock are privately owned and can be inherited, the means of production belong to the state, and individuals cannot control the labour power of others through the private ownership of land and capital, since this is forbidden. Thus there is no explicit unearned or property income with the exception of the nominal interest rates accruing to savings deposits, although in practice private incomes are derived from unregistered lettings of apartments and holiday homes, and state employees may unlawfully use the state's assets to perform private work.

Third, the Soviet tertiary income distribution (see table 2.1) is modified, as in the West, by the central authorities through the provision of free social goods such as medicine and education, although private health provision and tutoring do exist and some jobs may give preferential access to the state's facilities.

Fourth, the distribution of real incomes is influenced by the provision of basic goods and services at very low prices, often insignificantly different from zero. For example, urban public transport is virtually free, state housing absorbs on average only 5 per cent of disposable income, and fuel and basic foods are heavily subsidised. A comprehensive comparison of Soviet and US consumer goods prices is provided by Bergson (1984, p. 1060), who confirms that basic foods are cheap, whereas 'luxury' items such as meat and alcohol are subject to high rates of turnover tax. Soviet clothing is very expensive, however, and it should not be forgotten that subsidised public services and consumer goods must be financed by deductions from enterprise profits or individuals' incomes.

For these four good reasons, the central authorities claim that the Soviet distribution of incomes is relatively egalitarian, but the next section considers objections to this thesis suggested by the work of Kornai.

SOVIET EQUITY – THE KORNAI VIEW

In a Kornai world, an economic system is subject to perfectly hard or soft budget constraints or something in between, and budgets may be supplemented by hard or soft administration. With hard constraints in a 'pressure' economy, enterprises must be innovative, responding to new technological opportunities and new consumer demands, but keeping production costs down at the same time. The penalties for failure in the buyers' markets of a pressure economy are loss of sales and the eventual liquidation of the enterprise. Goods markets are characterised by excess supplies and sellers are always competing for new buyers. Inputs like labour and capital are also in excess supply, although fully utilised *within* the enterprise. Unemployment outside the enterprise is a characteristic of hard budgets.

Kornai considers centrally planned economies to exhibit relatively soft budget constraints. Enterprises must achieve their gross output targets if the co-ordinated plans of the central authorities are to be achieved, but enterprises and the central authorities bear *co-responsibility* for the achievement of targets. This means that targets may be flexible downwards at the last minute, enterprises may not be disciplined for producing the wrong assortment of output, and enterprises may use inputs in a profligate way without severe penalty. Above all, enterprises are instructed to achieve a mixture of output plans that suits the vertical hierarchy above the enterprise: the ministries, planners and other central authorities. Only by coincidence or exhaustive market research will this mixture match the individual demands of consumers. Given the universal softness of the budget, administrative constraints on enterprises, and the hoarding of labour, capital and materials, buyers must largely accept the mixture produced for them. Even where consumers refuse to buy the assortment of output produced, differential taxes and subsidies can keep loss-making enterprises in business. Of course the central authorities can administer hard constraints in a few priority sectors, but complexity and limits on administrative capacity must prevent their universal application in a centrally planned economy.

Although Kornai himself kept his theory of shortage quite separate from considerations of 'justice', it is pertinent to ask: what are the implications of these relatively soft budgets and administration for income distribution? There are three. First, Kornai would echo the official view in the sense that soft constraints give every man or woman the chance of earning a wage or salary income.

Second, excess demands for consumer goods (or certain *qualities* of goods) at the planned pattern of production and prices, together with a fairly egalitarian central wages policy, will leave state enterprises *unwilling* to produce more, since they can stay in business with existing production, and *unable* to produce more, since fairly egalitarian wages may be set too low to enable the enterprise to attract further labour or induce labour to work harder or longer. Excess demand provides an incentive for state employees to divert resources into private production which may embody quality improvements. This could involve legal private services or the unlawful use of state assets for private production. The *private incomes* earned could substantially modify the pattern of wages and pensions set by the central authorities (see row 1(g) in table 2.1).

Third, chronic levels of over-demand for crucial supplies of labour and materials will tend to generate hidden price increases (see chapter 4 below). In addition, however, enterprises unable to pay above-plan wages to attract key personnel may resort to offering *higher fringe benefits and perquisites* to labour (see row 1(f) in table 2.1). In some cases it may be possible, given the co-responsibility felt by enterprises and the central authorities for the achievement of targets, for recruits to key positions in an enterprise to enjoy preferential access to social goods provided by other branches of the state. The Party could provide the link, say, between the recruitment of an enterprise manager and the accelerated movement of the new manager's name to the top of a local authority's housing list. More probably, the enterprise itself could take to building apartments, holiday homes and health clinics for its own employees. All these actions will substantially modify the distribution of tertiary incomes, and the extent of local 'wage drift' will depend on 'whether the central authorities are capable of *enforcing* the wage policy and the observance of wage discipline'. (Kornai, 1980, p 405).

It can be seen therefore that Kornai's perspective on central planning suggests that 'perks' and private incomes may substantially modify the income distribution legislated by the central authorities. The next section of this chapter now looks at the available Soviet evidence in order to evaluate the views of Kornai versus the official orthodoxy.

EVIDENCE ON SOVIET INCOME DISTRIBUTION

It is particularly easy with the Soviet income distribution to confirm one's preconceptions. This chapter will try to give a balanced view, but it has already been shown in table 2.1 that there are at least three major income definitions, and many components such as the value of perquisites and private incomes cannot be estimated accurately. In addition, the careful choice of observations for particular years can bias results, and the use of household units instead of individuals always leads to the relative over-estimation of income inequality (see Morrison, 1984, p. 123). On top of all this, official Soviet earnings and income statistics are extremely flimsy. Only broad statistics of the dispersion (spread) of the income distribution are published for selected years, as opposed to the underlying frequency distributions themselves, and statistics such as percentile ratios and Gini coefficients are ambiguous. Above all, the Soviet statistics on earnings and net incomes are based on sample surveys and there are grave doubts about the rigour of the sampling procedures involved. It is clear that elite groups are mostly left out of the surveys, together with collective farmers, but it seems probable that Soviet sampling techniques may involve other forms of bias.

This section analyses primary, secondary and tertiary Soviet income distributions and overall conclusions follow at the end. The evenness of the distribution of average real incomes *across republics* is left until chapter 9, as one aspect of living standards.

Primary ('Gross') Incomes

The components of primary income are listed in table 2.1. In this section we concentrate on wage and salary earnings, perquisites and private incomes. With regard to earnings, the data are restricted to employees in state enterprises, farms and other institutions, but excluding collective farmers and full-time officials in the Party and trade unions. As a result, the data cover about 70 per cent of all employees, and exclude most elite groups.

It was explained in the first section of this chapter that official attitudes to earnings distributions have changed since 1953, and McAuley (1979, pp. 174–213) catalogues the efforts since 1955 of the State Committee on Labour and Wages (Labour and Social Questions since 1976) to convert Stalin's wide earnings differentials into a more egalitarian system. A full reorganisation of wage tariffs by occupation, industry and skill level was achieved in 1957–61, and a minimum wage of between 27 and 35 roubles per month (depending on industry) was introduced in 1956, and subsequently raised to 40–45 roubles in 1959, 60 roubles in 1968, 70 roubles in 1974/5 and 80 roubles in 1985. In 1967, a five-day week and 12–15 days of holiday pay per year were also introduced. These changes are reflected in table 2.2, although it must be emphasised that all measures of dispersion in an earnings distribution are subjective. For example, only two deciles are shown in table 2.2 and in *absolute* terms the gap between (D_1) and (D_9) has increased for each year quoted. It is more usual, however, to look at *relative* measures of dispersion (see the decile ratios in column (4) of table 2.2, where a lower decile ratio represents an 'improvement' in the earnings distribution in terms of the value-judgement favouring greater equality made at the start of this chapter). Despite small increases in the decile ratio for 1972 and 1976, there is overall evidence of a substantial narrowing of the earnings distribution since 1956, reflecting the reform of the wage structure and increasing minimum wages.

International comparisons of earnings distributions are even riskier than measures of equality within one country, but Pryor (1985, p. 253) shows that the Soviet distribution is not typical of, but is much more unequal than, the earnings distributions of other 'socialist' countries in Eastern Europe. Despite this conclusion, the selection of Western comparisons shown in table 2.2 implies (with the exception of the UK in 1976) that even the Soviet earnings distribution is relatively egalitarian compared with those in the West, but not dramatically so. Pryor (1985 p. 254) confirms that centralised wage scales are responsible for this outcome, as the central authorities have tried to reduce the gap between wages and salaries in different industries and especially between blue- and white-collar jobs.

One complication with these earnings (and, later, income) data, however, is that measures of relative dispersion have been seen to be reduced universally with rising living standards. Bergson (1984, pp. 1094–6) and Pryor (1985, p. 253) try to 'standardise' Soviet income levels for comparisons with the West, and the Soviet Union's relatively low real income makes its earnings distribution appear even more egalitarian. Pryor feels able to conclude that 'Legal monetary labor incomes are more equally distributed in the socialist than the capitalist nations . . .', (1985, p. 252), but Bergson is more guarded, concluding that after standardisation '. . . wage inequality in the USSR, especially in the early seventies, may have been somewhat low relative to that in the West' (1984, p. 1066). These conclusions seem reasonable, although the Soviet decile ratio did *increase* in 1972 and 1976 despite rising incomes, and in any case the Soviet authorities would probably reject all efforts to make allowance for low Soviet incomes as patronising in this context. In addition, the data are clearly restricted to official earnings in non-elite groups and omit any perquisites or private incomes. These omissions are corrected below. So far, however, the official view on income distribution stands unrefuted.

Perquisites and fringe benefits can refer to lawful and unlawful payments in kind to workers in agriculture, industry, services and administration. In practice, it is very difficult to distinguish perks from private income. For example, if a policeman takes a bribe to ignore a traffic offence, is that an illegal perk or private income? We would arbitrarily suggest that benefits received as a direct result of state employment are perks. This definition would cover the whole spectrum of fringe benefits from the bottom end, where illegal bribes may be paid to policemen, shop

Table 2.2 Average Soviet state wage and salary earnings and decile ratios, 1961–80 (with Western comparisons)

Year	Soviet Union					Japanese decile ratio	UK decile ratio	US decile ratio
	Average earnings (roubles per month)	*First decile, D_1 (roubles per month)*	*Ninth decile, D_9 (roubles per month)*	*Decile ratio (D_9/D_1)*	*Official Western estimate*[a]			
1956	73	30	131	4.44				
1961				4.02	3.92			
1966	99	49	161	3.26	3.26–3.36		3.5[c]	
1968	113	62	175	2.83	2.78–3.17	3.7		
1972	130	67	208	3.10	3.00–3.15[b]			4.5
1976	151	74	248	3.35			2.8	4.0[d]
1981				3.00				

The first (ninth) decile D_1 (D_9) shows the highest earnings in the lowest 10 per cent (90 per cent) of earnings. The decile ratio (D_9/D_1) shows the ratio of D_9 to D_1 (i.e. column 3 divided by column 2). Of course high ratios denote high inequality.

[a]References to sundry Western estimates can be consulted in Bergson (1984, p. 1064). It can be seen that these estimates broadly correspond with the official Soviet data.

[b]These estimates are for 1970.

[c]This estimate is for 1964/5 and includes all farm workers. The Soviet estimates include only state farm workers.

[d]This estimate is for 1975.

Sources: Table compiled from Bergson, 1984, pp. 1063, 1064, 1077; and Chapman, 1983, p. 410.

assistants and housing officials, for preferential treatment, through the middle of the income distribution, with the fairly general provision of improved health, housing, recreation and holiday facilities by state enterprises and institutions and income-in-kind for farm workers, to the top end of the spectrum, with the perks to members of elite groups by virtue of special shops and eating facilities within government departments, access to travel in the West, the provision of cars and chauffeurs, and even the special 'fifth lanes' on Moscow boulevards, which are kept clear for senior members of elite groups. The holding of multiple official jobs should also be mentioned.

The existence of these perks supports the Kornai view on income distribution. Despite centralised, relatively egalitarian, wage scales, labour is fairly free to move between jobs, apart from difficulties with residential permits in the big cities. To recruit and hold labour in the many occupations that experience over-demand, especially those jobs involving heavy responsibility for others, state institutions must raise wages towards their market-clearing rates by offering perks or at least turning a blind eye towards certain well-known practices. Feldbrugge (1984) explains how many perks support official state activities and are tolerated, or even encouraged.

So, the existence of substantial perks strengthens the Kornai, and weakens the official, view on income distribution, but any final judgement involves measuring the value of perks in the Soviet economy. This is difficult. For example, how can the value of an official car or house be estimated, when prices are kept far below market-clearing levels, and long waiting-lists are normal? In any case, how can comparisons be made with a different pattern of perks in the West? Indeed Ellman (1984, p. 115) argues that access to information is a most valuable perk for elite groups, and this cannot be valued at all. For the purposes of this chapter, we must leave any final judgement until after some discussion of the related topic of private incomes.

Private incomes, like perks, may be legal, simply tolerated by the state, or illegal, depending on whether they support or compete with the state sector's activities (see Feldbrugge, 1984). In the Soviet Union, high-income groups have legal access to private tutoring and health care, and an intelligentsia of artists, writers and entertainers is able to command large private incomes. The private production of such items as food, flowers and handicrafts is legal or tolerated, but in addition there is a network of small-scale producers of consumer goods who manufacture at home or behind the facade of a state job. The repair of cars and domestic appliances depends heavily on the private sector, and building skills or materials can be obtained privately. The private production of alcohol seems to have accounted for about 28 per cent of total Soviet consumption in 1979 (Treml, 1982, p. 70).

Kornai would view all this private activity as a response to sellers' markets in the state sector. State enterprises have relatively soft budgets and their existence does not depend upon their ability to match the quantity or quality of consumers' demands. Thus a television can be fixed more promptly and effectively by a private repairer than through the state repair network. It has been estimated by Ofer and Vinokur (see Bergson, 1984, p. 1068) from their survey of Soviet émigrés that, in 1972–4, private income constituted 11–12 per cent of all household income, although their sample did not include elite groups. To this extent Kornai's view is vindicated, but it must be remembered that illegal and/or unreported incomes are common in the West. Gutmann (1985, p. 3) estimates that the US 'subterranean' economy in 1981 amounted to 14–15 per cent of legal official GNP, and reports that 'Others have produced a range of estimates, the highest over 30 per cent, the lowest about 3.5 per cent, with some grouping of estimates at the midpoint' (p. 123). Presumably, this 'subterranean' economy must substantially modify official Western estimates of the distribution of income and wealth.

It was provisionally concluded above that the Soviet distribution of state monetary wage and salary earnings was relatively egalitarian and that this could be viewed as a positive achievement. Does the existence of substantial perks and private incomes in the Soviet economy weaken this conclusion, even if it is recognised that the same phenomena are common in the West? It is suggested that, to answer this question, attention should be focused on *elite groups* in the Soviet Union, since the existence of perks and private incomes lower down the income scale will not affect our conclusion that the Soviet earnings distribution is relatively egalitarian.

Elite groups have received much attention in the literature on the Soviet economy (see Matthews, 1978; Morrison, 1984; and Bergson, 1984, pp. 1085–91). Matthews (1978) identified the elite as all recipients in 1971–3 of at least 400–500 roubles per month of official earnings, which was between 3.1 and 3.8 times the average 1972 pay (Bergson, 1984, p. 1085). The subsequent list of 227,000 elite personnel (Matthews, 1978, p. 31) comprised :

80,000 full-time Party officials;
60,000 other government, Komsomol and trade union officials;
17,000 managers of large enterprises;
40,000 in an intelligentsia of writers, artists, etc.
30,000 diplomats, police and military.

Matthews' list therefore amounted to a very small proportion (below 0.3 per cent) of the Soviet population, and in the USA a similar proportion would be delineated by a salary over eight times the national average leading to an extremely high standard of living. In fact the *median* US income would be equivalent in absolute terms to the Soviet income that qualifies for membership of Matthews' elite (see Matthews, 1978, p. 176). He concluded that 'the Soviet elite family in the early seventies enjoyed a standard of living roughly equal to or perhaps somewhat below, that of an average American household. This would fit our own observations and those of émigrés who have lived in both societies. There is nothing surprising about it' (p. 177).

In contrast with Matthews' position, it has been pointed out that in 1981 Party membership stood at about 17.5 million, although 'instructors' in the factories and other junior Party members could not be included in the elite. Matthews himself drew attention to the *nomenklatura*, or list of posts for which the Party provides nominees, and observed in relation to the elite that 'In so far as it is covered by nomenklatura listings the Soviet elite is virtually State registered' (Matthews, 1978, p. 34). It is now known that the number of persons on Party *nomenklatury* amount to over 2 million (Miller, 1982, p. 21), but it would be wrong to identify the elite as all Party-nominated job-holders. For example, the headmaster of a small school nominated by a small local Party committee would not have access to many privileges, whereas, on the other hand, many who are not on the list enjoy elitist life-styles, especially those receiving multiple incomes (see Bergson, 1984, pp. 1087–9). On balance, it does not seem unreasonable to accept Morrison's (1984, p. 126) judgement, based on Soviet and Polish experience, of an elite comprising 1.5 per cent of the population enjoying fringe benefits and additional incomes worth up to 100 per cent on top of official incomes. The effect of these assumptions on the distribution of Soviet net incomes is described in the next session.

Secondary ('Net') Incomes

Table 2.1 showed the importance of pensions, stipends and taxation when converting individual earnings into household net income data. Table 2.3 looks at the Gini measure of the dispersion of incomes, a measure which is most sensitive to high incomes within the top decile of incomes ranked by households, an appropriate choice since we are interested in testing the hypothesis that elite incomes in the Soviet Union have the effect of making the distribution of incomes relatively inegalitarian.

The results in table 2.3 place the Soviet Union in an intermediate position between two groups of Western nations, although it must be emphasised that the Gini coefficients are not adjusted for levels of economic development, an adjustment that would surely lift the Soviet Union up the list in table 2.3, if it were made. Results like those in table 2.3 prompt Gregory and Stuart (1981) to conclude that the Soviet post-tax income distribution 'was more unequal than in other planned socialist economies

Table 2.3 Gini coefficients of Soviet and Western post-tax household net incomes

	Gini coefficients[a]
Denmark (1963)	0.225
Sweden (1970)	0.266
UK (1978)	0.296
USSR (1975)[b]	0.299
USSR (1975)[c]	0.342
Canada (1969)	0.344
FRG (1969)	0.352
France (1973)	<0.370
USA (1970)	0.364
USA (1976)	0.377

[a]Gini coefficients measure the difference between an actual income distribution and an 'ideal' egalitarian one. A high coefficient denotes high inequality.
[b]Without adjustment for the non-monetary incomes of elite groups, see text.
[c]After adjustment for the non-monetary income of elite groups, see text.
Source: Morrison, 1984, pp. 131–2.

of Eastern Europe, was about equal to the distribution of income in the "capitalist welfare states" (the UK and Sweden), and was more equal than in the capitalist nonwelfare states (US, Canada, Italy)' (1981, p. 353). It should also be noted from table 2.3 that the second measure of the Soviet income dispersion incorporating Morrison's (1984) estimate of elite-group non-monetary income does lower the Soviet Union's position towards the United States, but does not affect our overall conclusions concerning the relatively egalitarian nature of Soviet income distribution.

One final complication involves the relative price structures of the Soviet Union and the West. Although Morrison (1984, n. 124) points out that Soviet indirect taxes are not progressive, apart from some inferior goods consumed by the poorest sections of the population, it seems clear from Bergson's (1984, p. 1060) list that the prices of Soviet consumer goods (when available) do favour the recipients of low incomes, overall. This influence cannot be measured, but reinforces the conclusion that the distribution of Soviet net incomes is relatively egalitarian. Such a conclusion, however, does not embrace the provision of 'social goods' provided by the state, which is discussed below.

Tertiary ('Total') Incomes

Finally, it is necessary to consider how the Soviet state's provision of 'public goods' such as child and health care, education and housing at low or zero prices affects income distribution. Since the state employs over 70 per cent of the population directly, Kornai would predict that, like any other employer, organs of the state might be tempted to administer public goods in such a way as to supplement the 'wage package' in order to attract labour to important jobs in sellers' markets. Ellman proposes the extreme view that 'Because important areas of consumption are determined by bureaucratic position and not by income, a policy of subsidies for basic goods and services may turn into a policy of increasing inequality, of taxing the badly off to subsidise the well off' (1984, p. 115).

Housing provides the classic example of a good supplied by the state at low prices in a fairly regressive way, although since about half Soviet housing is owned individually or by co-operatives the subject could easily be considered in the discussion of perks or private incomes, above. A Hungarian sociologist, Szelenyi (1983) illustrates the Kornai view in relation to housing in Eastern Europe 'The basic point is this: inequalities in administrative allocation, and inequalities arising from it, probably become inevitable when the wages policy is set . . . scarce goods are always likely to be allocated to the most meritorious citizens in the most essential jobs, who tend to be those with the highest incomes. It could scarcely be otherwise. How could the state say to its rising managers and bureaucrats, 'If you get promoted you will *reduce* your housing chances?' (p. 10).

Morton (1980) provides an analysis of Soviet housing and explains (p. 256) how families in elite groups live in favoured locations close to city centres and enjoy housing subsidies applied to square metres of accommodation. This implies that richer families enjoy larger subsidies in *absolute* terms, given their greater living space. Linked with the administration preference shown to elite groups in housing allocation, this clearly constitutes a regressive element in income distribution, although housing subsidies still represent a lower relative share of higher incomes than lower. McAuley (1979) confirms that for pre-school child care and housing 'their detailed administration has resulted in the perpetuation of substantial inequalities' (p 288). It is also true that the children of elite personnel enjoy considerable preferential access to higher educational facilities (Bergson, 1984, pp. 1089–90), and different grades of state medical treatment exist.

Overall, however, it is difficult to sustain the Kornai-type position in relation to public goods in the Soviet Union. The Ofer–Vinokur survey, 1972–4 showed that the value of publicly supplied education and health care represented 14.7 per cent of net income at the first decile and 9.2 per cent at the ninth decile (see Bergson, 1984, p. 1075). It is difficult to argue with Morrison's conclusion (1984, p. 124) that the distribution of Soviet state expenditure on public goods is very similar to the pattern found in Western countries. Their distribution therefore should not interfere with estimates of the Soviet income distribution vis-à-vis their Western equivalents.

Nevertheless, the foregoing analysis of aggregate incomes should not be allowed to obscure large variations in the distribution of incomes between different groups of citizen, for example between *males and females* or *peasants and industrial workers*.

Women are formally guaranteed equal rights to education and occupations in the Soviet Union, and equal pay for equal work. This conforms with Marxist philosophy and the achievements have been real: women now form 51 per cent of the workforce, the female participation rate in 1979 was 83.1 per cent (Pietsch, 1986, p. 179), and women are supported by generous childcare facilities, maternity leave and the right to resume work after giving birth. Women participate widely in higher education and provide 79 per cent of all teachers, 70 per cent of doctors and 40 per cent of engineers.

As in the West, however, formal equality conceals actual discrimination. Women are over-represented in the lower grades of most occupations, providing only 29 per cent of secondary-school heads and fewer than half the head physicians, for example (Brown et al., 1982, p. 381). Two-thirds of women provide manual labour and casual observation suggests that they perform the most monotonous and exhausting tasks. Gregory and Stuart (1981, p. 207) report that the hourly pay for Soviet urban women is roughly 68–70 per cent that for men.

The formal lack of discrimination can be explained by the state's nominal adoption of a Marxist philosophy, but more practical reasons must have contributed. For example, the Second World War decimated the ranks of males of working age and Kornai-type labour shortage also prompted attempts to raise female participation rates.

To a large extent, sexual inequality in the Soviet Union is comparable to that in the West. Women tend to be involved in low-level work and the wage differentials quoted above are similar to Western levels. The important differences are, first, the relative absence of efficient contraception, but the ready availability of abortions to encourage women to continue working; second, the fact that many Soviet women are required to perform heavy manual work; and third, the 'double shift' work of Soviet women with full-time jobs and a home to run. (Harrison (1986, p.

79) reports that Soviet working women perform weekly about 27 hours of shopping, cooking, cleaning and washing at home compared with just over 6 hours for men. Housework is performed without labour-saving devices on a Western scale, see chapter 9 below.) Nevertheless, Soviet women probably feel that their relative position has improved significantly over time.

A gradual improvement can also be noted for *peasant/worker* inequalities. To the extent that peasant/worker ratios differ between republics, these inequalities are reflected in the regional differences reported in chapter 9 below. Until Stalin's death in 1953, it could reasonably be claimed that raising the living standards of agricultural workers had a very low priority in the Soviet Union. Between 1953 and 1967, however, agricultural prices increased, and despite a 10 per cent reduction in the number of farm workers, the total income of the agricultural population from wages and the output from private plots doubled (Gregory and Stuart, 1981, p. 239). Official statistics show that between 1970 and 1982 the real incomes of collective farm workers continued to grow by 4 per cent per annum compared with only 3 per cent for manual and white-collar workers in industry (*Narodnoye khozyaystvo* SSSR, 1982, p. 380).

At the same time, however, these relative improvements for farm workers have not been able to stem the tide of emigration from the land to the cities, which still have to use residence permits to control numbers. Perhaps the reason for this flow is the relatively poor provision of services in rural areas. Cole (1984, p. 359) reports how in rural Novgorod, an area south of Leningrad with snow cover for up to five months a year and little car ownership, the percentage of the population living more than five kilometres from services was 31.1 per cent for eighth-year school, 15.1 per cent for hospitals, and over 50 per cent for the repair of electrical and other appliances. The direction of migration is a very reliable indicator of relative living standards and in a country like Hungary the flow away from the land has been reversed since 1980, after a thorough reform of agricultural prices and the distribution of public services.

CONCLUSIONS

A consideration of primary, secondary and tertiary incomes suggests that the distribution of incomes in the Soviet Union is relatively egalitarian and that this is due mainly to the virtual absence of property income and to a national earnings structure that, compared with the West, is not significantly modified by the existence of transfer payments, perks, private incomes and public goods. Elite groups do exist in the Soviet Union but on a scale insufficient to overturn our conclusions. Sexual and urban/rural inequalities still exist, but these have been reduced.

If the values and judgements made at the beginning of this chapter are accepted, concerning the desirability, other things being equal, of a more equal distribution of income, then the Soviet Union can be proud of its achievements in this field. Of course, 'other things' may be *un*equal and equity may interfere with the allocation of resources. It must be left until chapter 9 to judge on Schroeder's conclusion in Bergson (1983, p345), that the Soviet Union has achieved 'a relatively low level of material well-being (real incomes) distributed rather evenly . . .'

CHAPTER THREE

ALLOCATION AND PRODUCTION

In this chapter we are concerned with the first group of efficiency concepts that appear in the top left-hand corner of figure 1.2. 'Fairness' or distributive efficiency is treated separately in Chapter 2, so that leaves 'X'-(or productive) efficiency and allocative efficiency for consideration in this chapter. The definitions of the two concepts in this introduction are followed by an explanation of why they are treated together; the structure of the remainder of the chapter is then outlined.

Both allocative and productive efficiency are concerned with the *micro-static* allocation of resources: it is *static* in the sense that the economy must manage within existing resources and constraints, and *micro* in the sense that our focus is on the activities of particular industries and the output of particular products rather than on the overall performance of the economy at the macro-level.

Allocative efficiency refers to *relative mixtures* in production rather than the *absolute* outputs of each good. In a utopian capitalist market economy, allocative efficiency would comprise the extent to which the actual mixture of production reflected the individual preferences of consumers. So, if individual consumers preferred two-storey houses to apartments in tower blocks at prevailing prices, the price of the former would tend to rise and the latter fall. Existing builders should respond by producing more houses and fewer apartment blocks. Some existing builders of apartment blocks could leave the industry and new firms could start to build houses, although it must be emphasised that an ideal world is being considered. In a centrally planned economy, allocative efficiency depends on the extent to which the preferences of the central authorities are reflected in the pattern of output, although the authorities may conduct market research surveys in an attempt to make their preferences match the demands of individual consumers.

Besides the proportions of final *outputs* like houses and flats, however, allocative efficiency refers also to the mixture of *inputs* chosen, and in a perfect market economy the pattern of inputs must match their prices, if allocative efficiency is to be achieved. For example, if labour were expensive and machinery relatively cheap, it would be appropriate to produce cement on site using mixing machines rather than manual labour with shovels and buckets. Labour would be attracted to those industries and firms able to offer the highest wages on account of higher labour productivity.

Once an appropriate mixture of inputs and outputs has been selected, however, a producer must turn to absolute productive efficiency and the problem of obtaining maximum output from the mixture of resources chosen. In other words, if a house-builder decides to produce two-storey dwellings with a certain number of machines and employees, productive efficiency now refers to obtaining the maximum number of houses from those inputs. This will clearly depend upon the quality of the management, the efforts of the workforce and the quality of the inputs.

If allocative efficiency and technical efficiency are so analytically distinct, why are they combined in this chapter? This is done for two reasons. First, it is usually impossible to measure allocative and productive efficiency separately. For example, statistics for the building industry would simply show outputs and costs. Costs could be higher because of the 'wrong', allocative choice of expensive inputs and/or because inputs were not productively employed to their maximum potential. Second, it can be argued that, even theoretically, there can be no basic distinction between allocative and productive efficiency. Looking at the labour force, for example, the 'correct' allocative choice of numbers of employees to match the availability of machines and buildings may have been made at prevailing wages and prices, but the workforce may not be fully utilised in production. This would be viewed as productive (or 'X'-) inefficiency by Leibenstein (1981), but in a quite different way by De Alessi (1983). Instead of being seen as sloppy management or shirking by the workforce (Leibenstein), De Alessi would interpret the low productivity of labour as being a result of the wrong allocative choices having been made at the contracting and monitoring stages of employment. Thus workforces respond to their contracts in a quite rational allocative way, since shirking on the job involves insufficient penalty under prevailing contracts. If on-the-job leisure is 'free' to the worker, why should more work effort be offered? The management have simply chosen to offer workers the 'wrong price' for on-the-job leisure. The effort that is put into alternative contracts by management should simply be viewed as just another input, according to De Alessi, along with labour and machines. If the wrong *allocative* choice of contractual effort is made, then this will show up as high costs and (apparently) as low absolute productive efficiency.

For these two good reasons, the third section of this chapter considers allocative and productive efficiency simultaneously. The shape of this chapter sets the pattern for the remaining chapters, with the exception of the final chapter. The official Soviet position in regard to allocative and productive efficiency in a centrally planned economy is explained. This position is exposed to a Kornai-type critique, and then empirical evidence is taken from the Soviet Union in an attempt to judge whether the official Soviet view or the Kornai view is a more accurate predictor of Soviet performance.

PLANNED PRODUCTION – THE OFFICIAL SOVIET VIEW

After chapter 1 it will be of no surprise for readers to learn that the official Soviet view is that central planning is capable of achieving the higher levels of efficiency in allocation and production, although the next section below will provide a contrasting Kornai view.

With regard to allocation, advocates of central planning could cite three main reasons for the superiority of central planning. First, resource allocation is *centrally controlled* and the central authorities are able to transmit *their* priorities into production instructions, although the central authorities will not deliberately ignore individual consumer preferences, if they can be accommodated at little cost. Central control is considered to be a great advantage and the preferences of the central authorities under planning generally replace the preferences of individual consumers under capitalism. Central resource allocation according to planned priorities is considered to be advantageous because it can take account of long-term development needs. It can ignore consumer demands for such items as fashionable goods that may be considered frivolous, and resource allocation under capitalism is in any case influenced (some would say determined) by monopolistic producers as well as by so-called sovereign consumers.

Second, resource allocation is *centrally co-ordinated*, as explained in chapter 1 above. Ex-ante resource allocation is supposed to achieve the internal consistency of plans so that the plans for one industry are never dislocated by shortages of inputs from another. This co-ordination should mean that Soviet industry should be able to enjoy economies of scale and avoid the 'wasteful' duplication of capacity that occurs under capitalism wherever the competitive process is active.

Third, central resource allocation is supposed to *internalise* costs and benefits that would otherwise lie outside the ambit of a decentralised enterprise. For example, underground railways in cities impose external costs and benefits for industry, government and individuals. The construction of new Metros for many large Soviet cities after 1985 is justified in terms of avoiding road traffic congestion and delays, even though each Metro system can be expected to make large financial deficits for the ministry.

In theory, this principle of social cost–benefit analysis can be extended to other industries, too. For example, where central planners are responsible for the co-ordination of outputs in different industries, they may realise that the pollution of the atmosphere and the water supply by one industry interferes with the output of agriculture and fishing, or that pollution makes it difficult to attract key workers to an area with a generally poor environment. The Soviet government ought, in theory, to be in a position to pay more attention to atmospheric pollution from its factories than a Western firm, which would be reluctant to bear voluntarily the costs of pollution control, which could enable a competitor to undercut its prices. Indeed Soviet enterprises participate in a range of 'external' activities that few capitalist firms could match, providing housing, transport, kindergartens, recreation, holidays, health care and financial services for employees. It is argued that these activities are theoretically easier to co-ordinate under central planning for enterprises, ministries and the state as a whole. Of course, theory is not practice, and the Soviet economy has experienced environmental disasters and an absence of co-ordination on many occasions, perhaps the most spectacular instance being the disaster at the nuclear power station near Chernobyl in the Ukraine in April 1986.

In relation to production, central planning is concerned with (a) collecting information as an aid to deciding what to produce, and (b) ensuring that enterprises actually produce the quantities chosen. The Soviet authorities would claim that their system offers genuine advantages for each of these processes. It is argued, for example, that the virtual abolition of property incomes (see chapter 2 above) and the state's ownership of the means of production generates a collective attitude to work, a sense of 'team spirit' that compares favourably with feelings of alienation and exploitation under capitalism. If this were the case, the behaviour of Soviet planners, ministries, enterprises and employees could be expected to be less opportunistic, and processes (a) and (b) would be characterised by candour, conscientious effort, and therefore higher productive efficiency. Supervisors at all levels of the hierarchy of industrial control would not have to monitor their subordinates strictly, since they should feel that they are 'working for themselves'. Horizontal or self-monitoring dispels the need for vertical monitoring from the hierarchy.

Paradoxically, however, the authorities could claim that under central planning they are in a stronger position to enforce whatever vertical monitoring is needed. They have access to *two* channels of information and instruction in the formal industrial chain of control and in the Party –

and it is easy to legislate for more work effort. For example, in September 1985 two public holidays, Constitution Day and Revolution Day, were declared work days. In addition there are a number of control devices borrowed from the West which may be expected to yield better results under central planning. For example, work study or 'Taylorism' was avidly seized on by the Soviet planners in an attempt to increase work effort, giving birth to the NOT (Nauchnaya Organizatsiya Truda, or the Scientific Organisation of Labour) movement of the 1930s, which is reflected today in the universal application of work 'norms' in production. Another example would be the adoption of the multidivisional form implicit in the association movement (see chapter 1 above), which allows central planners to observe and compare the productive efficiency of equivalent production plants at different locations.

So the official Soviet view on productive efficiency has it both ways: less formal control over production is needed under central planning, but the control that is exerted can be more effective. These assertions must now be exposed to a Kornai-type criticism.

PLANNED PRODUCTION – THE KORNAI VIEW

In contrast with the smooth industrial administration portrayed by the Soviet authorities, a Kornai perspective would see the centrally planned economy as a series of complex vertical hierarchies with different levels separated by distance, in both the physical and communications senses. This distance inhibits the efforts of those higher up the hierarchy to monitor the activities of those lower down, and the outcome is soft constraints or weak penalties (rewards) for bad (good) performance.

Before looking at the implications of soft budget and administrative constraints, it should be noted that in the Soviet Union three other factors besides the communications 'distance' between planners and the planned (see chapter 1) have contributed to their softness. First, and despite efforts at economic reform, *gross-output targets* remain the dominant success indicator for Soviet enterprises and ministries. This implies that enterprises may inflate their demands for inputs beyond profitable levels in their attempts to raise gross output. Second, input and output targets are not calculated in some objective way at the centre and then passed down the hierarchy to enterprises. Rather, they are *negotiated* with enterprises, who may be expected to 'pad' their input needs for a 'quiet life'. Third, it seems likely that adjacent levels of the hierarchy develop a sense of *co-responsibility* for enterprise performance. For example, a new factory may be planned and built on joint initiatives from the ministry (ministries), the Party and local authorities. They determine its location, buildings, technology and workforce and appoint a management team to run it. The management are charged with the task of operating the plant, but are, to some extent, able to count on the *co-operation* of at least local Party, ministry and local authority officials, if threatened with failure. It is possible to operate central planning with hard constraints in particular sectors like the Soviet defence industry, but hard constraints involve close supervision and such an administrative burden on the central authorities that it is probably not sustainable for more than a few priority sectors. Large capitalist firms in the West are massive vertical hierarchies too, but market transactions can take a lot of the pressure off the central controllers in resource allocation. Soviet planners can try to harden constraints by marking output targets up and input targets down on actual levels achieved, but this gives rise to ratchet effects and *more* 'padding' of costs (see chapter 1 above).

As was also explained in chapter 1, relatively soft constraints create a state of chronic excess demand as enterprises procure inputs, relatively uninhibited by cost penalties. Although enterprises may be able to negotiate reductions in higher output targets, the Soviet system does penalise plan underfulfilment more than it rewards overfulfilment. This asymmetry of rewards and penalties means that enterprises become risk-averse and *hoard* materials, rather than convert them into gross output, just in case supplies are subsequently disrupted. The planners may try to discourage such hoarding and harden the budget constraint by increasing output targets by a certain proportion, but this has the effect of creating more 'slack' in enterprises loath to overfulfil plans and risk higher targets next year.

These phenomena of relatively soft constraints, excess demand and a suction economy have implications for allocative and productive efficiency. Soft constraints interfere with allocative efficiency because enterprises experiencing excess demand for their products have little incentive to cater either for the needs of the central planners or individual consumers and other buying enterprises. This implies two things: first, enterprises will produce undemanded outputs, and second, they will leave other demands unsatisfied.

In the first case, unwanted production occurs when, because of communications 'distance', physical output plans are specified in insufficient detail. (For example, the 'big nail' story in the Soviet Union mentioned in chapter 1, which began as a cartoon in the journal *Krokodil*, has now assumed almost legendary proportions in the West (see Miller, 1984). Here, a nail factory's output plan denominated in tons of nails is satisfied by the production of one enormous nail!) This leads to the so-called *'assortment' problem*, or the inability of the planners to secure the mix of production they desire, and allocative inefficiency occurs in the form of discrepancies between the planned and actual mix of production.

In the second instance, even if planned production is achieved, this may not coincide with the demands of individual consumers and other enterprises. This constitutes a kind of allocative inefficiency which the Soviet authorities, with their emphasis on *planner* sovereignty, would play down. Nevertheless if it does occur, they must expect to have to contend with the pressures that excess individual demands create. These pressures will tend to manifest themselves in the form of black markets and private incomes as the informal sector responds to excess demands for goods not supplied by the state. In addition, excess demand for state produce will tend to encourage fringe benefits, perquisites, bribes, price premia and other devices designed to ration out inputs or finished goods that experience shortage.

Thus soft constraints imply allocative inefficiency in the form of production, which may be unwanted by the central planners and/or unwanted by individual firms and citizens. Administrations cannot cope with the complexity of detailed decisions and (in the Western sense of the word) 'irrational' prices prevent the market mechanism from taking over effectively. In chapter 1 it was explained that Soviet prices were intended for use as yardsticks in order to add together quantities of unlike items such as milk and beef in state agriculture and in order to achieve a desired pattern of *income distribution*. So, for example, cheap bread influences the real incomes of workers, although all subsidies must be paid for out of taxes elsewhere.

Soviet prices are not designed to deal with resource-allocation decisions, but if the central planners are unable to administer detailed allocations like individual bread consumption, then buyers must choose in the light of prevailing prices. Thus, if the price of bread does not even cover the cost of the grain that goes into it, farmers may buy bread instead of grain and feed that to the pigs. If enterprises are rewarded to some extent according to their profits, they will tend to produce outputs and buy inputs according to their relative prices. Project planners and engineers who must design dams and railways cannot make 'rational' investment decisions without central direction or prices that reflect relative scarcities.

Soft constraints also impair productive efficiency. On the face of it, shortages should encourage enterprises to husband their resources carefully, and with gross-output targets all input capacity should be utilised fully to secure bonus payments. As explained above, however, the structure of rewards and penalties is asymmetrical and encourages risk-aversion, so inputs are hoarded. Although central plans are adjusted for consistency in advance, the planners cannot forecast the future perfectly. Supply uncertainties arise and enterpises cushion their positions by hoarding inputs paid for out of soft budgets. High-cost enterprises are kept in operation by subsidies and soft loans financed out of the profits of low-cost enterprises. Thus the paradox is created whereby shortage and excess *demand* outside the enterprise is matched by hoarding and excess *supply* within it. Indeed, the two phenomena feed on each other.

So Kornai would predict that enterprises with soft budgets will hoard all inputs, and soft administration yields the same outcome. Stocks of materials and finished goods will be high and plant capacity will not be fully utilised. In the case of inputs bought in from other enterprises where hoarding is not possible, enterprises might resort to self-production in small in-house workshops which involves the sacrifice of all scale economies. Labour is a uniquely human input and the hoarding of employees for peak production can demoralise a workforce, leading to poor workmanship, lateness, absenteeism and alcoholism.

ACTUAL SOVIET PRODUCTIVE PERFORMANCE

It has been seen in the previous two sections that the official and Kornai views of Soviet allocative and productive efficiency are diametrically opposed to one another, and it is the purpose of this section to see which predicts more accurately. Apart from a few ingenious attempts by economists to separate allocative and productive efficiency, it will be necessary to resort to synthetic measures. For example, some time ago Campbell (1967, pp. 150–2) constructed 'materials conversions ratios', which were intended to isolate productive efficiency by relating the output of electricity to a given input of fuel, or the output of metal castings to given quantities of sheet metal. These physical comparisons between Soviet and US industry were supposed to avoid the problem of different resource endowments in the two countries, and they came out in favour of Kornai's prediction of low productive efficiency under central planning. Although central planning should economise on stock-holding by planning and sequencing operations, Campbell (1958) also found that the Soviet economy devoted relatively more of its resources to current stocks. Ofer (1973) reports the relative technical efficiency of the Soviet retailing industry however, which has fewer employees than retailing in Western countries at comparable levels of development. Centrally planned retailing enjoys substantial economies by avoiding the 'duplication' of similar competitive stores, but Pryor (1985, pp. 212–15) has shown that the labour resources saved in production are almost exactly matched by the time wasted by Soviet shoppers searching out and queuing for supplies. An econometric study of productive efficiency in the Soviet cotton industry by Danilin et al. (1985) showed that it varied between different factories very little from Soviet 'best practice' levels, but international comparisons were not possible. Desai and Martin (1983) found that in 1955 around 3 per cent more output could have been achieved among eight branches of Soviet industry by switching resources to branches with the highest efficiency, but by 1975 their 'gap' had increased to about 10 per cent. Again, international comparisons were not possible, and Desai and Martin's study could not entirely separate technical efficiency from allocative influences.

The separation of production from allocation is a general problem, as was explained at length at the start of this chapter. The rest of this section therefore considers technical and allocative efficiency together in general terms and then in two case-studies, foreign trade and agriculture.

We begin with a general view, and try to judge the efficiency of Soviet production and allocation by examining factor productivity or the value of output per unit of labour or capital. There are two fundamental problems with such comparisons across countries, however. First, the values (prices) of goods and services in a centrally planned economy are largely determined by the preferences of the central authorities and not by individual consumers. Second, resource endowments may differ, and one would expect higher capital (labour) productivity in an economy with relative labour (capital) abundance. Thus it would be easy to pick capital-intensive industries in the Soviet Union (like the railway network, for example) and demonstrate the higher productivity of track and rolling-stock in terms of passenger and ton-miles of output (see Campbell, 1974, pp 149–53) or low labour productivity in relatively labour-intensive industries such as Soviet agriculture or coal-mining (see Campbell, 1974, pp. 109–13). Overall, however, it has been found across all industries that the amount of *extra* capital required to produce an additional unit of output (i.e. incremental capital–output ratios) does not differ significantly between the USA and USSR (see Cohn, 1982, p. 169), although *trends* in *average* capital productivity are poor relative to the West (see chapters 6 and 8 below). Regarding labour productivity, Hanson (1981, p. 193) found that Soviet manning levels in thirteen imported chemical plants were between 1.5 and 1.7 times normal Western levels. Cohn (1982, p. 173) reports low levels of Soviet labour productivity between 1974 and 1978, and Soviet official statistics no longer show Soviet labour productivity as catching up on US levels, despite the release of labour from agriculture (see table 3.1).

Despite these trends, in the strategic programme of the CPSU announced on 15 October 1985 it was planned that industrial output would be *doubled* by the year 2000, largely on account of an increase in labour productivity of up to 150 per cent (an annual compound rate of over 6 per cent). It is currently increasing at an annual rate less than 2 per cent (see Cohn, 1982, p. 173).

Comparisons of aggregate *combined* labour and capital productivity for

Table 3.1 Labour productivity in agriculture and industry, USSR as a percentage of the USA

Year	*Labour productivity (%)*	
	Industry	
1950	less than	30
1960		44
1970	approximately	53
1980	more than	55
1982	more than	55
	Agriculture	
1966-82	approximately	20–25

Source: Narodnoye khozyaystvo, 1982, p. 57.

the USA and USSR have been attempted, but the resulting indices reflect all kinds of assumptions regarding the form of production functions and weightings. For what they are worth, these studies suggest Soviet productivity per factor input to lie in a range between 28 per cent and 56 per cent of the US level (see Buck, 1982, p. 138).

Apart from comparative statistics, however, it is possible to examine the allocative and productive efficiency of the Soviet economy in relation to its own standards rather than risk doubtful comparisons with the West. From our standpoint, it is easy to criticise Soviet resource allocation in terms of its failure to satisfy individual consumer demands. For example black market activities are surveyed in chapter 4 and also in chapter 2. They seem to demonstrate that state industry is not satisfying the demands of consumers. Such a view is supported by anecdotes concerning resource misallocation. The Soviet motor industry seems incapable of producing wiper-blades to match the number of cars, and *Izvestia* (18 July 1985, p. 3) reported how the state record store 'Melodia' in Moscow's Kalinin Prospekt is heavily stocked with seven-inch, 45 r.p.m 'extended play' records, while there is demand only for twelve-inch albums. Binyon (1983, p. 161) noted that one town had a glut of 40-watt, but a shortage of 100-watt light-bulbs, while a neighbouring town had the opposite problem. He also provided one of the more colourful anecdotes (Binyon, 1983, p. 170): 'And the most painful shortage of all is the lack of toilet paper, a commodity that has achieved an almost mystic value to those who tire of the discomfort and irony of using *Pravda*.'

Anecdotal evidence may be considered as cheap and partial, and may in any case be irrelevant to resource allocation in relation to central priorities, not individual demands, although by seeking to fix both quantities *and* prices at the centre, it is unlikely that markets will clear unless perfectly co-ordinated (see Kornai, 1985, p. 23). It makes more sense to evaluate Soviet resource allocation not by reference to individual demands, but in relation to the extent to which production reflects *central* preferences and plan intentions.

On this criterion, resource misallocation is occurring on a wide scale. Bornstein (1985, pp. 14–17) shows how ministries have been unable to obtain the assortment of output from the *enterprises* that they demand, and how (pp. 11–14) the quality of industrial output has been consistently misgraded to higher categories. Central preferences have also changed frequently, disrupting the allocation of resources. In a Soviet economist's survey of plan changes in 175 enterprises over the period 1970–8,Levine reports: 'Of his almost 1,600 observations, 63 percent involved significant changes in the plan, during the plan year; 37 percent were decreases in plan targets, and 25 percent were increases in plan targets. Failure to achieve plan fulfilment was reported in only 6 percent of the cases, whereas in actuality, 32 percent of the cases failed to fulfil the original versions of their plans' (1982, p164).

Hanson (1984b, p. 40) reports significant amounts of lost production as a result of the unauthorised absences and materials shortages that Kornai would associate with a soft budget regime. Finally, it is obvious that the central authorities have been unable to obtain planned outputs at the aggregate level from the *ministries*. Figure 3.1 is intended to present a balanced picture from a fairly typical sector, the Soviet fuel industry. Although the natural gas industry has fulfilled the targets of the central authorities, this cannot be said of the oil or coal industries, and even more dramatic pictures of underfulfilment could have been drawn from steel or fertiliser production, still high-priority sectors compared with light industry, and services such as retailing.

Although this is interesting and suggests low Soviet levels of allocative and productive efficiency, we have no way of providing realistic comparisons with Western industries at equivalent levels of development. The next two sections therefore examine case-studies in more detail.

Foreign Trade

On the face of it there can be no justification for granting a separate section to foreign trade. Foreign tastes may be unpredictable and currencies and other barriers to international trade produce additional uncertainties, but these are only differences of degree compared with domestic trade. On the other hand, foreign trade provides an area in which different economic

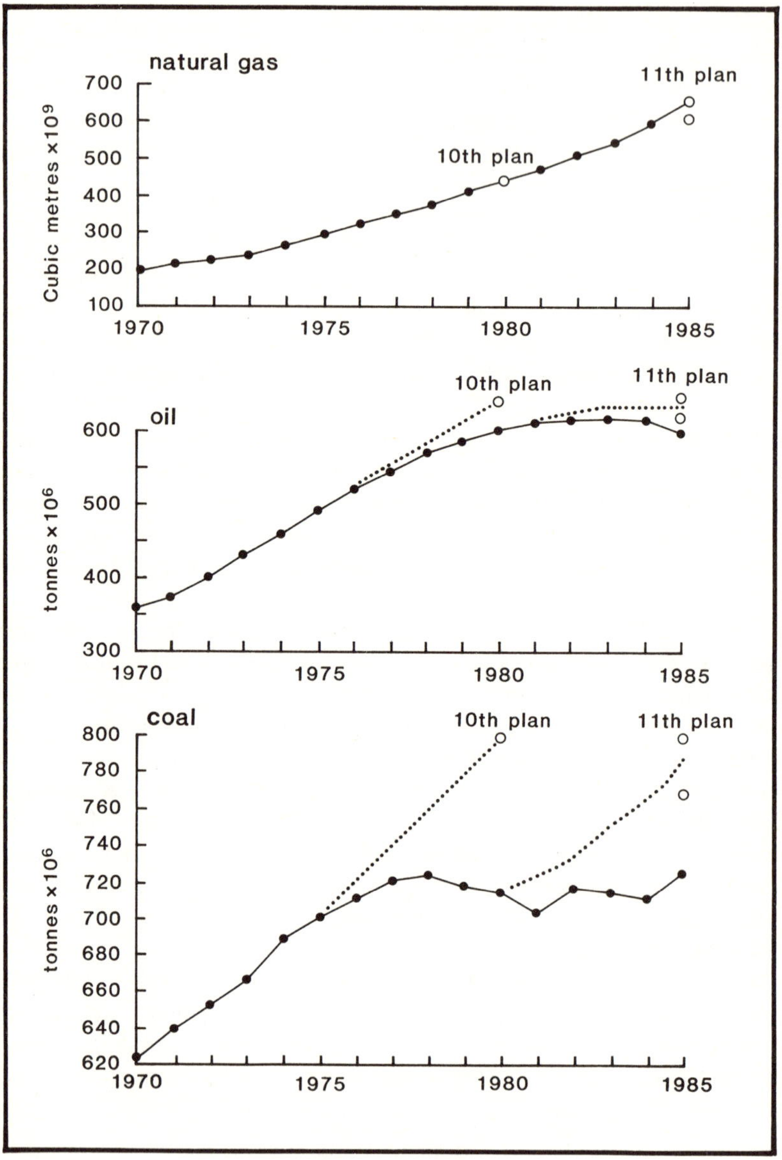

Figure 3.1 Soviet production of the major fossil fuels and five-year plans. *Sources*: various numbers of *Narodnoye khozyaystvo SSR* and *Ekonomicheskaya gazeta*, No. 6, Feb. 1986, for 1985 data. See also Cole (1985), p. 377. *Note*: actual production is shown by unbroken lines.

systems interact with each other, and trade patterns may highlight their distinguishing characteristics. Imports may be goods that one system cannot produce for reasons of resource endowment or they may represent a relative weakness that has developed over time; exports may imply relative strengths. As with other chapters and sections, this section will examine actual Soviet foreign trade performance in the light of Kornai's theories and the contrasting Soviet official view on foreign trade. We deal with these subjects in reverse order.

Centrally planned foreign trade offers a number of advantages. The Ministry for Foreign Trade can specialise in international opportunities and transactions, while other ministries have their hands full with production and distribution. This specialist body can identify products that seem to possess a comparative advantage in international terms (e.g. through economies of scale), and stable, long-term contractual arrangements can be made with other centrally planned economies or Western corporations. In these arrangements the Ministry for Foreign Trade, or its subsidiary Foreign Trade Corporation (FTC), can wield substantially more bargaining power than individual enterprises or branch ministries. To reinforce their view, the Soviet authorities could point to the international marketing divisions of multinational enterprises (MNEs) and the general trading companies (GTCs) like Mitsubishi and Mitsui in Japan. These institutions specialise in foreign trade and deal in the products that other divisions or companies design and produce. They can therefore be seen as Western efforts to exploit the benefits of specialist foreign trade institutions. In relation to a planned economy's imports, FTCs can observe the priorities established by the central authorities in relation to their overall plan.

As usual, Kornai provides an entirely opposite perspective. With relatively hard budgets and excess supplies in the West, capitalist corporations are anxious to discover and exploit overseas markets offering the best price for their products. If necessary, they may be willing to re-design processes and products specifically to meet the needs of foreign buyers. It is likely therefore that producers in buyers' markets will have to establish close relations between their production and marketing departments, especially for technologically sophisticated goods. This implies the integration of marketing and production and no separation into divisions or companies for foreign trade.

By way of contrast, Kornai sees centrally planned economies as being characterised by relatively soft budget and administrative constraints and excess demands at all levels, including excess demands for imported foreign goods. Given excess demands for domestic production too, it is unlikely that enterprises and ministries will volunteer goods for export in return. Their soft constraints generate uninhibited demands for all materials, labour and equipment, but other enterprises experience the same excess demands, leading to the diversion of inputs and supply uncertainties. Given supply uncertainties, and perhaps the need to offer some goods as barter in order to sweeten the price offered to secure input supplies, above-plan production may be concealed and hoarded rather than offered for export. Enterprises and ministries are unlikely to offer to tailor their products for overseas sale, given that they are already experiencing excess demand for existing products at home. Central planners may succeed in generating a surplus for export only in those industries where they can impose hard budgets or otherwise penalise poor performance severely. Given the complexity of monitoring performance by administrative methods, the central authorities are likely to concentrate their efforts on homogeneous goods like gold, oil, gas and other minerals, where quality variations are easy to monitor.

Unfortunately, an economic system that generates an excess demand for imports and a reluctance to export is inviting a balance of payments deficit and currency depreciation. Devaluation is, however, an unattractive prospect for a state that is trying to keep down the cost of its imports and to maintain the impression that its living standards are high. (For example, an average monthly wage of 200 roubles represents £200 per month at an official exchange rate of 1 : 1, and £50 per month at four roubles to the pound, the approximate black market rate in 1984.) FTCs may choke off import demands by forbidding enterprises and ministries to buy directly from overseas, and rouble rates of exchange with hard currencies may be kept artificially high. If this is the case, however, overseas exporters may respond by inflating their prices to compensate for the unconvertible currency or undesirable goods offered in exchange.

If one turns to the *evidence* on trade that may shed light on these competing hypotheses, one first notes that there have been universal trends *away* from specialised foreign trade institutions outside the Soviet Union (see Brada and Jackson, 1978). MNEs in the West have gradually abandoned their international marketing divisions, giving product divisions their own marketing functions, and in Japan the GTCs have declined, with large manufacturers like Sony, Toyota and Nissan now exporting directly. CMEA countries other than the Soviet Union have gradually diversified their exports into more sophisticated products, simultaneously decentralising their foreign trade institutions, drawing them closer to the manufacturer. In Hungary in 1985, enterprises were permitted to export directly to the West and were rewarded with permission to raise their domestic prices as much as they had successfully raised their hard-currency prices.

The significance of foreign trade to the Soviet Union should not, however, be overemphasised. The USSR has about 5.8 per cent of the total population of the world and about twice that share of the total world production of goods and services. In contrast, in the last fifteen years its share of all exports in world trade has been steady at about 4 per cent and its imports have been about 3.5 per cent of all imports. Imports and exports are each equivalent in value only to about 5–6 per cent of the total production of goods and services in the USSR. The comparatively small size of trade (in terms of value) is illustrated by the fact that total Soviet foreign trade is not much larger in value than that of the Netherlands.

Soviet foreign trade is relatively limited in scale for at least three distinct major reasons. First, very large size, other things being equal, minimises the need to trade, a feature shared with the USA, China and India, all of which have low import coefficients. Secondly, Soviet leaders have been preoccupied with the prospect of hostile neighbours, the risk of economic sanctions and the threat of military attack, reasons enough to encourage considerable economic self-sufficiency at both national and regional levels. Third, since the USSR has a centrally planned economy, imports and exports have to be allowed for in national plans. It is not easy, however, and in some cases not even possible at all, to allow for, let alone control, the prices and requirements of Soviet products in foreign countries, and to guarantee the availability of products that need to be imported. The co-ordination of plans within CMEA, however ensures a reasonably captive and predictable market for much of Soviet trade.

Soviet foreign trade with CMEA and the West will be briefly described below, and then an analysis of official and Kornai interpretations will follow. The Soviet Union is so large and diverse and its economy so varied that the composition of Soviet foreign trade cannot be described in simple terms. Virtually all broad classes of products are both imported and exported. Moreover, during quite short periods of time marked changes have taken place in emphasis. Contrary to what one might have expected with the emergence of an industrial giant, primary products account for about two-thirds of the value of Soviet exports, while manufactures make up about half of the value of imports.

Eight categories of products, which together account for nearly all of Soviet foreign trade, are ordered in table 3.2 according to the ratio of imports to exports of each class in 1983. Thus food comes first, since it accounted for over 20 per cent of the value of imports in that year, but only 1.5 percent of exports (a ratio of about 13 : 1). Fuels are last with a ratio of about 1 : 10. Thus the products for which the USSR most depends on foreign suppliers head the list, whereas its principal export by far, fuels, comes last. Some items are not included in the eight sectors in table 3.2, among them trade in arms and in gold, both of which are of considerable international importance, although they do not reflect Soviet economic performance in a straightforward way. The position of food at the head of

Table 3.2 Soviet imports and exports by major classes, percentages of total value in selected years from 1950 to 1983

	1950	*1960*	*1965*	*1970*	*1975*	*1980*	*1983*
Imports							
Food	17.5	12.1	20.2	15.8	23.0	24.2	20.5
Consumer goods	7.4	17.2	14.2	18.3	12.9	12.1	11.5
Machinery	21.5	29.8	33.4	35.5	33.9	33.9	38.2
Textiles	7.7	6.5	4.4	4.8	2.4	2.2	2.1
Chemicals	6.9	6.0	6.2	5.7	4.7	5.3	4.6
Ores, metals	15.0	16.8	9.8	9.6	11.6	10.8	8.8
Wood-paper	3.8	1.9	1.9	2.1	2.2	2.0	1.3
Fuels	11.8	4.2	2.5	2.0	3.9	3.0	5.6
Exports							
Food	20.6	13.1	8.4	8.4	4.8	1.9	1.5
Consumer goods	4.9	2.9	2.4	2.7	3.1	2.5	1.8
Machinery	11.8	20.5	20.0	21.5	18.7	15.8	12.5
Textiles	11.2	6.4	5.1	3.4	2.9	1.9	1.4
Chemicals	4.3	3.5	3.6	3.5	3.5	3.3	3.1
Ores, metals	11.3	20.4	21.6	19.6	14.3	8.8	7.5
Wood-paper	3.1	5.5	7.3	6.5	5.7	4.1	2.8
Fuels	3.9	16.2	17.2	15.6	31.4	46.9	53.7

The official Soviet trade statistics omit important items like diamonds, platinum and defence goods.
Source: Various years of *Vneshnyaya torgovlya SSSR*.

the list underlines the disappointing performance of Soviet agriculture, which is discussed below.

In spite of attempts to increase the availability and raise the quality of consumer manufactures, the USSR has been importing substantial quantities of consumer goods for several decades. In relation to the total home production of such goods, however, the amounts are small, and there is no justification for inferring that the consumer manufacturing sector is unsatisfactory solely on the basis of this evidence.

The same is not true for the trade in capital goods, defined broadly in Soviet publications as 'machines, equipment and means of transport'. Ever since 1928, when the first five-year plan was launched, great emphasis has been put on the importance of the engineering industry. For a socialist country to be mature, independent and prosperous, it should have the means to supply many of its own producer goods, yet in virtually every year since 1960 the machinery category has accounted for between 30 per cent and 40 per cent of the total value of Soviet imports. Whereas most of the food imported comes from developed 'capitalist' countries (particularly the USA, Canada, Australia, France, Argentina), most of the machinery is imported from CMEA partners in East Europe, although a considerable proportion comes from West Europe and Japan. East Europe and certain developing countries are the main markets for Soviet exports of machinery, but the poor quality, reliability and suitability of the products of the Soviet engineering industry presumably account for the lack of enthusiasm to buy them in the Western industrial countries.

The four categories of textiles, chemicals, ores and metals, and wood-paper are comparatively small sectors of foreign trade and are all roughly balanced. A gradual decline in the share of raw materials among Soviet exports may, however, be noted.

Since the early 1980s more than half of the value of Soviet exports has been accounted for by fuel and energy, the category consisting almost entirely of oil, natural gas, coal and electricity. The sudden rise to prominence of fuels can be related to a considerable extent to the worldwide rises in oil prices in 1973–4 and in the late 1970s. While the USSR has sold oil and oil products at favourable prices to its CMEA partners, it has been able to benefit in its sale of oil elsewhere from the oil crisis. Almost all the oil going to non-CMEA countries ends up in West Europe and Japan, although the collapse of world oil prices after 1985 may upset this trend.

From the evidence in table 3.2 it is clear that fuels are a vital item in Soviet foreign trade, with oil in 1983 accounting for 41.6 per cent of the value of all Soviet exports and natural gas for 9.3 per cent. The dependence on oil and oil products is particularly marked and there are at least two reasons for concern here. First, the gradual decline in oil prices in the 1980s will be worrying to Soviet planners. Second, the failure to expand oil production as planned for nearly a decade is even more serious. Data for 1985 (*Ekonomicheskaya gazeta* No. 6, February 1986) show that oil production at 595 million tonnes was considerably down on that for 1984, while 1984 production was lower than the peak of 616 million tonnes in 1983.

Can natural gas fill the gap, if the surplus of oil available for export drops? Certainly there is no shortage of natural gas in the USSR, but the large deposits are a long way from the western boundary of the USSR. The rest of Europe can absorb large quantities of natural gas and the construction of pipelines to deliver it is progressing. Oil, however, has advantages over natural gas in both its wider range of uses and its transportability by sea. So serious has been the shortfall in oil production that substantial quantities have been imported from Libya and smaller amounts from Saudi Arabia in the last few years.

The Soviet economy is fairly well insulated from major upheavals in the

Table 3.3 Value of total Soviet foreign trade (imports plus exports)

Average annual value of total trade (million roubles)	*Percentage of total trade with:*				*Year*
	Socialist Countries		*Capitalist Countries*		
	CMEA	*Other*	*Industrial*	*Developing*	
6,669	54.5	23.1	16.1	6.3	1950–60
15,552	57.2	11.1	20.1	11.6	1961–70
53,605	53.0	5.2	28.9	12.9	1971–80
109,739	47.6	5.2	32.2	15.0	1981
119,576	49.1	5.2	31.6	14.1	1982
127,476	51.2	4.8	30.1	13.9	1983

Soviet trade statistics omit important items such as diamonds, platinum and defence goods. In addition, the fairly arbitrary prices applied to CMEA trade distort its value compared with hard-currency trade.
CMEA includes Cuba and Viet Nam.
Source: Various numbers of *Vneshnyaya torgovlya SSSR*, 1956–83.

world economy such as the 1973–4 oil crisis and the recession of the 1980s on account of its low import coefficient and the reliance on fellow socialist countries for much of the total trade (see table 3.3). Before the Second World War most Soviet foreign trade was with the leading industrial countries of the time, especially the UK, Germany and the USA. By 1950, when the allegiance of various socialist countries had been sorted out, with Yugoslavia taking an independent line, but China entering the Soviet bloc, over 80 per cent of all Soviet foreign trade was with socialist partners, none of which, except the German Democratic Republic (as Germany), had been a partner of significance previously. After the decline of trade with China, from about 1960, dependence on socialist partners declined and the role of other partners increased. By 1980–1 almost half of the value of Soviet foreign trade was with non-socialist countries, the 'developed capitalist group' accounting for a third of all trade. Soviet intervention in Afghanistan provoked varying reactions in the West including sanctions, and may have persuaded Soviet leaders that they and their CMEA partners in Europe had gone too far in committing their fortunes to the fluctuations of the world economy. Several long-term agreements have been worked out to increase again the mutual interdependence of CMEA members and the effect seems to have been felt quickly, since all CMEA partners (including Cuba and Viet Nam) accounted for 52.1 per cent of total Soviet trade in 1984 compared with 47.6 per cent in 1981. There is frequent reference in Soviet material to the value of the international division of labour, but such CMEA trade will not ensure overnight the supplies of food and sophisticated capital goods needed by the USSR.

What conclusions can be drawn from this description of Soviet foreign trade in relation to the official and Kornai views? There are two. First, centrally planned trade *with CMEA* countries is substantial at over half of total Soviet trade, and this trade conforms largely with the official view above, although it could be described as foreign trade between pairs of 'excess demand' economies. CMEA trade (and most Soviet trade with other countries, too) is obviously influenced by political considerations, however. In the long run, trade links with countries with which politically motivated trade has been developed may prove the most desirable on economic grounds, too. In the short run however, better economic returns could be secured by the USSR selling its exports in the markets offering the highest price and buying imports from countries offering the lowest. The short-run loss of net foreign trade earnings brought about by politically motivated trade is linked with the Soviet Union's reliance on barter, 'buy-back' and 'counter-trade' deals (see below).

Second, Soviet trade *with the West* has generally conformed with the predictions suggested by Kornai's work. Excess demands for Western imports have been limited by the FTC's restrictions, and Soviet exports have generally been of the reluctant 'make-weight' variety, consisting largely of primary products. Even the export of primary products requires some conscious planning, however. The steady increase in primary exports has been possible only with the improvement of transport facilities, especially seaports, many of which have been modernised to handle containers. One reason for constructing the BAM (Baykal-Amur Magistral) railway to run parallel to the Trans-Siberian line in East Siberia and the Far East has been to speed up and increase the flow of goods between the western and central parts of the USSR and the Pacific coast. In European USSR, several oil and gas pipelines have been built specifically to take fuel to both East and West European customers.

Soviet planners do not appear to have been greatly concerned in the past over catering for the export sector, and cannot be said to have behaved like Western firms with hard budgets desperately designing new products or seeking new overseas markets for survival. To be sure, at various times food (in the 1920s), raw materials (especially in the 1930s and immediately after the Second World War), and more recently fuels have been exported in large quantities, but only items such as furs, crabmeat and other luxury goods have been specially prepared for Western markets. One bizarre export for an officially atheist country was reported in the *Financial Times* (7 June 1982): Christmas cards! More recently there have been conscious efforts to improve the quality of potential export items, while a top priority now must be somehow to cope with the internal oil crisis, preserving oil for export by using coal, natural gas and nuclear power where possible instead of oil, as for example in the generation of electricity. It may be noted, also, that the reluctance to allow the widespread ownership of private (personal) cars has saved oil. More than a quarter of all Soviet oil is exported. Very approximately, a level of car ownership in the USSR similar to that in West Europe would just about use up the oil exported.

Given the need to economise on hard-currency imports, the FTC has often been driven to arrange barter-type deals with overseas exporters, which seem consistent with a Kornai explanation. Thus suppliers of gas pipeline technology in the German Federal Republic have agreed to take gas supplies in exchange for their equipment, and 'counter-trade' deals have required Western exporters to accept Soviet goods to the value of a sale denominated in hard currency. Such trades are rarely optimal. Western exporters inflate their selling prices to take account of the (often low-quality) goods offered in return and both parties suffer. As with politically motivated trade, barter implies that Soviet exports (imports) are rarely sold (bought) in those markets offering the highest (lowest) price. Brada (1974) estimated that income lost in this way amounted to up to 8.6 per cent of GNP in Hungary's case, although no calculations for Western countries were presented for the purposes of comparison. Murrell (1981) demonstrated that the foreign trade characteristics of CMEA countries compared with the West were as follows (p. 355): a slowness to react to changes in world demand conditions, a handicap in sophisticated products for which innovations are important, and the choice of goods for export determined according to artificially low wages or temporary excess supply in the home market. Perhaps significantly, Hungary was seen to assume the characteristics of Western foreign trade when the budget constraint facing Hungarian industry was 'hardened' after 1968.

Although conscious central planning and a Kornai interpretation of Soviet foreign trade are *both* correct, in the senses described above, the long-run foreign trade prospects of the USSR seem reasonably bright. The country has about 6 per cent of the world's population, but (Cole, 1983) very roughly 15 per cent of the bioclimatic resources and non-fuel minerals and 30 per cent of the more accessible energy reserves. Many of the proven and inferred mineral reserves are at present difficult to reach on account of the lack of suitable transport links in most of Siberia and the Soviet Far East region. An increasing number of countries in the Third World are industrialising, and West Europe, Japan and the USA are already heavily industrialised. Most of the countries are large net importers of primary products. Canada, Australia and Siberia are especially well endowed with regard to primary products, while enjoying the benefits of modern industry and a high level of mechanisation. If Soviet planners could remove the irritating need to be a net importer of agricultural products and if the CMEA partners of East Europe could collaborate more effectively to cope with the production of high-quality and high-technology capital goods, then an end might come to the present state of production failing to meet targets.

Soviet Agriculture

Soviet agriculture is considered separately here because of its unique character as an industry, because of its reputation as the least successful sector in the Soviet economy, but at the same time the sector that propelled Mikhail Gorbachev to power and that was largely responsible for the demise of Nikita Khrushchev. This section is intended to review the peculiar features of Soviet agriculture, to reflect on Soviet agriculture in the light of the contrasting economic theories of the Soviet authorities and János Kornai, and to provide a general evaluation of the allocative and productive efficiency of Soviet agriculture with particular reference to wheat yields, which are likely to cause massive disruption in world grain markets and aid to poor countries for years to come. It will be assumed throughout that Soviet agriculture is centrally planned. State and collective farms account for about 95 per cent of the total sown area, but only about 75 per cent of all livestock, the rest being taken up by private plots tended by state farmers, collective farmers and urban households. State farms are generally larger than collective farms and offer guaranteed wages in a factory-like environment, with a director appointed from outside. Since 1966 collective farmers have received a minimum wage and pension rights like the state farmers, although the incomes of collective farm workers do fluctuate more above this minimum. A chairman is ostensibly elected by the collective, but Party and ministerial support is often needed. State procurements only account for about a third of total agricultural output. In the case of collective farms, above-procurement output can be sold on collective-farm markets at prices far above the state level.

On the face of it, the nature of agriculture as an industry should support the official view on the static efficiency of central planning, outlined in the first section of this chapter. Central planning has the ability to mobilise and co-ordinate massive resource inputs, securing economies of scale. Agriculture's share of total Soviet investment (which has itself tripled in real terms between 1965 and 1980) shows the scale of inputs to the industry (see table 3.4). Agriculture's share of investment in the twelfth five-year plan, 1986–90, is reported to be 33 per cent. These figures compare with about 5 per cent for the United States. Table 3.5 also reveals massive increases in inputs of fertiliser, tractors and land between 1960 and 1983; the increase in land is due mainly to the cultivation of the 'virgin' and 'long fallow' lands of Kazakhstan and West Siberia, which started in the mid-1950s. Besides resource mobilisa n, central planning would seem ideally placed to achieve rapid technological advance at central research institutes and to co-ordinate crop rotations and massive irrigation projects, including the possible diversion of whole rivers from the Barents to the Caspian Sea or from the Arctic Ocean to the Aral Sea (see Cole, 1984, p. 95). The latter schemes have, however, been shelved, if not abandoned, as they are extremely costly and also could produce adverse effects on climate in the Arctic.

Table 3.4 Soviet agriculture's share of total capital formation

Plan		*Percentage to agriculture*
7th (seven-year) plan,	1959–65	20
8th (five-year) plan,	1966–70	23
9th (five-year) plan,	1971–75	26
10th (five-year) plan,	1976–80	27

Source: Cole, 1984, p. 133.

Kornai's work encourages an entirely different view on centrally planned agriculture, however. Agriculture is an industry that is open to the skies, and the uncertainties of disease and climate demand quick, on-the-spot reactions to the needs (and precise timing) of fertiliser application, harvesting, machinery repairs, the protection of harvested crops from the weather, and the transport of crops and livestock. Such a delicacy of touch is difficult to achieve with central control and relatively soft constraints. Artificially low agricultural prices ensure that more than half of all collective and state farms make financial losses (Rumer, 1984, p. 29), although it is ironic to note that artificially *high* prices in the West keep many smaller farms 'profitable'. Soft budgets must result from persistent losses, however, and Ellman (1981, p. 987) reports that excess demand for farm equipment ensures that only 60–70 per cent of requisitions are supplied. Soft budgets mean low allocative and productive efficiency (see the first section of this chapter).

An appraisal of these official and Kornai views must take into account the unique agricultural resources of the Soviet Union, which are very easy to misrepresent. Overall comparisons with the United States are fruitless, given the exceptional soil and climate of the Middle West in relation to grain. In terms of rainfall, temperature and soil, it seems fairer to compare Siberia with Canada, and European and Central Asian USSR with the

Table 3.5 Trends in Soviet agriculture, 1940–83

	(1)	(2)	(3)	(4)	(5)	(6)	(7)	(8)	(9)	(10)
						Tractors			*Fertiliser*	
	Total sown area	*Total population*	*Population to sown area*	*Population employed in agriculture*	*Agricultural population as % of total employed*	*Total*	*To sown area*	*To agricultural population*	*Output*	*kg per hectare of sown area*
1940	151	194	128	39.5	50	531	3.5	13.4	760	5
1960	203	212	104	38.4	39	1,122	5.5	29.2	3,280	16
1970	207	242	117	30.2	26	1,977	9.6	65.5	13,100	63
1975	218	253	116	26.0	21	2,334	10.7	89.8	21,200	97
1980	217	265	122	22.0	16	2,562	11.8	116.5	24,770	114
1983	213	271	127	19.8	15	2,697	12.7	136.2	29,730	140

(1) Sown area (*posevnyye ploshchadi*) in millions of hectares.
(2) Total population millions.
(3) Number of persons per 100 hectares of sown area.
(4) Economically active population in agriculture in millions.
(5) Economically active population in agriculture as a percentage of total economically active population.
(6) Tractors in use in thousands.
(7) Tractors in use per thousand hectares of sown area.
(8) Tractors in use per thousand persons economically active in agriculture.
(9) Output of fertilisers in thousands of metric tons of conventional (effective) units.
(10) Kilograms of fertiliser applied per hectare of sown area.
Sources: Various years of *Narodnoye khozyaystvo SSSR* and various years of UN *Food and Agriculture Organization Yearbook*.

western half of the USA (see Cole, 1984, p. 98). Even then, however, Ellman reports that:

> only a small part of the country has the combination of soil, temperature and precipitation necessary for low cost agriculture. The USSR has by far the world's largest and best soil resources. Nevertheless, in general where the soil is excellent the rainfall is inadequate, and where the rainfall is (barely) adequate the soil is usually poor. Only about 1% of Soviet farmland (mainly the eastern coast of the Black Sea) receives 28 inches or more precipitation a year. Much of the western United States and practically all the area east of Nebraska receives more than 28 inches. Hence vast areas of the USSR are too dry for normal agriculture. (Ellman, 1984, p. 64)

At a *general* level, Soviet agriculture has been severely criticised, both inside and outside the USSR. Some 2 million farm workers in the USA in 1975 produced about one-sixth more than 20 million in the USSR (Cole, 1984, p. 138), and Milton Friedman (1984) is still proposing the 'old chestnut' that private plots in the USSR produce 26 per cent of total agricultural output from 3 per cent of the arable land. Grain harvests have been disappointingly low since 1973 in each year except 1976 and 1978, and grain imports since 1972 have increased from the USA and (latterly) Argentina, until in 1983 they amounted to over a third of domestic production. Despite massive investments (see table 3.4), the release of labour from Soviet agriculture has been disappointingly slow, with agriculture still using about 15 per cent of the total labour force in 1983.

On the other hand, gross agricultural production in 1980 exceeded that of 1960 by over 50 per cent, although that probably says more for the chronic state of the farm sector after Stalin's acute neglect of the industry; however the total population of the USSR (to be fed) grew during those two decades by nearly 25 per cent or by more than 50 million.

Table 3.6 shows the relative performance of the meat and grain sectors for the USA and USSR: two countries with populations of 231 million and 275 million respectively. The percentage of the total Soviet workforce employed in agriculture halved between 1960 and 1983 to 15 per cent, representing 19.8 million. The high productivity of private plots referred to above follows from the heavy consumption of state fodder by private livestock. Indeed it was the conscious decision of the leadership in 1972 to sustain meat production and consumption that led to subsequent imports of grain. Previously, the livestock sector had borne the burden of adjustment to poor grain harvests, but after 1972 hard currency was sacrificed to keep the livestock in feed. Massive levels of food imports by countries like the UK are not considered to be disastrous. On the other hand, Canada (with similar resource endowments to those of the USSR) has been able to increase grain *exports* over the same period and has increased its share of increasing Soviet grain *imports* from 14 per cent in

Table 3.6 Production of grain and meat, USA and USSR, 1960–82

	1960	*1965*	*1970*	*1975*	*1978*	*1979*	*1980*	*1981*	*1982*
Grain production (kilograms per capita of total population)									
USA	1,003	944	910	1,154	1,242	1,345	1,184	1,450	1,461
USSR	586	524	769	551	908	681	712	n.a.	n.a.
Meat production (kilograms per capita of total population)									
USA	71	74	110	106	112	104	107	107	103
USSR	41	43	51	59	59	58	57	57	56

Source: CIA, *Handbook of Economic Statistics*, 1983, p. 25.

1978/9 to 26 per cent in 1982/3 (see Tarrant, 1984, p. 398). Beyond these observations, however, general conclusions are difficult and it is suggested that the *wheat* sector of Soviet grain production provides a case-study that can give useful insights into Soviet agricultural efficiency.

Wheat accounts for about half of total Soviet grain output, but about 80 per cent of grain imports. Table 3.7 shows the relatively low Soviet yields and the slow rate of improvement compared with other countries. Kornai-type shortages have often been blamed for this poor performance, emphasising unreliable supplies of fertiliser and equipment, poor transport facilities and labour shortages, together with low levels of motivation on state and collective farms accustomed to soft constraints. (Certainly, Soviet attempts to reform agriculture through autonomous work-groups and the encouragement of private plots, inter-farm co-operation and agro-industrial diversification may be interpreted as attempts to harden the farm budget constraint.) Labour is still grossly underpaid on Soviet farms, presumably as a result of the artificially low price of food, and wages are not allowed to reflect the excess demand for labour on the farms. Indeed, Stuart (1984) blames low Soviet wheat yields on low farm incomes: yields tend to rise when expensive labour has to be replaced (not complemented) by machines, although the Soviet authorities would be unwilling to accept such a patronising explanation of low yields in terms of relative Soviet poverty. Of course in the West, labour is expensive, but displacement is inhibited by governments who ensure that wheat prices are artificially *high*.

Low yields are not the major cause of plan dislocation or massive grain imports into the Soviet Union, however. Rather, the *variability* of Soviet

Table 3.7 Yields of wheat in the USSR and the rest of the world (selected countries) (kilograms per hectare)

	1974–6	*1981–3*
Denmark	5,030	6,230
UK	4,390	6,160
France	4,080	5,060
Mexico	3,660	3,950
USA	1,980	2,460
Canada	1,820	2,030
World average	*1,690*	*2,030*
India	1,310	1,720
USSR	1,360	1,490

Source: Food and Agriculture Organization Yearbook, 1983, tables 16, 17

wheat yields seems to be the culprit (see Tarrant, 1984). This variability is *not* found to be a result of soft budgets on the farms, but rather of the *central decisions* to choose wheat as the most important cereal crop and to push the frontier of production into the north and east of the USSR. Wheat production is now conducted in marginal conditions where modest variations in weather at critical periods produce great variations in wheat yields and substantial repercussions for grain imports, world prices and thus for poor countries relying on food aid.

To be fair, however, one ought to concede that soil and climatic conditions are often unique and make it difficult to isolate the effect of central planning. The low level and variability of Soviet wheat yields are largely attributable to the cultivation of *spring wheat* in the marginal conditions experienced in Kazakhstan and West Siberia. Spring wheat has a very short growing season that can be easily disrupted by fairly minor, temporary variations in temperature and rainfall. In the case of Kazakhstan, spring wheat is grown on the 'dry margin' where precipitation is on the verge of being too low, as in parts of Australia. The right-hand side of table 3.8 shows, however, that, before wheat-yield statistics for Kazakhstan were suspended in 1974, average yields in that republic were 42 per cent below Australian levels and 50 per cent more variable, in terms of standard deviations. Spring wheat in West Siberia is on the 'cold margin' of cultivation, as in Canada, but table 3.8 shows yields to be 52 per cent lower and 32 per cent more variable.

The central decisions that have been blamed for variable cereal yields in the USSR can be traced back to Lysenko's advice on genetics to Stalin and

Table 3.8 Spring wheat yields on dry/cold margins (kilograms per hectare)

	Cold margin		*Dry margin*		
	West Siberia	*Canada*	*Kazakhstan*	*Australia*	
1961	960	750	690	1,130	
1962	710	1,420	650	1,250	
1963	360	1,760	390	1,340	
1964	990	1,360	990	1,380	
1965	480	1,540	310	1,000	
1966	1,320	1,870	1,100	1,510	
1967	760	1,320	610	830	
1968	1,160	1,480	830	1,370	
1969	850	1,840	860	1,110	
1970	1,250	1,790	960	1,240	
1971	1,480	1,830	1,160	1,190	
1972	1,800	1,680	1,380	860	
1973	1,330	1,690	1,120	1,330	
1974	930	1,490	790	1,330	
1961–74	1,027	1,560	846	1,205	mean yield
1961–74	393	298	301	200	standard deviation

Sources: Various years of *Narodnoye khozyaystvo SSSR* and various years of UN *Food and Agriculture Organization Yearbook*.

Khrushchev in the 1950s. Despite the higher priority given to agriculture since Stalin's death in 1953, the farms have been saddled with the burden of these central decisions. Of course, the margins of agriculture have been pushed back too far in most countries at some stage. (For example see the 'dust-bowl' experience of Kansas.) In less centralised economies, however, mistakes have been quickly appreciated, though adjustments have nevertheless been painful. In the Soviet Union, the real influence of soft budgets in agriculture has been at the *centre*, where leaders have oversold experiments like the 'virgin lands' programme and have been unwilling to accept responsibility for their decisions. In consequence, individual farms have been unable to change their crop patterns and there has been a degree of co-responsibility between the farms and the centre which has obstructed the penalties for poor performance that are central to Kornai's hard budgets. In fact, the marginal conditions of Kazakhstan and West Siberia would have been fairly hostile for *any* crop as an alternative to spring wheat.

Conclusions

It is most difficult to make firm conclusions on Soviet allocative and productive efficiency in relation to the predictions of the official Soviet and Kornai views outlined in the first two sections of this chapter. Certainly, statistical studies of factor productivity, of foreign trade with the West, and of agriculture provide support for Kornai, but Soviet foreign trade with other CMEA countries does conform with official expectations.

In general, it is very difficult for Western commentators to make balanced judgements on static Soviet efficiency, given the different subjective weights applied to static and dynamic efficiency. One of the authors found great difficulty in justifying to a party of visiting Russians the existence in a typical British suburban shopping centre of similar, often adjacent, branches of banks, building societies and retail shops, usually providing apparently identical goods and services.

Pryor (1985, pp. 188–91) echoes the observation that capitalism involves static duplication and waste. In the West, research and development programmes and production capacity always overlap and compete to some extent. Advertising campaigns compete and may promote 'frivolous' product differentiation, and expenditures may appear extravagant in the areas of finance, insurance, real estate and the provision of legal services. Pryor (1985, p. 190) reports that such 'extravagance' may have amounted to 10 per cent of measured GNP in the West.

Capitalists would contend that the process of market competition in product, labour and capital markets *always* involves static efficiency losses in the form of duplication and waste, almost by definition, and Kornai would insist that excess supplies are a precondition of hard budget constraints. These static losses could be justified in terms of certain *dynamic* benefits in the areas of investment (chapter 6), innovation (chapter 7) and hence economic growth (chapter 8).

Although the techniques of central planning seem particularly suited to the static allocation of given resources, we would have to conclude that, both in relation to our Western prejudice in favour of *individual* preferences and to the Soviet emphasis on *planners'* preferences as expressed in production targets, Soviet allocative and productive efficiency has been relatively low and can be explained reasonably in terms of Kornai's theories.

CHAPTER FOUR

EXCESS DEMAND AND INFLATION

After living with inflation in the West, it is somehow reassuring in Soviet shops to see prices stamped indelibly on cartons or even on the product itself. This contrasts with our paper price-tags on the shelves next to the products, which can be easily changed (increased). In the case of metal items like scissors, the Soviet price is often stamped in the original casting.

This feeling of reassurance conforms with the state's official position regarding the virtual absence of inflation under the Soviet system. In this chapter, this official Soviet stance in relation to inflation is reviewed, followed by Kornai's very different predictions regarding excess demand in economies with relatively 'soft' constraints; the third section consists of subjective estimates of actual inflation in the Soviet Union. In practice, Western visitors often find that the 'indelibly stamped' price is ignored.

The definition of inflation used in this chapter is arbitrary, like its official measurements. A retail price index should be familiar to all readers, but this only covers sales to the final consumer. Our definition of inflation is taken to be that price index which, when applied to the whole of national income, allows one to calculate 'real' income changes as a residual. In other words, inflation is identified with what is called in the West the 'GDP deflator'.

Of course, Gross Domestic Product (GDP) is not measured in the Soviet Union, although the CIA does estimate this magnitude. When using official Soviet data, Net Material Product (NMP) must be taken as a measure of national income. This concept includes income in the form of consumption goods and capital goods minus depreciation, but is restricted to what is called the 'material' sector. This embraces all physical goods and 'material' services. The latter include services in the distribution of physical goods, like storage, transport and the retail sector, but omits general administration, finance and credit, education, health, culture, housing services, passenger transport, household communications and personal services like hairdressers, bath-houses and cemeteries. All these 'non-material' services are considered 'unproductive', following Marx, and are therefore excluded.

SOVIET INFLATION – THE OFFICIAL VIEW

The attitude of the Soviet authorities towards inflation is paradoxical: on the one hand, inflation has been successfully eliminated from the Soviet economy, but, on the other, inflation does not really matter in the context of a planned economy anyway. Inflation is seen to be a disease of anarchic capitalism, where profit-seeking producers who have managed to shelter themselves from competition are able to raise prices and profits at will. This capitalist inflation reduces the value of the apparent growth of incomes. It favours those with large stocks of physical assets (like property) and hurts those on fixed monetary incomes or with monetary assets (like pensioners with savings). In a planned economy, however, state price and income control can ensure that any inflation does not have these undesirable consequences, and individual property ownership is lower, so inflation is less important in the Soviet Union than elsewhere.

At the same time, however, the authorities are proud of their achievement of zero officially-measured inflation. To a large extent, this achievement has been made easier by the fact that the Soviet Union is a fairly self-sufficient economy, although the valuation of the USSR's foreign trade is always difficult. Foreign trade probably accounted for less than 6 per cent of national income in the 1980s, with less than a quarter of this trade being with the developed West. The Soviet Union is therefore able to insulate itself from most of the inflation in the outside world.

Nevertheless, the Soviet authorities have been anxious to eliminate inflation, because it seems to be a symbol of the anarchy of capitalist markets. With central planning, all resource allocations are supposed to be rationally co-ordinated in advance, so open inflation is an admission that planned supplies have proved inadequate to meet planned demands. In practice, the Soviet enterprise has little power to influence prices, which are largely fixed centrally, but subject to changes in turnover taxes and subsidies. Inflation can, in theory, therefore be legislated away.

Table 4.1 shows the official retail price index which, like many official series, is infuriatingly based on 1940. It seems clear that the Soviet system is not inherently immune from inflationary tendencies, although all the inflation shown from 1940 to 1950 in fact occurred before the currency reform at the end of 1947, and prices generally fell from 1948 to 1954. After 1954, the official rate of inflation was approximately zero until

Table 4.1 Soviet state retail price index, 1940–83 (1940 = 100)

Year	*Retail price index*
1950	186
1960	139
1970	139
1975	139
1980	143
1981	145
1982	150
1983	151

Sources: Narodnoye khozyaystvo, 1970, p. 602, and 1983, p. 472.

1978, although since then an annual rate slightly in excess of 1 per cent has been conceded, until 1983. Table 4.1 does reveal a non-negligible inflation rate of 5 per cent for the single year of 1982, but this was due to the introduction of price 'reforms' (that is largely increases), which should strictly be spread over the period of the eleventh five-year plan (1981–5).

Official Soviet claims of actual inflation rates below 2 per cent per annum are supported by Portes (1977), who asserts (p. 113) that, since Western estimates of the annual growth of real Soviet consumption between 1955 and 1975 have been around 4 per cent, compared with official estimates of the growth in money disposable incomes of 5 per cent per annum, inflation cannot have been sustained at several percentage points annually. The same author has, however, later conceded (in Brown et al., 1982, p. 363) that inflation seems to have accelerated during the 1970s.

This chapter is more concerned with the overall inflation in national income than with the retail index alone, but here Soviet official statistics are less than helpful. Table 4.2 shows an attempt to deduce the USSR's NMP deflator from the data in columns (1) and (2), adapted from official publications. Column (3) shows that our estimate of the official NMP deflator (general rate of inflation) fell in the 1970s, and reductions in the recorded price of capital goods could reconcile this result with table 4.1. Since 1980, however, the NMP deflator has risen by rates of 1.7, 3.4, 0.9 and 1.6 per cent in successive years, largely on account of the increases in retail prices announced in 1982. Column (4) shows that the outcome for official real income per capita was *zero* growth between 1981 and 1982, although official real income has never been defined precisely. (For example, it is not known if housing subsidies are included, and how.

Table 4.2 Soviet national income growth, 1970–84 (1970 = 100)

Year	*(1) NMP utilised per capita at current prices*	*(2) NMP utilised per capita at 1973 prices*	*(3) Implicit NMP deflator*	*(4) Real income per capita*
1970	100	100[a]	100[a]	100
1975	121.3	127.4[b]	95.2[b]	124
1980	145.5	159.2	91.4	146
1981	151.8	162.9	93.1	151
1982	161.4	167.3	96.5	151
1983	167.4	171.8	97.4	154
1984	172.7	174.4	99.0	159

[a]These figures relate to the period 1966–70 and not to 1970 alone.
[b]These figures relate to the period 1971–75 and not to 1975 alone.
Sources: (1) *Narodnoye khozyaystvo SSSR*, 1982, p. 380 and 1984, p. 426.
(2) *Narodnoye khozyaystvo SSSR*, 1982, p. 379 and 1984, p. 426.
(3) Calculated as (1) divided by (2).
(4) *Narodnoye khozyaystvo SSSR*, 1982, p. 380; 1984, p. 426 and 1922–82, p. 418.
Mid-year population figures are from *Narodnoye khozyaystvo SSSR*, 1983, p. 5.

Incomes in kind from collective farms are valued at state prices, whereas incomes from private plots are valued at actual prices received.)

From these comparisons, it can be seen that official indices do show a significant degree of price stability compared with the West, and to this extent the official position is vindicated. Official inflation has not been negligible in the 1980s, however, and the implications of Kornai's view on inflation in centrally planned economies will now be considered.

INFLATION IN A 'SUCTION' ECONOMY

Kornai does not refer explicitly to the Soviet Union as a 'suction' economy or even as an economy employing 'soft' constraints, but this is implicit in his theoretical work and in his discussion (Kornai, 1983) of Hungary's attempts to transform its economy from one using Soviet-style 'soft' constraints to a system where poor performance is severely penalised automatically. In the Soviet Union, the survival of an enterprise does not usually depend upon profitable sales or the fulfilment of cost or output targets. Because of the coincidence of interests between the enterprise and the hierarchies of planning and politics, cost increases can be passed on in the form of higher prices, the state can modify taxes and subsidies to aid particular enterprises, credits for investment are available without stringent conditions, and defaults are permitted, with the state effectively sharing in the risks of enterprises. These characteristics were summarised in chapter 1, above as being typical of 'soft' budget constraints.

It is argued that soft constraints give the Soviet Union all the characteristics of a 'suction' or excess-demand economy. In the case of capital goods, soft credit creates an investment 'hunger' in all enterprises and suppliers of capital and other producers' goods find themselves in sellers' markets subject to excess demand. This over-demand feeds off itself in the sense that enterprises cannot be sure that they will obtain the capital inputs that have been authorised since other enterprises also demand them. Rational enterprises therefore over-demand and try to hoard capital goods even more to allow for supply uncertainties, which in turn become greater. A similar picture can be drawn for labour inputs, except that labour inputs, unlike machines and buildings, can move between enterprises and areas of their own volition (see chapter 5 below). Labour will be attracted to high-priority and large enterprises where budget constraints are softest, and the rest of the economy will experience chronic labour shortage. Pietsch (1986, p. 177) calculates that the Soviet Union exhausted all effective reserves of labour in about 1970, and a general over-demand for labour has existed ever since. In the case of labour, capital and other inputs, buyers with relatively soft budgets, on account of the nature of Soviet hierarchies and an emphasis on gross output targets, must generate excess demands and inflationary tendencies, although these may be hidden or repressed.

The sale of enterprise outputs to the final consumer is slightly different from the circumstances in relation to inputs, outlined above. On the face of it, consumers *are* constrained by the size of their budgets and cannot sustain demands in excess of their incomes for long. In addition, the authorities try to insulate different sectors of the economy from supply and demand imbalances in others. Producers of capital goods with soft budgets are treated separately from lower-priority producers of consumer goods and separate banking institutions deal with transactions between state enterprises, on the one hand, and the transactions of individual households, on the other. In theory, it is possible to avoid excess demand for consumer goods, despite the shortage of inputs.

In practice, however, excess demands for labour, capital and other material inputs spill over into the demands of consumers for outputs. The excess demand for capital diverts resources from the consumer-goods industries and creates shortage there, too; the payment of higher incomes to labour in short supply inflates household budgets, and informal, unplanned transactions enable state enterprises to inflate demands in grey and black markets (see pp. 89–90). Black markets, in turn, attract state assets illegally, and in 1986 a Soviet campaign of exhortation was intended to reduce industrial theft by employees. Finally, enterprises anxious to secure scarce labour offer credit facilities to employees and so individual and enterprise banking becomes interdependent, too.

The outcome of these observations is that excess demands for most consumer goods exist beside shortages of capital goods, labour and other inputs, and this tendency is exacerbated by the reluctance of enterprises to overfulfil their output targets for consumer goods significantly because of 'ratchet' effects, explained in chapter 1. The degree of shortage in consumer goods is probably less severe than for capital goods, where both buying and selling enterprises have soft constraints. The consumer must still spend within the available budget, unlike many firms, and in the mid-1960s Soviet consumers *did* revolt against poor-quality textiles and garments, leaving the authorities with massive unsold stocks. This revolt contributed to demands for the economic reforms of 1965, discussed in chapter 1.

According to Kornai (1982, p. 34), chronic shortages and unused resources always co-exist. Materials are hoarded within soft budget enterprises, and in addition producers do not generally need to cater for consumers' demands to survive. Consumers are forced to substitute unsatisfactory goods for the ones they really need, but may baulk at totally unsatisfactory items.

Excess demand (accompanied by some excess supplies of unwanted goods) need not be reflected in the official price index, however. Central price-fixing may prevent overt inflation, but excess demand can lead to rationing devices of various kinds, price increases for 'new' goods that are unwarranted in terms of their quality, and other forms of what may be considered tantamount to inflation.

It can be seen that Kornai's perspective on 'suction' economies gives predictions that conflict directly with the official Soviet view, discussed above. 'Resource-constrained' economies like the Soviet Union are in sharp contrast to the 'pressure' economies of the West, which are characterised by excess supply, not demand, in product, labour and capital markets. One would therefore, on this view, expect *more* inflation in the Soviet Union, not less, although this may be hidden or repressed. The next section considers the possible refuges of excess demand in the Soviet Union and presents subjective empirical estimates of the inflation the authorities there may have concealed.

ACTUAL SOVIET INFLATION

'Hidden' and 'repressed' inflation cannot be analysed without understanding a simple identity (something which is true by definition) in macro-economic theory. Ignoring statistical niceties like property income from abroad and transfers between foreign governments,

$$C_D + S + T = C_S + I + G + (X-M)$$

where C_D is expenditure on consumer goods (demand), S is savings and T is taxation. The left-hand side of the identity – $C_D + S + T$ – measures national income from the expenditure side. C_S is the production of consumer goods (supply), I is net investment (including changes in stocks), G is government expenditure and $(X-M)$ is the balance of trade – the difference between exports (X) and imports (M). The right-hand side of the identity above – $C_S + I + G + (X-M)$ – measures national income from the production side. Each item of expenditure in the identity can change in real or money terms.

In aggregate, *actual* total expenditure must equal the *actual* value of goods available for purchase net of stock changes and foreign trade, although this does not mean that *planned* expenditures and outputs need be equal. For example, Keynesian theory emphasises that, from a state of equilibrium (where planned and actual expenditure and production are equal in total), if consumers suddenly plan to spend less (C_D falls), then in the short run, unspent incomes accumulate in (S), restoring the identity. Despite the identity, this is not an equilibrium position, however, as producers have planned to produce too much ($C_S > C_D$) after C_D has fallen. Undemanded production ($C_S > C_D$) accumulates in stocks (I increases), but this is just a transfer from C_S to I on the right-hand side of the identity. In an attempt to reduce unsold stocks, however, production may be reduced, and these cuts will ultimately reduce the incomes of consumers, who are also wage-receivers, through a 'multiplier' effect. In the long run, incomes (HT2 132) fall and thus expenditures (C_D), until the identity is secured without any tendency to shift again.

What is the purpose of this excursion into macro-economics? Simply that it provides the basis for an analysis of hidden and repressed inflation. The identity at the beginning of this section shows the possibilities. From an initial equilibrium, if excess demand for consumer goods ($C_D > C_S$) is generated by soft budgets, ratchet effects, bonus payments or price subsidies, then the following situations may occur.

1 In an economy where market prices are left free to move to market-clearing levels, *inflation in consumer goods markets* will occur. C_S is thus inflated until it equals C_D.

2 When investment (I) increases to cater for excess demand or in response to the higher prices that can be demanded, overt and/or hidden *inflation in capital-goods markets* may result.
3 Where prices are not allowed to move to market-clearing levels, demand may be choked off by non-price-rationing devices such as queuing and forcing consumers to substitute less satisfactory alternatives. These phenomena amount to *hidden* inflation and are allowed for in the next two subsections below. In the limit, however, consumers may not be able to find *any* suitable alternatives and may resort to the ultimate substitution of savings deposits or cash holdings for desired expenditure. *Repressed* inflation in the form of forced savings (S) may therefore be the final refuge for excess demand ($C_D > C_S$).
4 Governments may siphon off excess demand ($C_D > C_S$) by raising direct or indirect taxes (T). Indirect taxes like the Soviet turnover tax will show up in the official price index, but direct, personal and (especially) enterprise taxes can be raised to reduce demand.
5 Governments may reduce their own expenditures (G) or *reduce exports* (X) in order to make goods available for domestic consumption (C_S), or they may consider *raising imports* (M). The Soviet government has been prepared recently to import food, especially grain for animal feed, and new equipment (e.g. pipelines for gas transmission), but in general this tends to bring dependence on the West. Imports are generally only considered as a cure for excess demand if they can be shown to remove a temporary bottleneck in domestic supply.

In the paragraphs that follow, a survey of the empirical evidence from the Soviet Union on the first three of these refuges of excess demand is presented. Care is taken to distinguish *hidden* inflation which could be represented in an all-embracing price index from *repressed* inflation, which represents unspent incomes which have no place in a price index proper. In addition, when estimating the inflationary equivalents of hidden and repressed inflation, one must distinguish the inflation-equivalent that would establish market-clearing at a stroke from the constant rate of inflation-equivalent that would preserve equilibrium over time.

Inflation in Consumers' Goods Markets

It may be remembered from the discussion of the figures presented in tables 4.1 and 4.2 that the rate of retail price inflation officially conceded between 1954 and 1978 was zero, and in excess of 1 per cent per annum between, 1978 and 1983. Portes (1977) supports official claims of recent annual inflation rates below 2 per cent, although table 4.2 does suggest a rate of about 2 per cent, between 1980 and 1984.

However, these official estimates do not take into account:

1 higher prices unofficially paid on authorised transactions
2 implicit price increases hidden by quality variations
3 inflation in so-called 'Grey' markets
4 inflation in black markets

Higher prices unofficially paid on authorized transactions

The first mechanism relates to transactions that are planned or otherwise authorised by the state. Unofficial premia paid in excess of the authorised price may involve cash or 'blat', (that is, the use of contacts, influence and favours to secure supplies). Since contacts must be cultivated and favours repaid however, there is little analytical distinction between cash and 'blat'.

Anecdotal evidence abounds on unofficial premia. The degree of shortage varies across markets, but Kornai (1980 p. 499) indicates particularly intense shortages in housing and private car markets in Hungary and 'for the consumer goods sector in a number of other Eastern European socialist countries'. For example, in Soviet housing, Morton (1980, p. 247) reports that in officially-sanctioned housing transactions the true rent on rooms let may be many times higher than the legally permitted and registered fee of a few roubles, but it is the latter that features in the offical price index. In the case of holiday homes, if we assume a room of 16 square metres, then Morton's figures (1980, p. 248) imply an actual rent of 200 roubles per week in 1977 for a room, which was ten times the official, taxable rent at that time.

In the context of inflation however, it is not enough to observe premia and 'blat' on goods that are officially cheap, but in chronic excess demand. For such phenomena, there must be consistent *increases* in such payments and favours if they are to constitute hidden inflation. There is no evidence to suggest that such increases have occurred on a scale that would significantly add to annual Soviet inflation rates over several decades.

Price increases hidden by quality variations

Quality reductions are a different matter, however. For example an émigré Soviet planning official (Kushnirsky, 1984, p. 50) notes that in the 1970s, meat products gradually contained more starch and water and less meat, and the proportion of boiled sausage in total meat products increased. In the period 1965–80, milk sales increased by 116 per cent and cheese by 119 per cent, despite the fact that farm deliveries of milk grew by only 25 per cent. This paradox is explained by the dilution of milk, lowering its fat content. In addition, the introduction of 'new' models of allegedly higher quality may hide inflation. Enterprises are empowered to raise prices temporarily on new products, which do not enter the official price-index comparisons.

Such real or illusory quality variations on consumer goods are tantamount to hidden price increases, but there is no concrete evidence on their contribution to the 'true' rate of Soviet inflation. There is, however, evidence on the inflation-equivalents of quality reductions in *capital*-goods industries, which are reviewed below. Given the relatively harder budget constraints of buyers in consumer-goods markets, these estimates may be taken as an unrealistically high upper bound on the possible contribution to hidden inflation of quality reductions in retail markets. In our judgement, Howard's (1976) estimate of the inflation-equivalent of price 'drift' (through the introduction of 'new' models) of 0.8–1.2 per cent per annum between 1956 and 1972 is realistic. For the remainder of the decade we would expect that the harder budget constraints in the retail sector would produce fewer hidden price increases than for capital goods (see the section entitled 'Inflation in capital-goods industries' below). At a guess, we would propose that consumer-good quality variations were responsible for an inflation-rate equivalent of 2 per cent per annum in the 1970s, that is at half the rate estimated by Hanson (1984a) for capital goods.

Inflation in grey markets

The Soviet retail price index does not cover all sales. In particular, it omits sales on the collective farm market (CFM) of produce from the private plots of collective farm workers and output from the collective farms themselves that is surplus after fulfilling planned deliveries to the state sector. Such sales only represent less than 10 per cent of total food sales and 5 per cent of retail sales in general, but for particular products, the CFM's share of total sales is high. Recent figures are unavailable, but in 1970 the CFM's share was 67 per cent for potatoes, 54 per cent for eggs and 35 per cent for meat (Gregory and Stuart, 1981, p. 162).

Until 1977 it was possible to calculate inflation in collective-farm markets. Dirksen (1981) estimated no significant inflation here until 1970 and then 20.9 per cent aggregate inflation over the period 1970–7. The CIA's Soviet retail price index also takes CFM prices into account, and table 4.3 shows significant inflation between 1960 and 1980, but none between 1980 and 1982, giving an annual simple average rate of about 1.5 per cent between 1960 and 1982. Although this CIA index embraces CFM sales and involves fairly independent comparisons of total sales at current and constant prices, it is probably fair to conclude that the index in table 4.3 still understates the 'true' increases in prices which must also take into account inflation in capital-goods industries and forced savings (see below).

Table 4.3 CIA's consumer price index for the Soviet Union, 1960–82 (1970 = 100)

Year	*Consumer price index*
1960	90
1965	97
1970	100
1975	110
1978	114
1979	116
1980	120
1981	122
1982	120

Source: CIA, Handbook of Statistics, 1983, p. 51.

Inflation in Black Markets

The phenomenon of Soviet black markets was discussed in chapter 3 in relation to allocative efficiency. They are extremely prevalent, but, as with 'blat' and price premia, the very existence of black markets does not demonstrate hidden inflation. Excess demand for 'official' output must exist in the first place for black markets to emerge, but once they are established, *increases* in black-market prices (and not just the existence of black markets) are a necessary condition for hidden inflation.

Culbertson and Amacher (1978) try to measure price increases in one large segment of the Soviet black market – that part where transactions are conducted in Western, fully convertible currencies such as US dollars. Excess demand in such transactions drives up 'black' prices and thus the demand for currencies such as dollars. Movements in black-market exchange rates are therefore taken by Culbertson and Amacher as indicators of black-market inflation. If the demand for dollars increases on the black market, the rouble : dollar black-market exchange rate depreciates by an amount that reflects black-market inflation.

Their calculations (p. 393) for 1960–70 suggest that black-market inflation in the Soviet Union was running at a compound annual rate of about 8.6 per cent, which compares with the official rate of zero for that period. A number of reservations must be entered, however, before concluding that black market inflation in the Soviet Union is high. First, Culbertson and Amacher (1978, p. 387) show that the rouble : dollar exchange rate *appreciated* between 1970 and 1973, implying price *reductions* on black markets. Since then, casual personal contact with black markets in the Soviet Union suggests that the black-market premium on hard currencies has stayed around the 1977 level of about 400 per cent (Pick, 1978, p. 39), implying that black-market inflation has been approximately zero since 1970. Second, it is wrong to generalise estimated black-market inflation rates to the whole economy. Presumably, excess demand in official transactions is siphoned off into black-market dealings, and transactions in hard currencies on the black market are a sub-set of such dealings in general. Even if 10 per cent of *all* market transactions were 'black' and in hard currencies (see chapter 3 above), 8.6 per cent inflation in these transactions would only constitute 0.86 per cent inflation overall. If there was a *general* level of excess demand in the order of 8.6 per cent, this could cause rates of inflation in the relatively minor, hard currency black markets of several times that figure.

For these reasons, we refuse to accept Culbertson and Amacher's (1978) conclusion that black-market exchange-rate depreciation in the Soviet Union implies significant levels of hidden inflation. Even if we accept their reassurances that institutional changes such as black-market 'crackdowns', booms in tourism, official devaluations and inconsistencies in 'cross' rates have not biassed their results, our interpretation of their findings would suggest that, at a maximum, black-market inflation contributed certainly less than 1 per cent per annum to the overall rate in the 1960s, and there is no evidence that it has made any contribution at all since 1970.

Inflation in Capital-Goods Industries

Early estimates of hidden inflation through unrecorded price increases and quality reductions were calculated for the CIA by attributing the difference between the official Soviet estimate of real industrial output and the CIA's to hidden inflation (Steiner, 1978). Steiner supported this procedure by quoting the findings of the Soviet State Price Commission's inspectorate that unapproved price increases had occurred in nearly half of the 7,000 enterprises sampled. Rosefielde (1983) proposed, however, that Steiner's statistical procedures were flawed and that the price increases detected by the inspectorate were insignificant.

Later CIA studies (see Leggett, 1981) concentrated on capital-goods industries, with particular reference to Soviet machine-building. Leggett applied hedonic price indices to try to estimate the inflation-equivalent of quality reductions. (These indices assume that every characteristic of a product has an implicit price. For example, the price of a particular house is determined by the number of rooms, the quality of the location and aspect, etc. By pooling observations on all house characteristics and the total price of each house, the 'price' of each characteristic can be found by regression techniques.) No price increases were found until 1967, but in that one year allegedly 'improved' machines were responsible for implicit price increases of about 30 per cent. The CIA estimates (Converse, 1982) that hidden inflation amounted to 1.5 per cent per annum in producer durables before 1980, if price increases on imported machines are included.

More recently, an independent academic (Hanson, 1984a) has proposed that the CIA estimates of hidden inflation on producer durables are too low. Hanson examines the work of Soviet economists on the increasing Soviet capital-output ratio, 1976–80. Of course, a given increment of output may apparently require more investment as a result of diminishing returns, costly raw materials and unfinished construction work. Nevertheless, Hanson (1984a, p. 578) finds plausible estimates of hidden inflation in producer durables of about 3 or 4 per cent per annum in the 1970s.

Given soft budget constraints, enterprises using producer durables for the production of output for sale to the final consumer are not obliged to pass on increases in machinery prices, because they can survive anyway. In addition, it was noted above that the market for consumers' goods should be less of a seller's market compared with sales of producers' goods between enterprises.

These factors make it very difficult to generalise estimates of hidden inflation in producer durables through 'new' products of about 3–4 per cent per annum in the 1970s to *all* goods, but certainly some significant examples of hidden quality reductions in the retail sector are reported above. (Another example would be the gradual disappearance of cheap brands of vodka.) It would not be surprising to us if they amounted to as much as 2 per cent per annum hidden inflation overall, from 1970.

Forced Savings

It has been explained that prices in the Soviet Union are usually not market-clearing prices, that is, prices that would equate supply with demand. Accommodation is underpriced, for example, at least officially. This causes waiting-lists, queues and other rationing devices that persuade consumers to *substitute* less desirable goods for products that are underpriced. In Hungary, for example, Kapitány, Kornai and Szabó (1984, p. 239) show that in 1977, 95 per cent of car-buyers who ordered a Skoda or Zhiguli model would have preferred another at prevailing prices, if delivery were possible immediately. When an inferior car is not available for substitution, demand might switch to entirely different alternatives like expensive vacations, or to black markets. Ultimately, however, consumers might be forced to *save* their disposable incomes in the absence of easily obtainable goods of reasonable quality. Goldman (1983, p. 98), for example, asserts that: 'the astonishing growth of savings bank accounts . . . is another sign that Soviet consumers cannot find enough ways to spend their money'. Nove (1979, p. 224) shows that Soviet savings bank deposits increased from 18.7 billion roubles in 1965 to 46.6 billion in 1970 and 91.0 billion in 1975, thus insisting that 'a large overhang of surplus purchasing power now exists.' Since then, however, economists have appreciated the need for a more than naive examination of Soviet savings statistics. For example, Durgin's (1984 p. 104) review of Goldman's (1983) book observes that in the United States personal savings doubled between 1965 and 1970, explaining that savings rates usually rise with income.

Econometric work has tried to isolate forced savings from savings dependent upon income, wealth and other factors. The results have been mixed, and again Portes (with Winter, 1980) provides a dissenting view, denying that savings conceal inflation in centrally planned economies. This view is supported by Ofer and Pickersgill's (1980) survey of savings by Soviet émigrés. They report that savings rates are, if anything, lower than in the West, but can be explained in terms of the same variables. They find no evidence of savings being 'forced' by a lack of consumer goods.

Ofer and Pickersgill's sample from Jewish émigrés was small and atypical, however, and Gardner and Strauss (1981, pp. 402–3) reckon that forced savings amounted to 33 billion roubles between 1965 and 1975. They estimate that if savers had been able to spend these funds, prices would have risen by 17.25 per cent between 1965 and 1975, or at a compound annual rate of 1.3 per cent. No estimates are available for recent years, although Grossman (1982, p. 280) reports a slowing down in the rate of growth of savings deposits in 1980 and 1981, despite strong suspicions (p. 277) of a substantial increase in the rate of currency issue in 1980.

There now seems to be a consensus that Portes and Winter (1980) did not demonstrate that the centrally planned economies of Eastern Europe do not repress inflation in the form of forced savings. Kornai (1982, p. 35) finds 'absurd' the notion that excess *supply*, not demand, is the dominant characteristic in these countries. Portes and Winter (1980) were unable to apply their analysis to the Soviet Union, but, elsewhere, Askansas and Laski (1985, p. 173) estimate that forced savings probably were responsible for 2.1 per cent repressed inflation per annum between 1964 and 1978 in Poland, when the official annual rate was 5.2 per cent, while Havlik (1985, p. 183) reckons that the corresponding rates for Czechoslovakia were 1.9 per cent and 3.3 per cent respectively.

On balance, it seems fair to agree with Gregory and Stuart's (1981, p. 364) conclusion that there is probably a significant overhang of unsatisfied purchasing power in Soviet savings. The views of Soviet economists on the subject are discussed in Schroeder and Severin (1976, pp. 637–9). There seems to be no doubt that accumulated cash and savings deposits do reflect postponed excess demand that could descend unexpectedly. It is paradoxical that if the supply of 'shortage' goods like motor cars and private housing is increased, consumers may voluntarily save *more* in the short run with a view to their eventual purchase.

CONCLUSIONS

This chapter began with the promise of a 'guestimate' of the 'true' rate of Soviet inflation. In table 4.4 we stick our necks out and produce a very subjective estimate of Soviet inflation, which embodies 'hidden' and 'repressed' excess demand. We would conclude that the 'true' annual rate of Soviet retail price inflation before 1970 was in the range 2.3–4.0 per cent, probably accelerating through the 1970s to produce a figure between 2.8 and 5.8 per cent by 1980. We are unable to produce estimates for an NMP deflator.

These subjective estimates are significantly higher than the official figures, which appear in the first column of table 4.4. How can our estimates be defended against the Portes argument (Portes, 1977; Brown et al. 1982, p. 363) that inflation of several percentage points cannot be reconciled with the annual growth of money disposable incomes of only 5 per cent, since living standards have manifestly risen, perhaps by as much as 4 per cent per annum? Rising living standards and inflation are compatible, however, if official estimates of money wages and private incomes, together with the inflation rate, are all understated. This is our contention (see chapter 9 below).

Contrary to official claims, Soviet inflation rates have not been negligible, and Kornai's view of the Soviet-type economy as exhibiting relatively soft budgets and a significant degree of excess demand is vindicated to some extent. It should not be forgotten, however, that inflation in Western industrial economies has been generally in excess of the 'true' Soviet level. For example, compound annual rates of change in the retail price index between 1970 and 1982 were 5.2 per cent (German Federal Republic), 7.9 per cent (United States), 8.1 per cent (Japan) and 13.1 per cent (United Kingdom) (CIA, *Handbook of Statistics*, 1983, p. 51). To fit in with Kornai's ideas, rapid inflation in the West must have occurred because of softening budget constraints or for reasons unconnected with excess demand. This must be true to some extent.

Table 4.4 Estimated 'true' rate of annual Soviet retail price inflation

	Official rate (%)	*Quality reductions (%)*	*Grey markets (%)*	*Forced savings (%)*	*Total inflation (%)*
1960					
1961					
1962					
1963					
1964					
1965		0.8–1.2			
1966					
1967					
1968	zero				
1969					before 1970, 2.3–4.0
1970					
1971			1.5		
1972					
1973				0–1.3	
1974					
1975					
1976		0.3–2.0			
1977					
1978					
1979					
1980	1.0				around 1980, 2.8–5.8
1981					
1982					
1983					

Inflation in black markets and inflation in unofficial premia are assumed to be zero, see text.
Forced savings: in our judgement, Gardner and Strauss's (1981) estimate of 1.3 per cent for 1965–75 can be extended into the 1980s.

Keynesian demand management policies have artificially primed demand in an excess supply system, and inflation in the 1970s was exacerbated by the realisation of trade unions that they could force up wages by imposing potential costs on large producers, and by the OPEC oil cartel.

On the other hand, even 'true' Soviet inflation rates may understate excess demand since they only embody forced substitution in its ultimate form, that is, forced savings. Presumably, if consumers 'make do' with inferior substitutes for goods in excess demand, this is hidden, even from the estimates in table 4.4.

CHAPTER FIVE

UNEMPLOYMENT

Unemployment is still a taboo subject in the Soviet Union. Soviet unemployment levels had received little attention in the West either, until the last few years. On the face of it, unemployment should prove a less controversial subject than other aspects of efficiency discussed elsewhere. One can never be objective about equity, economic growth, inflation or technological progress but at least one can be sure that less unemployment is desirable, other things being equal. The measurement of unemployment is quite another matter, and Wiles (1984 p. 29) has called it 'the most arbitrary magnitude in a capitalist economy'. The British government reduced measured unemployment by 439,000 between 1982 and 1986 by four different administrative adjustments.

What is unique about labour? Why should unemployment be treated to a separate chapter, when labour could be bracketed with investment as just another input? There are two distinctive features of labour that demand separate treatment. First, labour is obviously *human*, has a mind of its own, and unlike other inputs will tend to walk away of its own volition from some occupations to others where demand is higher or conditions better. Where such mobility is officially restricted, labour may be attracted to unofficial activities. Second, and because it is human, labour is more *heterogeneous* than other inputs. Different skills, personalities, genders, locations and attitudes all help to make labour very complex to allocate from the centre. The uniqueness of labour makes its separate treatment advisable. In this chapter, therefore, unemployment will be considered on its own.

SOVIET UNEMPLOYMENT – THE OFFICIAL VIEW

After carefully explaining that labour is unique, it is strange to realise that the Soviet Union would claim to have eliminated involuntary unemployment because labour inputs can be *planned* like any other (see chapter 3). Labour can be allocated and controlled from the centre.

Labour Allocation

Material balances are the best-known aspect of Soviet central planning and are discussed in chapter 1. For important goods, the central planners draw up balance sheets of the planned production and uses of different materials to ensure the consistency of plans. Labour (and financial) balances are also calculated, but are less widely known. Since 1979 they have been calculated at all ministry levels and at the levels of the Union, republic, region and local authority. The demand for labour is not exposed to competitive forces and is therefore far more predictable than in the West. It is, in theory, not difficult for the authorities to identify potential pockets of excess supply and to manipulate the flow of investible funds to prevent local unemployment arising. There should be no danger of demand-deficiency unemployment in the USSR.

Labour Control

When the central allocation of productive funds has been determined with a view to preventing involuntary unemployment, the central authorities have further powers to prevent labour mobility from impeding their plans. Of course, labour input authorisations, wages and prices are mostly centrally determined, thus limiting mobility. In addition, however, labour-market institutions and the law further restrict mobility, and hence unemployment.

We will look first at labour-market institutions. These generally have the effect of discouraging the movement of workers between jobs and areas, although high-priority projects such as the BAM railway are a different story. When Stalin formally 'abolished' unemployment in 1930, employment exchanges were dispensed with, and they still do not exist in the Western sense. Enterprises needing labour can still advertise locally, and since 1970 job recruitment agencies have operated, but only at the (low-priority) republican, and not Union, level. There now remains little *direction* of labour, although Wiles (1984, p. 27) estimates that about two million prisoners are still serving 'corrective labour' sentences. Students in higher education are required to give an undertaking that they will work as directed for the first two or three years after graduation, although the best students are exempted as an incentive for better performance. It should also be remembered that the Communist Party acts as a 'labour exchange' for about two million *nomenklatura* posts for which it must provide nominees (see Hough, 1969, p. 156). Finally, appeals from the Party and Komsomol for volunteers for harvesting or other urgent duties may be difficult to resist.

The law is also effective in preventing unemployment. As might be expected, the state does not provide unemployment benefit. In addition, rights to pensions, extra vacations and housing benefits may be reduced if 'continuous employment' is interrupted by more than three weeks or more than once a year (see Helgeson, 1986, p. 150). It is the right, but also the duty, of every adult male to work and there are severe penalties for 'parasites' (including dissidents) who are out of work for more than four months. Nevertheless, many artisan trades are permitted outside the state sector, and unwilling workers do not find it difficult to register for jobs in the fourth month of unemployment, have the new employment registered with the police in a work-passport and then absent themselves (see Binyon, 1983, p. 32). Residence permits are still required for the big cities and in practice such permits limit labour mobility, although ingenious avoidance measures have been devised. Job security in existing posts is almost total, and Berliner (1976, p. 158) explains that technological unemployment is avoided by requiring innovating firms to provide displaced employees with alternative work. 'Good cause' dismissal is very unlikely, although a tightening-up of labour discipline in general has been attempted since 1979. Alcoholism and laziness may now result in a less attractive type of work for miscreants.

With this wide range of devices, central allocation and control of the labour market should be able to prevent the familiar forms of involuntary structural, regional and demand-deficient unemployment, although a small amount of frictional unemployment is inevitable. The Soviet authorities stress the *right* to work in their country whenever Western critics remark on the absence of other human rights to dissent and so on. They would claim that central planning has eliminated involuntary unemployment, and this official view on unemployment is to some extent *reinforced* by the Kornai perspective.

UNEMPLOYMENT IN A SUCTION ECONOMY

There must be grave doubts over the ability of central planners to allocate and control jobs and workers in a way that eliminates all unemployment.

It was explained at the start of this chapter that labour is often uncontrollable and is in any case a very complex input to plan. Kornai would suggest, however, that relatively soft budgets in industry 'rescue' the planners from any errors that they may make. This leads to over-employment in labour markets outside enterprises and internal unemployment within enterprises.

Over-employment

Over-employment is predicted by Kornai for all suction economies and is exacerbated by institutional characteristics in the Soviet Union. It has been noted that soft constraints result when great communications distance exists between the planners and the planned, and this phenomenon ought to be exaggerated for an input like labour, which is uniquely complex and difficult to plan from the centre. Soft budgets are reinforced in the Soviet Union where different levels of the economic (and Party) hierarchies feel co-responsibility for each others' actions. Given that central planners find it difficult to co-ordinate more than gross outputs, it seems inevitable that gross output targets will dominate at the levels of ministry and enterprise and cause them to over-demand all inputs, including labour. Communications distance, co-responsibility and gross-output targets inevitably produce labour balances that are likely to err on the side of over-demand and a tendency for enterprises to press for above-plan labour and wages-fund authorisations. In addition, over-demand for labour will increase with over-investment, if labour and machines are complementary, and with the supply uncertainties which are an inevitable consequence of soft budgets: labour may be hoarded for production 'storms' when materials finally arrive, and to cover for sudden requisitions of labour for 'shock' work (for example, on harvests) by local Party secretaries, who must help others to meet output targets elsewhere.

In addition to the above theoretical consequences of soft constraints, labour demand in the USSR is further stimulated by institutional features of the system of planning. Bonus schemes generally use the size of the wages fund as the basis for bonus calculations for workers and managers, and the basic salary (and quality of 'perks') for Soviet managers is a direct function of the numbers employed.

For these reasons, demands for labour may be more unconstrained than for any other input. Kornai would therefore support official claims to have eliminated all involuntary unemployment outside the enterprise, apart from a small frictional element. Indeed, his perspective would suggest an aggregate level of *over*-employment, the implications of which are discussed below.

Internal Unemployment

Although Kornai recognises that soft budgets eliminate unemployment in the labour market outside the enterprise, this does not guarantee full employment inside factories. On the contrary, soft budgets lead inevitably to 'internal' unemployment, or unemployment on the job.

There is no paradox involved here. Excess labour demands outside the enterprise and supply uncertainties force managers to hoard labour to avoid falling short of their output targets. This may involve spare resources being retained in case the *self*-production of scarce inputs in dire emergencies is needed, or to produce unreported output which can be used to secure supplies unofficially. In addition, labour hoarding may allow for the possibility of labour 'poaching' by other enterprises that are in dire straits in relation to their output targets. Here, the degree of hoarding will vary with the degree of priority of an industry, which determines the softness of the budget constraint. To quote from Kornai (1980, p. 255): 'The more frequent and intensive the labor shortage the greater will be the internal slack, namely the unemployment on the job.' And again (p. 256): 'The hoarding tendency increases labor shortage and unemployment on the job at the same time.'

The implications of internal unemployment with external shortage contrast with capitalist economies, where competitive forces like the threat of dismissal, redundancy and bankruptcy persuade firms and workers to raise productivity, although unions will press to preserve jobs when external unemployment is high. By way of contrast, there are three main implications of external shortage.

First, hoarding implies 'feather bedding' and low labour productivity. Given the capacity of human beings to keep themselves busy, this slack may not be easy to eliminate when circumstances change. For example, many Soviet hotels have manageresses or 'key ladies' on each corridor as well as a central reception area. *The Times* reported on 14th January 1986 that this post was finally abolished in 1986, after a nineteen-year campaign to do so by the Ministry of Housing and Communal Services. Time will tell whether they will reappear under a different guise.

Second, surplus labour inside the enterprise may have indirect effects. Low worker or management morale and discipline may further inhibit productivity gains where there is no effective threat of dismissal for poor performance and where alternative employment can in any case soon be found. At the same time, industrial accidents and labour turnover may be high for enterprises where morale is low.

Finally, the external excess demand and the internal excess supply of labour produce inevitable pressures for unofficial transactions in products and labour services. Private work may be performed on the enterprise's premises, or workers may absent themselves to go shopping or in pursuit of some other leisure activity, for example a visit to the steam-baths.

ACTUAL SOVIET UNEMPLOYMENT

In the light of the foregoing predictions, this section presents the available evidence on external unemployment and internal unemployment in the USSR. This is followed by a brief review of Soviet labour-market policies to see if they reveal the nature of the problems perceived by the central authorities.

External Unemployment

There is no question that the adoption of central planning ended mass external unemployment in a period of only eighteen months in 1929 and 1930, at a time when the capitalist world was collapsing into the depression of the 1930s. It is true that Stalin 'massaged' the unemployment statistics during this period. For example, 'bogus' unemployment was twice deducted from the figures where the unemployed were 'alien', 'déclassés', had refused jobs offered or because they were registered for trades not in demand (see Davies, 1986, p. 29). On the other hand, employed persons outside agriculture increased by 3.1 million to 13 million between 1928 and 1930. In construction alone, the feverish activity prompted by the 1928–32 five-year plan raised employment by 77 per cent in the single year of 1930 (see Davies, 1986, p. 29). The scale of this achievement should not be forgotten during the rest of this chapter.

It is widely accepted that demand-deficiency, structural and technological unemployment no longer exist in the Soviet Union, with the possible exception of Central Asia. Here, Pietsch (1986, p. 85) estimates that unemployment is around 4 per cent, but recognises that this is only a local phenomenon that contradicts both the official and Kornai predictions. Overall, Pietsch considers that full employment in the USSR as a whole persisted until about 1970, but that after this year all external labour reserves were exhausted. She judges that over-employment has persisted ever since.

This conclusion is quite consistent with the existence of some *frictional* unemployment for persons 'between jobs'. Compared with estimates for the West of about 3–4 per cent (Bornstein, 1978, p. 39), estimates of frictional unemployment in the USSR are somewhat lower, varying between 2–3 per cent (reported in Ellman, 1979, p. 494) and 1.3 per cent (Wiles, 1972, p. 626). Labour turnover at about 20 per cent per annum seems about the same as in the UK and USA (Wiles, 1984, p. 29), although wide variations are reported between Soviet enterprises by Malle (1986, p. 124), since large enterprises in priority industries can retain employees by the provision of substantial fringe benefits.

Minor Soviet investment 'cycles' are noted in chapter 9, but they have made no impression on full or over-full levels of employment. The fear of losing one's job and the associated anxieties of unemployment are quite absent from the Soviet economy (Ellman, 1979, p. 498), but one can never judge to what extent this undoubted achievement can be attributed to effective central planning or to relatively soft budgets in industry.

Internal Unemployment

Internal unemployment is quite a different matter. Effective central planning could achieve full external employment *and* high rates of internal labour utilisation. This has not been the case, although one must always remember that the USSR is a relatively labour-abundant, capital-scarce economy and could be expected to show low levels of labour productivity for this reason alone. This factor cannot explain variations on Soviet labour productivity over time, however, especially since external labour shortage has increased (see above).

Labour productivity is low and increasing at a declining rate in the Soviet Union, although increasing faster than in the USA and not so abysmally low as Soviet capital productivity (see figure 8.3 below). It is not possible to disentangle the extent to which low productivity is a direct result of over-manning or of its indirect consequences such as low morale and motivation. It has already been reported in chapter 3 that Hanson (1981, p. 193) found manning levels in thirteen Soviet chemical plants to be between 1.5 and 1.7 times their equivalents in the West. Schroeder (1982c, pp. 7–8) found that more than 10 million people are engaged in Soviet loading and unloading work and in intra-plant transport, compared with only 3 million in the USA.

It would be possible to provide an extensive analysis of lost working-time and machine down-time in the USSR, but the fact is that such an analysis would be meaningless without comparisons with Western industries. Ellman (1979, p. 503) reports that 25 per cent of all Soviet working-time is lost through supply uncertainties and Hanson (1984 b, p. 40) found that 'materials shortage' was the dominant cause of machine down-time in 1973, 1975 and 1982. Labour shortages are also an important cause of idle machinery (Hanson 1986, p. 103), but tended to diminish between 1973 and 1982, perhaps as enterprises learned to hoard labour internally as external labour shortages developed after 1970. Safety statistics in industry are not published, but Gidwitz (1982, pp. 27–8) does catalogue reasons for believing that safety standards in the Soviet Union are relatively low through poor morale, periods of output 'storming', and the fact that trade unions bear joint responsibility with management and the local Party for the enterprise's output performance. Harrison (1986, p. 77) reports from a survey of 800 enterprises in the Moscow area that 73 per cent took time off work to shop or for other personal business in preference to working and earning bonuses.

The evidence of internal unemployment and its consequences in the previous paragraph is fragmentary and omits any rigorous comparisons with the West. It is impossible to separate the contributions of poor planning and soft budgets, which are linked in any case. It may, however, be possible to deduce the causes and nature of labour-market problems by implication from the policies and solutions attempted by the Soviet central authorities.

Labour-market Policies

A number of productivity campaigns have been conducted in Soviet industry, apparently with a view to raising labour morale and efforts, and reducing unemployment on the job (see Rutland, 1986). These include bonus payments in general, 'socialist competition', the Shchekino experiment, work-study, and attempts to improve work discipline through administrative methods.

About 1975, basic wages accounted for around 70 per cent of total wages (Rutland, 1986, p. 195) although 55 per cent of the workforce are still on piecework (Malle, 1986, p. 134), and piece-rates may embody premia for individual effort. The remaining 30 per cent comprised bonuses which in 1975, for manual workers, ranged from 4.9 per cent in the timber industry to 20 per cent in the engineering and metal working, with an average of less than 9 per cent, and up to 40 per cent for technical workers and managers (see Malle, 1986, pp. 134–5).

Bonuses may be seen as a market supplement to a system of central planning that is less than totally effective, and to the extent that good performance is rewarded, bonus payments constitute a hardening of the budget constraint. The consensus seems to be that they have not been successful in raising productivity (see, for example, Rutland, 1986, p. 196). The scarcity of consumer goods and the complexity of schemes have proved barriers to effective bonuses.

Cash bonuses are intended to motivate individual selfish efforts. On the other hand, 'Socialist competitions' between individual workers, groups of workers or even entire cities have been used in moral appeals for team effort and a socialist spirit. Visitors to Soviet factories are usually confronted by rows of enormous photographs outside the main office block, depicting the most heroic workers. It seems likely, however, that

Rutland (1986, p. 197) is right in suggesting that these campaigns are fairly ritualistic with workers barely aware that they are competing.

Prompted by the relative ineffectiveness of traditional bonuses and moral appeals to groups of workers, the Shchekino experiment has tried to combine the two. Shchekino is an otherwise insignificant town about 100 miles south of Moscow, whose chemical plants were subjected in 1967 to an experiment whereby the combine could distribute 90 per cent of the wages saved by reductions in manning levels amongst remaining workers as a productivity bonus, with association directors enjoying an extra month's salary per annum for introducing the scheme (see Rutland, 1984). By 1970, spectacular successes were claimed for the experiment, which was extended to cover 70 per cent of the chemical industry and 21 million workers in all by 1982. Gradually, however, the proportion of savings retained by the factories declined, because managers could not attribute savings to acceptable categories, and only about 30–55 per cent of savings were ever distributed (Rutland, 1984, p. 351). The experiment has now become institutionalised, with many local variations, in the form of rules determining how jobs that have been rated by work-study engineers may be combined. Soviet enterprises are obliged by law to find alternative work for surplus labour 'saved' and this must have limited the impact of the experiment. If it had achieved its objectives, the hardening of the budget constraint implied by the Shchekino experiment could have helped to alleviate external labour shortage, and ultimately could have led to external unemployment. This may be considered an unavoidable consequence of hard budgets.

The Shchekino experiment and the payment of bonuses to individuals and to 'brigade' work-groups are all heavily dependent upon the evaluation of job-contents by work-study engineers, or members of the NOT movement. Such 'scientific management' involves a massive drive to establish work-norms using time-and-motion techniques that are now discredited in the West. Rutland (1984, p. 354) reveals that the Ministry of Tractor and Agricultural Machinery has alone established four million norms for its plants and hopes to revise 350,000 each year. These norms are usually written into the operating instructions (or 'passport') attached to each machine and are the basis for piecework payments. They appear to reward good performance and thus harden budgets, but they have been found to alienate workers in the West, leading to widespread abuse and low morale. If evidence from Hungary is anything to go by, norms and the 'machine-passport' system are resented by workers even more in a centrally planned economy (see Haraszti, 1977).

Finally, there have been successive campaigns under Andropov in 1982/3 and Gorbachev since 1985 to improve labour productivity by increasing the penalties for poor work performance, which is another way to harden soft constraints administratively. There have been reports of tighter controls on absenteeism and drunkenness, and spot checks on shoppers and clients at steam-baths to see if they should have been working. One of the authors has seen road-blocks set up by the militia to inspect drivers' work and vehicle documents at random. Overall, however, it is difficult to disagree with Hanson (1984b, p. 39) that the penalties involved are mild. Moral crusades for work discipline have been a regular feature of Soviet life. They have always been a temporary phenomenon. It is unlikely that the administrative resources exist for a consistent campaign, which would in any case breed contempt and avoidance in the long term.

CONCLUSIONS

The elimination of virtually all external unemployment for decade after decade is one of the major achievements of the Soviet economic system. On the other hand, a succession of productivity campaigns has revealed that levels of what Kornai calls on-the-job (or internal) unemployment have been a matter of great concern for the central authorities. These exhortations and incentive schemes are needed to replace the threats of redundancy, bankruptcy and unemployment, which force capitalist employers and workers to seek productivity gains. Indeed some Western governments have arguably increased unemployment to harden everybody's budget constraint and raise productivity.

In 1986, only 86.5 per cent of the British workforce was employed, according to the published statistics, but those fortunate to have a job were working relatively hard. Value-judgements are needed to decide whether it is better to live without any anxieties about job security. Soviet citizens find it very difficult to understand why capitalist economies leave large proportions of their workforces idle and on social security at the state's expense. Soviet factories may employ marginal workers whose pay exceeds their marginal contribution to the value of production, but at least they make *some* positive contribution to gross output, however trivial. Alternatively, one could view the Soviet system as one where 'dole' is paid by factories and not the welfare agencies of the state. Either way, the Soviet Communist Party's strategic objective, announced in 1985, for a 3.5 per cent increase in labour productivity per annum until the year 2000 seems heroic in the light of the historical trends noted in table 8.3. Harder budgets via dismissals for poor performance and ultimately the liquidation of unsatisfactory enterprises could boost productivity without any significant amounts of unemployment, when over-employment is so chronic. Unfortunately, Soviet prices do not approach market-clearing levels and so financial performance is difficult to appraise. In the circumstances, it is very difficult for the central authorities to decide which enterprises should be closed down or otherwise penalised.

CHAPTER SIX

INVESTMENT

In the previous chapter on unemployment, it was explained that labour was just like any other productive input with the addition of human characteristics. Capital is just another input too, so this chapter need not repeat at length the properties of the official Kornai views in relation to all inputs, discussed in chapter 2.

Capital's distinctive quality is *time*, or its dynamic content. Investment projects have a long gestation period and then generate output only gradually as more 'roundabout' methods of production are used. Marxists see capital as 'crystallised labour': that is, buildings and machines are composed of labour time which makes possible greater output in the long run compared with more primitive production with little capital. Besides adding to output in the long run, capital may also incorporate new technologies (see chapter 7).

In the West, measures of 'capital' include profits enjoyed by the suppliers of capital goods, as well as labour time. Whenever it takes place, however, the consumption of any good (like guns) involves sacrifices to others (like butter) and capital is no different. Although it may help to raise future consumption in the long run, investment must involve short-run sacrifices to current consumption and living standards. The rate of interest charged on investment finance partly reflects the need to reward the lenders who postpone their consumptions.

As with unemployment in chapter 5, it is very difficult to distinguish the predictions of the Kornai and official views on capital investment, since soft budgets may *reinforce* the characteristics of centrally planned economies in relation to many aspects of investment. Nevertheless, and as usual, we try to distinguish the official and the Kornai views on investment, and then present a review of actual Soviet investment characteristics.

SOVIET INVESTMENT – THE OFFICIAL VIEW

High levels of investment are absolutely central to the Soviet model of economic development, based on the rapid growth of heavy industry and on the holding down of consumption levels, at least in the short run, to make room for investment. Marx distinguished between 'Department I' and 'Department II' industries, and these categories correspond with the 'Group A' and 'Group B' distinction that appears in modern Soviet statistics. This distinction separates outputs (e.g. steel or machines) that are produced for consumption by another *producer* ('Group A') rather than for the final *consumer* ('Group B'). In practice, 'Group A' tends to comprise the 'heavy' industry that has repeatedly enjoyed a high priority in Soviet plans. A high proportion of 'Group A' output is made up of capital goods.

High shares of capital investment in national income are predicted by the official view on account of the alleged properties of centrally planned economies that are common to all inputs and outputs, and properties that are specific to investment. The first concept requires little explanation, as capital is no different in this respect from all inputs and outputs (see chapter 3) and labour (chapter 5). It is claimed that the central co-ordination of investment plans avoids the wasteful duplication of investments, internalises any external costs and benefits, and facilitates co-ordinated investment programmes determined by planned priorities rather than by frivolous individual preferences. In addition, investment in machines and factories may be highly productive, because workforces with job security do not protest against new capital projects.

The foregoing section implies more investment and higher capital productivity for the USSR because of the attributes of central planning in relation to capital or any other input. Central planning may also offer advantages specific to investment. An ideological preference for high levels of investment, and low levels of consumption in the short run, has already been noted. In addition, CMEA countries offer the stability of political and economic leadership that promotes a long-term view and lower interest rates. Interest rates are also kept down by the virtual absence of private property, which means that industrial investment does not have to compete with land speculation and opportunities overseas. Low interest rates encourage high rates of investment.

SOVIET INVESTMENT – THE KORNAI VIEW

As with the official view, capital attracts the usual observations from the

Kornai perspective that are common to all industrial inputs. Like labour, the Kornai view reinforces, rather than contradicts, many of the official predictions, this time in relation to the quantity, though not the quality, of investment.

Broadly, Kornai predicts for centrally planned economies an insatiable investment 'hunger', which is caused by relatively soft budget constraints rather than by ideological preferences. As with other inputs, an emphasis on gross output targets will encourage enterprises and ministries to over-demand capital. This over-demand will tend to be either permitted by the political and economic hierarchies, which feel a co-responsibility for enterprise performance in relation to output targets, or ignored by them because of the communications distance between the planners and the planned. In other words, the lack of (hard budget) penalties/rewards for poor/good performance in relation to investment encourages enterprises to err on the side of over-investment. Kornai explains:

> how the intervention of the bureaucracy prevents a firm manager from being penalised when he makes a wrong investment decision. Since there is no risk of penalty by financial failure, why not invest? The result is what we call 'investment hunger'. There is an almost insatiable demand for investment resources. You see that's exactly the symmetrical opposite of the Keynesian problem of insufficient demand for investment. In the command economy you have an ever-insatiable, never-satiable investment demand. (1985, p. 29)

In this respect investment is no different from other material inputs or labour. The uncertainties that enterprises experience concerning the supply of labour and materials in a shortage economy spill over into the demand for capital as enterprises seek spare capacity in the form of machines and buildings to 'storm' towards the end of a planning period when inputs become available. As with labour, an over-demand for capital outside the enterprises co-exists with spare capacity, or excess supply, within it. Indeed, the two feed off each other. This implies low capital productivity.

In addition, capital has five special features that may be expected to produce greater over-demands for investment goods than for other inputs to Soviet industry. The first feature is related to the existence of relatively soft budget constraints. As far as the enterprise or association is concerned, investment expenditures are essentially not financed out of their own income, but out of their ministry's budget. The reforms of 1979 did try to establish 'self-financing' principles for investment at the levels of ministry and enterprise (see Bornstein, 1985, pp. 20–2), but Bornstein shows that even at the level of the industrial ministry, the state budget cannot secure the sums to which it is entitled (i.e. planned profits minus ministry retentions for investment, research and development, interest charges and incentive funds). Many ministries are not even *planned* to earn enough profit to cover their planned investments, profit plans are often reduced during the period of the plan, and actual profit earned is often below the planned level due to supply uncertainties. This means that even ministries, let alone enterprises, must receive *grants* for investment from the state budget to cover their investment plans, financed largely out of taxes on profitable enterprises. Bornstein points out (p. 21) that self-financing is even more difficult at the enterprise level, where insufficient planned or actual profit is more likely. For this reason, the industrial ministries have always opposed the application of 'self-financing' at the enterprise level.

The second feature of Soviet industrial investment is also designed to make budgets for capital softer than for other inputs, and relates to the standard formulae for investment appraisal (see Gregory and Stuart, 1981, pp. 208–18, and Dyker, 1985, pp. 107–9). The Soviet authorities have consistently shown a great reluctance to apply hard investment-appraisal techniques. In part, this has been a symptom of ideological fashion and the interpretation of Marx, although it has also been argued that Soviet investment decisions involve intangible social costs and benefits that cannot be represented in any formula for marginal projects.

Throughout the Stalinist period, the public ownership and control of capital was felt to dispense with the need for interest rates in the comparison of projects. Under capitalism, interest charges were seen as just one of the means by which capitalists justified their exploitation of labour. With public ownership, there was no need for the working classes to pay interest to themselves, and so before 1960 investments were chosen administratively according to the priorities of the central plan. Where calculations were made as an aid to investment decisions, they amounted to preference for the system with the lowest *operating* costs. This led to 'gigantomania', since operating costs could often be reduced by massive investments, which substituted capital for running expenses. Gradually, 'payback period' calculations were applied to individual sectors, and they became standard after 1960.

Payback-period calculations did not originally include an element of interest charges. They simply compared the reduction in operating costs to the increase in the capital costs that a new project offered. A 'coefficient of relative effectiveness' divided the latter into the former and compared the resulting coefficient with a norm that varied across sectors. If the reduction in operating costs was sufficient in relation to the increase in capital costs, the norm was exceeded and the investment sanctioned. The inclusion of capital costs (or depreciation) was justified in terms of the project's consumption of labour-time 'stored up' (or 'crystallised') in the capital assets. No attention was paid to the *timing* of the operating and capital costs, and until 1969 there was no attempt to equalise norms across all sectors.

In 1969, discount rates of 8 per cent were introduced to calculate the present values of operating and capital costs on the grounds that long-term projects postponed the enjoyment of the fruits of crystallised labour-time. By 1979, it was recognised that enterprises should pay amounts to the state budget for 'especially favourable natural conditions', and Soviet investment appraisal came very close to capitalist techniques involving charges for land rents as well as capital. Dyker (1985, p. 108) surveys the 1981 methodology for investment appraisal, which involves the calculation of 'effectiveness coefficients' for whole blocks of investment projects. There is still no attempt to achieve a uniform rate of return across all industries, however, and the minimum rates are soft for priority industries. Overall, the required rates of return are still too low to eliminate an excess demand for investment from the enterprises and ministries, and in practice investments are still authorised according to 'branch priorities' and 'administrative procedures'. This is a recipe for soft budgets, on the Kornai view, especially for high-priority industries.

Administrative procedures are also responsible for the third feature of Soviet investment that is likely to cause softer budgets for capital than for other inputs: capital is so much more complex to plan than other factors. For example, Dyker (1985, p. 111–17) outlines the administrative procedures involved for the construction industry, although similar accounts could be developed for machine building, which also takes place in separate specialist ministries. In construction, a production ministry wishing to invest in new buildings must apply to the Design Organisation of the appropriate ministry (for construction, heavy construction or industrial construction). These ministries (together with the Construction Bank, which finances projects, and the state Operationalisation Commission, which monitors their implementation) all come under the control of the State Committee for Construction. The resulting designs, which usually involve minor adjustments to standard buildings, are costed by the Design Organisation, under considerable pressure from the production ministries to keep their estimates low. Under-stated capital costs make it easier for the production ministry to obtain approval from the centre for large projects, and in some cases to keep the cost of projects below the maximum limit (3 million roubles by the 1979 decree) that enables ministries to authorise projects without higher approval and pay for them out of their block investment votes. They also mean more work for the construction ministries. Each tier of this administrative process involves more complexity and information 'decay'. Once projects are approved, a reverse process is set in motion and the cost of projects tends to rise rather than fall. It is very difficult to value construction work in terms other than the actual cost of work done. If gross output (measured in terms of costs) is the measure of the construction industry's performance, then pressure to produce 'more' leads to what Dyker (1985, p. 116) calls 'cost maximisation' or 'the more costly, the better'.

As with other aspects of poor Soviet economic performance, the central authorities have been aware of this tendency and have tried to reform it. 'Cost reduction' was used as a success indicator between 1959 and 1965, and profit was introduced in 1965 as a basis for performance evaluation and bonus payments in construction, as in all other industries. In 1970, it was emphasised that the output of the industry must be sold, as opposed to just built, and 'marketed output' became the successor to the gross value of work done. During the 1970s a certificate of work completion from the Operationalisation Commission was needed, if production ministries were to be required to pay for construction work, either in stages or in total. Since the 1979 decree, labour productivity (measured usually in terms of normative net output per head) has been added to marketed output, profit and operationalisation as performance and bonus indicators, but the emphasis on gross output remains. From a Kornai perspective, such administrative procedures are unlikely to secure relatively hard budgets across all industries in an economy of the size and complexity of the USSR.

The fourth unique feature of capital inputs is tied up with the characteristic that distinguished investment goods from other inputs: the *time* taken to design and prepare investment goods and then to enjoy their benefits. Despite attempted reforms in the construction industry, funds have usually been made available when projects have been authorised and begun. Subsequent cost escalations and delays are unlikely to jeopardise the whole project when so many costs have been 'sunk'. Kornai himself provides a telling commentary:

> A particular *investment money illusion* develops. It appears as if financial investment quotas, i.e. money, were distributed by central organs: by the planning office, by financial authorities, and by banks. In fact they allocate *permission to start* the physical actions of investment. And, if action has begun, it cannot stop, not even if it costs much more money than has been planned. Money supply passively adjusts to the money demand generated by the physical inputs of the investment actions. The budget constraint of investment is also soft and ineffective. (1979a, p. 814)

Fifth, and finally, capital is unique because, unlike labour and other material inputs, capital is subject to more flexible *resource* constraints when budget constraints are soft. In the case of labour and raw materials, soft budgets and excess demands eventually hit strict resource ceilings. In the case of labour, general shortage was not achieved until about 1970 in the USSR (see p. 100). With physical materials, the rapid depletion of European fossil fuel and non-fuel mineral deposits has led to increasing dependence on distant Siberian sources, often at prohibitively high costs. In the case of capital, however, although labour and physical materials are required for plant and machinery, investment can always be increased at the expense of current consumption, if the population is not in a position to protest. A growing national income makes it particularly easy for investment levels to increase.

It only needs to be added that the five features of Soviet investment outlined above suggest that the budget constraint for investment might be expected to be even softer than for other inputs. A Kornai perspective would suggest that capital investment (and especially construction) is not determined by a balanced rational consideration of the needs of different sectors. Rather, the prevalent ideology and the self-interests of ministers and managers drives on the mobilisation of all possible resources for investment, uninhibited by soft budgets. High-priority industries are likely to enjoy the softest budgets and in the USSR this is likely to mean an emphasis on industrial construction at the expense of infrastructural support like transport and communications, of housing and of services in general. Construction starts (but not completions), project-cost over-runs, capacity under-utilisation (including low-asset retirement rates) are all stimulated by soft budgets. Soft budgets also discourage the embodiment of best-practice technologies in new capital, but this is the subject of chapter 7. The rest of this chapter is concerned with testing these predictions in terms of the quantity, not quality, of investment.

ACTUAL SOVIET INVESTMENT

This section makes observations on levels of Soviet capital formation and then tries to disentangle the official and Kornai explanations of the trends observed. There seems little doubt that Soviet investment's share of national income is relatively high compared with Western countries, and it is also growing faster than most, with the exception of Japan, which does not have the USSR's defence burden (see Pryor, 1985, p. 76).

Table 6.1 shows the USSR's commitment to investment in terms of (a) official Soviet and (b) CIA definitions. On either score, the devotion of around one-third of GNP to investment represents a large sacrifice. It compares with gross investment's shares of about 16 per cent in the USA and 31 per cent in Japan (Ellman, 1984, p. 176). According to Ellman (p. 177), investment takes an even larger share of national income in other CMEA countries and the rate of growth of investment in these countries was faster between 1950 and 1979 than in the USSR (see Pryor, 1985, p.

Table 6.1 Soviet investment's share of national income: (a) Soviet definitions; (b) US definitions

(a) Ratio of gross fixed capital formation (GFCF) to NMP, at 1976 prices

Year	*(1)* *Ratio (%)*	*(2)* *Annual % change in GFCF*
1976–80	30.3	3.9
1980	29.7	2.4
1981	29.9	3.8
1982	29.7	3.5
Plan 1983	29.7[a]	3.2
1983	30.0[a]	5.0
Plan 1984	30.3[a]	3.9[a]
Plan 1981–5	28.4[a]	1.5[a]

[a]Provisional estimate.
Source: Taken from *Economic Survey of Europe in 1983*, UN Commission for Europe, New York, 1984, p. 159.

(b) Total investment's share of GNP, at factor cost

Year	*Investment's share (%)*
1960	24
1965	27
1970	28
1975	31
1978	32
1979	33
1980	33
1981	33
1982	33[a]

[a]Provisional estimate.
Source: Taken from CIA, *Handbook of Statistics*, 1983, p. 62.

76). The magnitude of the gap between Soviet and US experience is emphasised in table 6.2, where the USSR in 1982 is shown to devote 16 per cent more to new fixed investment in absolute terms, despite having a GNP which is only 56 per cent of the US level.

Bergson (1982) was sufficiently encouraged by the reductions in the rate of growth of the Soviet volume of investment shown in column (2) of table

Table 6.2 Gross national product by end use, USA and USSR, 1982

	USA[a]	*USSR*[a]	*USSR as % of USA*
GNP	1,931.7	1,077.4	56
Consumption	1,363.4	572.0	42
New fixed investment	325.4	376.2	116

New fixed investment is approximately 80 per cent of total investment, USSR, shown in table 6.1(b)
[a]Billion US$, 1976 prices.
Source: Taken from CIA, *Handbook of Statistics*, 1983, p. 34.

6.1(a) to talk about a 'new-growth model' for the USSR. It now seems clear, however, that, despite the efforts of the central authorities, investment's share of GNP between 1980 and 1984 and increases in investment volume since 1983 (see column (1) of table 6.1(a)) show that there has been no abandonment of previous trends. Durgin (1983) provides a critique of the 'new-growth model' and suggests that little has changed in this respect since Stalin.

The only question mark over the measured volume of Soviet investment concerns inflation and capital goods. It has already been noted in chapter 4 that hidden inflation exists in the Soviet economy and that Hanson (1984a, p, 578) reports hidden rates of between 3 and 4 per cent per annum for capital goods in the 1970s. A compound annual rate of four percent over ten years amounts to 47.8 per cent overall, and thus almost half of Soviet investment may be illusory. On the other hand, hidden inflation is a universal phenomenon (though it is probably higher in the USSR than elsewhere) and hidden inflation outside the capital-goods sector means that the estimate for investment's share of national income is likely to be unaffected.

If we accept that Soviet investment levels are extremely high by Western levels, can this be interpreted as a result of relatively soft budgets or of a planned strategy of development? It seems clear that the death of Stalin precipitated a decline in the rate of growth of investment volume, and that during the 1970s a more rapid growth of consumers' rather than producers' goods output was planned. For 1986–90, NMP was planned to grow at 4 per cent per annum, consumption by 5.4 per cent and investment by between 3.4 per cent and 3.9 per cent. The latter range is not high by recent standards (see column (2) of table 6.1(a)), but it remains to be seen whether the traditional priority of investment in heavy industry reasserts itself, as it did in the previous three five-year plans. The plan for 1986–90 encourages re-equipment at the expense of new construction, but it emphasises once again the need for investment in the old, heavy, priority industries around Moscow and Leningrad and in the Ukraine and the Urals. Ambitious projects to divert southwards rivers flowing into the Arctic Ocean have been abandoned. Although *some* relaxation of a development model based on high levels of investment in heavy industry has been attempted in the past, these attempts have not yet proved stern enough to withstand the pressure from old institutions, which include relatively soft budgets in industry. It is interesting to compare the comments of two recent General Secretaries in their addresses to the CPSU Congress. In 1982, Andropov called for an increase in the share of investment going to reconstruction and modernisation, as opposed to 'more of the same' in terms of buildings and machines, and demanded a reduction in the number of new construction projects (see *Pravda*, 1982). By 1986, one could find Gorbachev making an almost identical plea (*Pravda*, 1986) for more reconstruction and re-equipment at the expense of construction projects, whose gestation periods should in any case be shortened by 50 per cent.

As with unemployment in chapter 5, however, soft budgets complement and reinforce ideological preferences, in this case for high investment levels. It is impossible to distinguish the effect of these two explanations from an examination of the *quantity* of investment alone. If the official view were correct, however, one would also expect to find in the USSR high levels of investment offering high levels of productivity. The evidence is not consistent with this claim.

At the aggregate level, table 8.3 shows the estimated contribution of Soviet investment to the growth of national income, compared with the US economy, which invests less in relative and absolute terms in fixed assets (see table 6.2). As might be expected, rows (2) of table 8.3(a) show that the quantity of investment has contributed more to Soviet GNP growth (by an average of about 7 per cent of GNP per annum between 1968 and 1982) than to US growth (around 2 per cent per annum for the same period). At the same time, however, this 'extensive' growth has been achieved at the cost of low and falling capital productivity. Rows (5) of table 8.3(a) show that falls in the quality or productivity of Soviet investment have *reduced* GNP growth by about 3 per cent per annum between 1966 and 1982. This compares with an approximately *zero* contribution of capital productivity growth in the USA between 1966 and 1980 through a period of oil and research and development crises, although negative contributions have been recorded for the USA in 1981 and 1982.

How can this relatively poor contribution of Soviet capital productivity be explained? A consideration of Soviet levels of innovation and the extent to which best-practice technologies are adopted must be left until chapter

7, but at this stage other explanations are considered. Overall, it has to be said that, industry-by-industry, there is *no* evidence that *new* Soviet investment projects, once commissioned, offer less output than their Western equivalents. For example, Cohn (1982, pp. 169–77) shows broadly similar incremental capital-output ratios across all sectors. At the same time, however, cost over-runs, long gestation periods for all investments, unfinished construction, overmanning and a reluctance to retire old assets all contribute to a low *average* productivity of capital, both old and new.

For example, Dyker (1985, p. 113) reports that, despite the attempted reforms of the construction industry noted above, clients are still financing 85 per cent of construction work in progress before 'operationalisation', that (p. 119) cost 'hikes' above 100 per cent after the approval of a project are not exceptional, but that (p. 115) 25 per cent of construction organisations still make financial losses. Goldman (1983, p. 40) notes that buildings like the Moscow Law School were still unfinished in 1983 after more than a decade in construction, and that the percentage of 1980 investment projects unfinished at the end of the year was 87 per cent compared with 73 per cent for 1970. Nove (1982, p. 162) reckoned that Soviet construction has tended to take twice as long as planned norms, and that the 'running in' of new factories once completed takes 1.5 times the norm. This would not be so bad if the norms themselves were not already double their Western equivalent standards. In a sample of Western chemical plants installed in the USSR, Hanson (1981, p. 190) again found lags between project commencement and commission at about double Western levels, despite their high priority.

Besides delays and cost-hikes, this question of priority, which itself determines the softness of budgets, is largely responsible for low average Soviet capital productivity. Old high-cost plant is retained by managements and ministries that are unconstrained by hard budgets and that simultaneously push for new factories. Cohn reports:

> On the average, fixed assets have been retained in service twice as long as those in the major market economies. This prolonged retention of obsolescent low productivity capital has been reinforced by the proportion of investment devoted to replacement of obsolescent assets. In recent years the replacement share has been about a fifth, compared with nearly half in the United States. Together these two policies account for about half of the negative capital productivity rate. Productivity has also been depressed by the rapid additions to the capital stock compared with additions to employment. (1982, pp. 169–70)

Hanson (1986, p. 102) added to this finding by pointing out that although new investment in industrial plant has the highest priority and the softest budgets in the Soviet economy, it also suffers the most acute labour shortages, since labour is tied up with overmanned, obsolete, old plant. Furthermore, a preference for industrial plant has meant the relative neglect of investment in housing, transport (despite the BAM 'hero project'), communications and services in general (see Pryor, 1985, p. 93). A lack of industrial infrastructure ultimately reduces the productivity of direct industrial investments and impedes innovation. For example, the computerisation of industry is hindered by the unreliability of the Soviet telephone system, and poor housing and other services erode a workforce's motivation.

CONCLUSIONS

Investment 'hunger' can be caused by ideology or soft budgets. They complement each other and nobody can prove that either cause has been dominant in the USSR. Certain phenomena such as low capital productivity and long gestation periods for projects do contradict the official position and support the Kornai perspective, however. Despite repeated attempts to raise consumption's share of GNP, it would appear that additional industrial investment is uncontrollable as long as budgets remain soft. In the area of Soviet investment, Kornai's theory has been found to provide an accurate explanation of performance.

The high levels of investment for decade after decade are another undeniable achievement of the Soviet system, but as with all achievements in all systems, it has not been achieved without its costs. If low capital productivity persists or accelerates, a population used to current consumption being repeatedly sacrificed for investment may not be able to protest openly, but it is likely to make its feelings felt through level of workplace effort, or lack of it.

CHAPTER SEVEN

INNOVATION

Together with investment (see chapter 6), the innovative ability of any economic system determines what is known as its micro-dynamic efficiency, which was explained at the end of chapter 1. Innovative ability refers to the *responsiveness* of enterprises on the demand-side (product innovation), and the supply-side (process innovation), and to the rate at which such innovations are *disseminated* throughout the economy. Chapters 2–5 were concerned with the static allocation of resources to existing production. Here the subject is *innovation*, or new products and processes, which are inventions that have been applied in regular production. Research and development (R & D) is the process that generates innovations. In many ways the innovative capacity of an economic system is its most important characteristic, since the force of human ingenuity is not so easily exhausted as other sources of economic growth.

On the face of it, innovation provides central planning with its biggest challenge. In chapter 1, it was seen how such a system grapples with the static allocation of resources: the planners must organise the *quantities* of inputs and outputs for industry, and then try to ensure that these plans are carried out. It was noted that enterprises cannot be relied upon to provide perfectly accurate information to the planners or to respond instantly to their instructions. Innovation, however, is concerned with the design of machines and products, or the *qualities* of inputs and outputs, which are even more difficult to represent in messages and instructions than simple quantities. This exposes planners and enterprises to massive uncertainties. For example, researchers may be tempted to overstate the benefits of new technologies and products to the planners; see, for example, Khrushchev's difficulties caused by Lysenko's agrarian schemes discussed above in chapter 3. In turn, these planners may be too optimistic in their attempts to convince enterprise managers of the benefits of innovations.

The first section of this chapter provides a background description of Soviet institutions for the research and development of new products and processes, explaining how R & D is basically centralised, but has been supplemented by decentralising incentive schemes and institutional reforms; the second section explains the official Soviet view on the desirability of centralised R & D; in the third section, the contrasting Kornai view on the relative advantages of such an arrangement is presented; and the final section considers whether the actual performance of Soviet R & D institutions conforms to the official or Kornai view.

SOVIET R & D INSTITUTIONS

Before going into institutional detail for Soviet R & D it is useful first to note the different stages of R & D, and their location in Western economies, with which the reader may be more familiar. Parker (1974, p. 21) distinguishes *basic research* ('pure' or 'fundamental' research or science) from *applied research* and *development work*.

Basic research is the search for new technical knowledge for its own sake and is not directed towards some existing need or technological problem, although of course basic research in fields such as laser technology has subsequently spawned new products in audio equipment and military weaponry. This kind of free-ranging work is carried out in Western universities or research institutes, and soft budgets seem appropriate, if apparently unpromising ideas are to be pursued by tenured academics. Basic research is not easily carried out by private firms with hard budgets because of its distance from commercial applications; in any case, private basic research would inhibit the dissemination of new knowledge if discoveries were made. Western governments have therefore been prepared to fund basic research in universities and research institutes, although sometimes the picture is confused by state-sponsored corporations like RAND in US defence research. This policy has yielded a fairly rich diversity of basic research unconstrained by the profit motive.

Applied research is consciously directed at new products and processes and the solution of industrial problems; Parker reports (1974, p. 21) that 65 per cent of applied research in the United States is carried out by private corporations. Most of the remainder is carried out in the universities and institutes on the basis of contracts from private corporations.

Finally, development work is concerned with the use in industry of the fruits of applied research in the form of new products, processes or applications. According to Parker (1974, p. 21), at least 85 per cent of US development work is located in private corporations.

Thus, to summarise the Western situation, applied R & D is largely conducted or sponsored by private firms. Although this depends on the level of industrial concentration, it seems likely that such a system of profit-based independent R & D will generate a relatively diverse set of technological responses. It is largely left to the market mechanism to weed out unsuccessful developments, although products like the Concorde may be cited as contradictions. Basic research is still the preserve of central governments, although the sheer proliferation of capitalist nations provides a wide diversity of projects.

Many parallels and contrasts can be drawn between R & D in the West and in the Soviet Union. In terms of sheer scale, Soviet efforts in the R & D field are considerable. Bergson (1983, p. 54) shows that in 1975 the Soviet Union devoted 3.7 per cent of its GNP to R & D, whereas the corresponding figure for the United States – the highest in the West – was 2.2 per cent. In the same year, Bergson reports that the Soviet Union employed 873,500 scientists and engineers in R & D (66.0 per 10,000 total workers) compared with 534,800 (61.5 per 10,000) in the United States.

In many ways, the organisation of Soviet R & D is similar to that in the West, with the major exception that in the Soviet Union technological change is predicted and embodied in economic plans. This should not imply, however, that Soviet R & D is totally centralised. Certainly, basic research is still the prerogative of the Academy of Science, which is directly responsible to the Council of Ministers, but of course the Academy has facilities at republican level as well as at the centre. Until about 1961 virtually *all* R & D was under the control of the Academy (Parrott, 1983, p. 167), and the R & D system could unambiguously be described as centralised, in the sense that R & D was controlled by one arm of the state. Although the universities and higher education institutions do employ 36 per cent of all scientists, they have until recently been concerned largely with teaching, and they account for only 5 per cent of total research in terms of expenditure (Brown et al, 1982, p. 261). The Academy has traditionally led R & D from the centre.

After 1961, however, a new State Committee for the Co-ordination of Scientific Research (now Science and Technology) was set up to break the stranglehold of the Academy on all R & D. The State Committee now initiates and co-ordinates much of the Soviet R & D effort and delegates some control to Gosplan and the Academy. Although it is without ministerial status, the Academy still leads in basic science and employed 150,000 workers and 88,000 scientists in 1976 (Brown et al., 1982, p. 260). About 45 per cent of the Soviet R & D budget is spent centrally, either by the Academy itself or through the co-operation of ministries in joint ventures.

The bulk of the R & D effort is carried out away from the centre, in the sense of the separate ministries and their enterprises, with the State Committee attempting to co-ordinate their efforts. Although Soviet enterprises are very large and in 1967 were already responsible for 33,000 laboratories (Berliner, 1976, p. 33), it seems that in practice they have probably made only a small contribution to Soviet technological advance in the form of 'product improvement or of minor changes in the basic production technology' (Berliner 1976, p. 54). Applied R & D in the Soviet Union has been dominated not by the enterprises (as in the West), but by the ministries and their sub-branches, which have set up research institutes or similar bodies. This has tended to isolate innovation from production, but it should be noted in passing that in the defence sector this has not happened, with R & D facilities attached to factories and pilot plants available for the production of prototypes by the ministerial design bureaux (Amann, 1982, p. 16).

The Soviet R & D organisations (largely research institutes) within the branch ministries and departments employ about 48 per cent of all scientists (Brown et al. 1982, p. 261) and have few equivalents in the West. The branch institutes numbered 1,700 in 1969 (Berliner, 1976, p. 39) and deal in the full range of applied research relevant to their particular ministerial branches. As innovations move closer to the production stage within the ministry, they pass through an engineering–design organisation to a construction-engineering organisation which produces the blueprints for a new plant.

Although R & D work within the ministries is not centralised in the Soviet sense of the word – a term restricted to the work of the Academy of Sciences and the State Committee for Science and Technology – most Western observers would still describe the ministerial research institutions as an example of central planning fairly distant from the managers of industrial enterprises. In addition, one should not ignore the power of the Communist Party in R & D. Miller (1985, p. 31) reports that the Party was only given the legal right to control the research institutes and universities in 1971, but it seems that effective control came much earlier. Most research institutes have a Party 'cell' and the more important ones a full-time Party secretary. As with industrial enterprises, Miller found that the standing of the institute's director *vis-à-vis* the Party secretary was decisive in the appointment of staff and the direction of research. Berliner (1976, p. 41) suggests that the Party's role in the factories is to encourage reluctant enterprise managers to adopt innovations that are the fruits of the research institutes. Parrott (1983, p. 293) emphasises that the Party's leadership has always preferred the degree of central control offered by the traditional R & D system and has avoided truly decentralising reforms that might undermine the political system.

Nevertheless, some reforms of centralised R & D have been attempted, with a view to resolving the need for the 'intensification' of the Soviet economy demanded by successive General Secretaries. These include:

(1) innovation incentive schemes;
(2) associations of enterprises;
(3) contract R & D.

Innovation Incentives

Berliner (1976, pp. 397–500) reviews a plethora of schemes designed to encourage enterprises to adopt innovations. Since 1965, bonus payments have been handed out for cost reduction via innovation, for improvements in product quality made possible by innovation, and for the adoption of specific planned innovations. Innovating enterprises have been allowed to raise product prices (and hence bonus funds) and scientists in research institutes have themselves been rewarded for innovations successfully carried out. On the other hand, innovations may appear threatening to risk-averse managements, who fear that the promises of innovation will remain unfulfilled, but that targets will increase anyhow.

It is difficult to evaluate the impact of these reforms. The 'economics of regulation' would predict great difficulties for such schemes in the area of R & D, where specialist researchers and enterprise managers have more information than ministers and central planners. The 'success' or otherwise of innovations has often been judged by the research institutes themselves to avoid the late payment of bonuses after the application of innovations, and a small inspectorate has been unable to ensure that the quality of goods sold has corresponded to the categories of quality embodied in certificates issued on the basis of trial production runs. A decree of August 1985 announced a new system of fines and rewards related to the quality of output, and enterprise managers have been given some discretion over their own construction and R & D budgets. Again, it is pertinent to reflect on the Soviet defence sector, where quality control has been carried out not in the form of infrequent checks by remote commissioners, but by military inspectors protected from the influence of factory directors (see Amann, 1982, p. 35).

Overall, however, innovation incentives have provided extremely small supplements to enterprise salaries (Berliner, 1976, p. 481) and they leave virtually undisturbed the Soviet system of centralised R & D, with all its virtues and faults. This conclusion is reiterated by Spechler (1983).

Associations

Since the decree of September 1968 two kinds of associations or groupings of enterprises have been formed in Soviet industry (see chapter 1 above).

Simple production associations ('corporations') are groups of enterprises that leave R & D functions firmly in the hands of the ministry or its branch, while *research-based* (or science-production) associations are essentially R & D institutes that have been expanded to embrace production. Gorlov and Baburin (1985) report that both kinds of association together accounted for about half of total enterprise sales and employment by the end of 1983, and associations are planned to be the normal form of industrial organisation in the future.

It seems possible, however, that the 'distance' between R & D and production may increase within the ordinary production associations, as enterprises become exclusively concerned with production matters. In the case of the research-based associations, the reform may reduce this 'distance' and decentralise R & D, but another development is possible: actual production may be seen as totally subservient to R & D. In the example of a research-based association of electrical engineering plants in the Moscow region described by Gorlov and Baburin (1985, p. 180), some low-order R & D is brought closer to the shop-floor in suburban plants, while high-order research and high-technology production is retained at the research institute and plants in Moscow. Problems remain with R & D and the association movement. In his address to the CPSU Congress, Gorbachev made special reference to it:

> Measures are also being taken to step up the work of branch research institutes and increase their contribution to the acceleration of scientific and technical progress. However, this process is proceeding at an intolerably slow pace. Many institutes remain extensions of the administrative apparatus of ministries, frequently play the role of advocates of departmental interests, and are mired in routine and paper-shuffling. At the June conference, the question of bringing science and practice closer together and including branch institutes in production and research-and-production associations was raised sharply. We must find out who is opposing this, what the position of the ministries and their Party committees is, and how they are reacting to life's demands'. (*Pravda*, 26 February 1986)

Contract R & D

As an alternative to formal associations of enterprises and research institutes, research contracts have been used since 1962 to bring R & D closer to production. Until this time, research institutes were allocated a budget from their parent ministerial branch and monitored by them. Research contracts were introduced in an attempt to weaken the ministerial influence on the relationship between science and production, and to allow researchers and enterprises to make decisions in a decentralised fashion.

This reform attempted to convert research institutes into business-like entities dependent on revenues from clients (usually enterprises) for their existence rather than the ministry's budget. These 'horizontal' links have made possible many forms of co-operation between research institutions and ministries that cut across previously rigid ministerial boundaries. For example, *science–production complexes* are fairly loose inter-departmental groupings of related enterprises and research bodies in particular city-regions held together by long-term contracts and agreements. In the case of Novosibirsk, such a complex was given a physical dimension in the form of a new 'academic city' (Akademgorod) made up of the research institutes of the ministries and the Academy at its corc, surrounded by research-based factories. Such complexes can also embrace the universities and colleges of higher education. Meshkov (1983) shows how subtle relationships between teaching, research and production have been achieved in Belorussia. Finally, contract research and inter-ministerial co-operation in R & D have made possible the *programme approach* to technical problems that affect more than one ministry. For example, the 1981–5 five-year plan was concerned with energy conservation, and 'mission-oriented' R & D has been used in a fashion familiar to the defence sector.

As with other reforms, however, it is easy to overestimate the extent of decentralisation in the Soviet economy. Despite contracts, the research institutes still receive the bulk of their funds in the form of budget allocations from the ministry, and contracts between enterprises and research institutes must in any case be submitted to the branch ministry for approval. Ambitious Party secretaries in enterprises and research institutes will always push for the current central R & D priority despite local preferences.

Furthermore, contracts are not easy to enforce in the R & D field, where outcomes are complex and uncertain. Berliner (1976, p. 118) reports that such contracts used to include a clause to the effect that 'a negative result does not free the client from paying the cost of the work'. In the West, the very nature of applied R & D work has caused it to be carried out 'in-house' by private corporations more often than through external contracts.

This concludes the review of Soviet R & D institutions. Our judgement is that the system can still be described as centrally planned, despite the reforms. The next two sections consider the relative merits of such a system.

PLANNED R & D – THE OFFICIAL VIEW

Although attempts to reform centralised R & D in the Soviet Union prove that there is a wide understanding of the shortcomings of such a system, the case for centrally planned R & D still dominates the leadership's thinking. This case rests on three elements, involving the 'socialisation of knowledge', economies of scale and the associated reduction of uncertainty.

In the West, it is unusual for any one person, group or institution to be seen as holding a monopoly of information on any subject, particularly new technology. We are used to the notion that all information is subjective and exists only in the minds of individual researchers and producers. Outside public R & D, the task of capitalist entrepreneurs is to judge which new technologies are likely to be profitable. New scientific developments have very uncertain futures and 'belong' to the individuals or companies who discover them. To encourage R & D efforts, patenting laws protect innovations at least for a limited period.

Soviet patents also exist in the form of inventors' certificates and a whole State Committee of Inventions and Discoveries is charged with the task of promoting innovations. Millions of scientists and engineers are members of voluntary societies that encourage inventiveness, and those who develop successful innovations are rewarded by a proportion of the economic benefit estimated as accruing to the innovation.

These bonus payments fall far short of the rewards offered to Western innovators, however, and the State Committee is often seen as keeping *down* the price that innovators can charge for new technologies (Martens, 1983, p. 534). This policy is justified by pointing out that researchers use the State's property for their work. *Knowledge is 'socialised'*, and bonus schemes only modify slightly the view that innovations belong to the state. This situation offers many advantages. For example, there is less need for secrecy compared with a situation where private inventors compete, and there are fewer barriers to the dissemination of new knowledge. If there is a common interest in new technologies, workforces may be less obstructive to new technologies and there may be generally less opportunistic behaviour in the field of innovation. A relative absence of positive incentives to impede innovations may not be enough to overcome inertia, however, and aversion to risk in Soviet industry will be considered below as a cause of unresponsiveness to innovation.

Centrally planned R & D should offer considerable *economies of scale.* Some projects could be too large for single enterprises, but practicable for a ministry: for example, nuclear power generation. Where technologies are interdependent, centralised R & D may be directed in a multiple attack on a particular objective or problem. Certainly, some duplication of research efforts can be avoided by centralised R & D.

These scale economies must inevitably be associated with some costs, however. A monolithic research effort may lack the diversity of approach of decentralised R & D, leaving too many 'eggs in one basket'. For example, Berliner (1976, p. 41) reports that the Soviet development of the turbo-drill in the oil industry met a great deal of resistance from the petroleum ministry and enterprises, but a strong central Party commitment to the turbo-drill ensured that by 1981 80 per cent of all Soviet oil-drilling equipment was of the turbo-drill variety rather than electric (Stein, 1981, p. 307). As explained in the section on past performance in chapter 1, however, the turbo-drill is only effective down to a depth of about 2.5–3 km and in the 1980s the unforeseeable occurred: massive new oil deposits in Western Siberia were discovered at depths beyond the turbo-drill, so it became necessary to consider the import of electric drilling technologies from the West. Compare this centralised approach with a new area of Western technology like the prop-fan, which harnesses propellers with up to sixteen blades to a gas-turbine aircraft engine. Prop-fans promise to be so much quieter and cheaper than conventional engines that at least four corporations (Pratt & Whitney, General Electric, Boeing and Rolls-Royce) are developing prop-fan variants. The engines will not be ready for service until about 1992 and the corporations are uncertain about the demand for air travel, fuel costs and noise regulations in that year. It is possible that only one variant will be successful and this will be chosen *ex post* by the market in terms of the engine's solution of certain technical problems and the successful corporation's 'right' combination of guesses about market conditions in 1992. Meanwhile, projects involve duplication in static terms.

In the West, competition always involves static duplication and 'waste'. (For example, petrol filling-stations often stand together on Western highways at frequent intervals, whereas their Soviet equivalents are bigger, but almost impossible for a visitor to find.) Many examples of static duplication in the West (for example, adjacent branches of competing banks) transfer costs to the producer from consumers, like bank customers who might otherwise have to queue at the state bank. Competing banks suffer the excess supply instead of consumers bearing the excess demand. Presumably the advocates of capitalism are prepared to accept static losses through duplication in favour of dynamic gains through competition. Western R & D managers have always known that half of their budgets are wasted, but, faced with an uncertain future, they have never known *which* half in advance. Duplicated research is only wasteful if the value of resources consumed by unsuccessful projects is greater than the expected costs resulting from a fairly randomly chosen, unique variant.

In one sense, however, Soviet R & D involves fewer guesses about 1992 and the future in general, and this *reduction of uncertainty* constitutes the third major benefit from centralised research. Soviet R & D can be conducted without competition from overseas, and future prices are centrally controlled. Demands for intermediate products like turbo-drills and aircraft engines (supplied to other enterprises) can be predicted from co-ordinated plans, final demands for something like clothing can be controlled, and there is no need for innovations to cater for consumers' demands for 'frivolous' product improvements. On the other hand, central plans may prove uncertain and subject to frequent revision. Central interference with plans and enterprises causes new uncertainties over supplies; in the next section, Kornai's view on the implications of general shortage for innovation is discussed.

PLANNED R & D – THE KORNAI VIEW

Many apparently unrelated criticisms can be made of centralised R & D, but in this section it will be argued that most of these criticisms can be seen as part of a wider view of R & D provided by Kornai's theory of the shortage economy. At the risk of repetition, it may be remembered from the end of chapter 1 that a case was made there for the description of the Soviet economy as one with relatively *soft budget constraints* in industry. This conclusion was based on two observations: first the Soviets have preferred vertical hierarchies to horizontal links between buyers and sellers, and this puts physical and communications distance between parties to a transaction; and second, many decisions that help to determine enterprise performance, such as factory location and technology, are decided centrally before the appointment of an enterprise director. This leads to a *co-responsibility* for enterprise performance between different levels of the hierarchy (e.g. branch ministry and enterprise management), which is reinforced by the influence of the Party. Co-responsibility inhibits effective monitoring.

For these reasons, it is concluded that poor Soviet enterprise performance is not punished as severely as it would be in the West, and Bergson (1983, p. 61) points out that 'enterprise liquidation is clearly an extraordinary rarity'. This does not mean that enterprises do not feel obliged to meet or overfulfil their targets. It is suggested in chapter 1, however, that an overriding concern for gross output is inevitable, if central planning is to co-ordinate resource allocation, and this generates additional enterprise demands for inputs that would not be justified if profitability were the criterion. Plans are often achieved because they are flexible downwards, because of the hoarding of inputs of all kinds to deal with supply uncertainties, through informal horizontal links between enterprises and by the informal self-production of inputs by enterprises.

Taken together, all these mechanisms generate excess demand at different levels of the Soviet economy, or what Kornai calls 'shortage'. What are the implications of shortage for Soviet innovation? We would identify low incentives for innovation, a lack of diversity in R & D and poor co-ordination between different research projects and between buyers and sellers.

Innovations may relate to new products or new processes. On the face of it, shortage provides an enormous *incentive for innovation* in relation to processes. Surely ministries and enterprises experiencing desperate shortages of labour, materials and other inputs will encourage researchers to come up with new processes that economise on these inputs? At the end of chapter 1, Stalin was quoted as having consciously chosen a shortage economy for the Soviet Union for this sort of reason.

The possibility that shortage (suction) encourages innovation contradicts Kornai's basic proposition (Kornai, 1976, p. 197) that the threat of extinction is the mother of invention for enterprises facing relatively hard budgets. Producers under competitive pressures must introduce new products to survive, let alone grow, and successful innovations are rapidly imitated by others. In other words, soft budgets discourage product innovation and inhibit the dissemination of new knowledge.

How can Kornai's prediction of low rates of *product* innovation under shortage be reconciled with the claim that suction encourages *process* innovation? Kornai concedes that 'Many recognise that suction is unfavourable for product innovation but add that it provides incentives for production innovation for careful economising of scarce resources' (1976, p. 198). His discussion that follows this quote implies, however, that there is no conceptual difference between a process and a product innovation. In other words, a process innovation is simply an innovation concerning an intermediate product for which there is a buyer and a seller, just as for a final product. Processes are the output of a supplier of machinery.

For example, consider a process innovation such as some application of robots in the motor vehicle industry. On the face of it, this process innovation will be encouraged in a suction economy experiencing chronic labour shortages. Kornai would probably emphasise, however, that at each stage of the production and sale of motor vehicles in a suction economy, sellers' markets are likely to impede innovation. It goes without saying that the massive pent-up demand for motor vehicles in the Soviet Union prevents the consumer from being choosy and demanding product improvements from the car manufacturers, but an enterprise in the Automotive Ministry is in exactly the *same* position when trying to buy its machinery from the enterprises of the Ministry of Machine Tools or Instrument Making. The automotive works is striving to meet its output target, but has a relatively soft budget and an insatiable appetite for existing machinery. New machinery that economises on labour could be a mixed blessing, if the factory has developed informal sources of supply of parts for the old plant and if its output is fairly predictable. The achievement of innovation bonuses is uncertain and output targets may be increased after innovation. In other words, the automotive enterprise (and ministry) may be averse to risks where supplies are uncertain, and may behave conservatively when survival does not depend upon process innovation.

Given the excess demand for the existing machines of the Ministry of Machine Tools, there is no great pressure there from the buyers' side to innovate. Indeed, one could go back even further in the chain of production: the research institute within the Ministry of Machine Tools is likely to experience an excess demand for *its* services as many ministries clamour for labour-saving innovations, and given the Soviet Union's desperate need to 'intensify' production (see chapter 8), many ministries and research institutes may experience an excess demand for their services from their 'client', the Council of Ministers and the Party's Central Committee.

Kornai (1976, p. 198) implies that many process innovations in the West are in fact product developments in industries facing over-capacity and crisis. In other words, hard budgets encouraged the chemical industry to convert plastics into synthetic fibres for sale to the textile industry. The chemical industry felt the need to widen its product range and new processes resulted.

It follows that hard budgets in all industries will produce a *diversity* of research efforts that does not occur under centralised R & D without massive administrative efforts. A car-buying public demanding improvements in the quality of products – i.e. pressure, not suction – will encourage those suppliers of materials and potential materials to the car industry, who are under similar pressure in all their markets, to pursue R & D projects which could enhance their sales to the car industry. (Of course capitalism does not guarantee hard budgets without competition, and monopolists may reduce product quality.)

A diversity of research approaches is difficult to arrange under centralised R & D except for a few high-priority projects such as defence or energy conservation in the 1980s. The same observation applies to the *co-ordination* of non-diverse projects relating to different stages of the process of production. According to Kornai (1976, p. 200), 'In a suction economy the buyer is burdened with a disproportionately large share of the cost of obtaining information', and (p 199), 'Suction places the consumer at the mercy of the seller'. The specialist engineer or scientist in a research institute 'sells' innovations to the ministry and may not be anxious to underestimate the potential benefits of an innovation. Expert knowledge produces communications 'distance' within a vertical hierarchy that obscures the real value of projects, and spatial distance may add to the problem. Siemaszko (1982, p. 251) describes how a process control instrument was developed at a research institute in Moscow whose prototypes are made at an experimental factory at Smolensk, 380 km to the west. Preparation for production was near Kazan, about 1,200 km from Smolensk and final production in the Western Ukraine, a further 2,200 km away.

To summarise, Kornai's perspective challenges the official Soviet preference for centralised R & D. Of course, if the buyer does assert close quality control and administered budget constraints are hard, innovative performance may improve, especially when objective tests on the product's quality can distinguish effective improvements, as in the defence industry with weapons evaluations. It may not be possible, however, for a centrally planned economy to sustain these conditions for more than a few years or a few priority sectors. A wide Soviet awareness of the drawbacks of centralised R & D is in any case amply demonstrated by the various attempted reforms, and the final section of this chapter will try to judge whether the Soviet Union's innovative performance compared with that of the West, conforms to the official or Kornai view.

SOVIET R & D PERFORMANCE

A Western economist attempting to appraise Soviet R & D performance is already prejudiced by the experiences of *capitalist* R & D. The R & D *efforts* of capitalist firms do increase with size and centralisation, but there is no evidence that economies of scale produce more *innovations* (see Kamien and Schwartz, 1982). They conclude that: 'The largest firms appear to be far less efficient motivators than smaller rivals' (p. 104). The hierarchies of larger firms find it more difficult to monitor the activities of their researchers, and innovations tend to reflect more the 'technology push' of the scientists and engineers than the 'demand pull' from user needs. Freeman (1974, p. 218–9) gives a similar emphasis: 'The freedom to criticise the management and establishment of existing institutions is a necessary condition for innovation, but it can only be really effective if new small innovating organisations can be set up independently'. So, the evidence from within capitalism tends to favour the decentralisation of non-basic R & D.

This section compares the performance of Soviet R & D with that of the West in three different areas: by trying to infer R & D performance from Soviet foreign trade; by trying to infer R & D performance from Soviet GNP growth analyses; and by directly observing technical progress in case studies of particular industries.

Foreign Trade and Technology

It is often suggested that the Soviet Union reveals its technological performance at home when it trades with the rest of the world.

'One of the most important results of this technology problem is to be seen in the structure of foreign trade. The USSR is now the world's second largest industrial country and what does it export to the West? Does it export sophisticated industrial products? No. It primarily exports raw materials, namely, oil, gas, gold and wood'. (Ellman, 1982, p. 27).

Table 7.1 Foreign trade by major commodity groups (percentage of total imports/exports)

	Imports			*Exports*		
	USSR (1983)	*Australia (1982)*	*Canada (1982)*	*USSR (1983)*	*Australia (1982)*	*Canada (1982)*
Machinery and equipment	38.2	39.2	47.9	12.5	3.8	32.2
Food	20.5	4.6	7.7	1.5	30.6	13.4
Fuel	5.6	14.4	10.1	53.7	18.2	14.3

Sources: Handbook of International Trade and Development Statistics, UNCTAD, New York, 1984, tables 4.1, 4.2. *Vneshnyaya torgovlya SSSR, 1983*, Ministerstvo Vneshnoy Torgovli SSSR, Moscow.

Reference to table 7.1 shows that in 1983 Soviet imports were dominated by machinery and equipment (38.2 per cent) and food (20.5 per cent), whereas only 12.5 per cent of exports were machinery and equipment and 53.7 per cent were fuel (of which oil claimed 41.8 per cent). The significance of Soviet machinery exports has also declined over time. In 1972 machinery was responsible for 23.6 per cent of total exports, compared with 12.5 per cent by 1983.

The obvious conclusion to draw from these statistics is that low levels of Soviet technology have hindered Soviet exports of machinery. Indeed the Soviet Union is heavily dependent on foreign countries for many kinds of capital equipment. In addition, food exports have declined and imports increased over a period during which Soviet agriculture has been substantially mechanised and able to take advantage of fertilisers. Poor technological performance may have contributed here, too.

These conclusions should not go unqualified, however, for three reasons. First, they are based on foreign trade, which embraces only a small sample of industries, representing only about 5–6 per cent of GNP, a similar proportion to that in the United States. Foreign trade is very difficult to plan centrally, especially for sophisticated goods which must be sold in extremely volatile overseas markets. Foreign trade may then be a special case, atypical of Soviet industry as a whole. On the other hand, it could be pointed out that since 1973 trade in fuel, gold and industrial diamonds has been subject to greater uncertainty than capital equipment.

Second, it could be argued that the Soviet Union's foreign trade structure is typical of industrialised, resource-rich countries. Exports of fuel and imports of food and machinery could still be rational, even with satisfactory technological performance at home. For this reason, table 7.1 includes an outline of the foreign trade of Australia and Canada. Many parallels can be drawn, although the Soviet Union's dependence on food imports and fuel exports is quite unusual, and neither Canada nor Australia has embarked on a Soviet-type development programme emphasising heavy industry and technological advance.

Third, more than half of Soviet trade is with other socialist countries and the structure of Soviet foreign trade could be interpreted as reflecting a 'master plan' to integrate socialist trade – that is, to insulate the socialist economies from Western trade sanctions and to make the economies of Eastern Europe and elsewhere dependent on the Soviet Union for imports of fuel and raw material, and exports of machinery.

Soviet Innovation and Economic Growth

The whole of chapter 8 is devoted to the analysis of Soviet economic growth. One of the most widely used tools of analysis is 'growth accounting', which tries to attribute increases in GNP to the generation of *more inputs* of land, labour and capital to the economic system and to *more output per unit of input*, or 'total factor productivity'. The technique and its limitations are explained in chapter 8, but table 7.2 shows one

Table 7.2 CIA estimates of aggregate Soviet factor productivity, 1961–82 (average annual percentage growth)

	1961–5	*1966–70*	*1971–5*	*1976–80*	*1981*	*1982*
Increase in factor inputs	4.5	4.1	4.2	3.6	3.2	3.1
Increase in factor productivity	0.5	1.1	−0.5	−0.8	−1.0	−1.1
GNP Growth	5.0	5.3	3.7	2.7	2.2	2.0

Figures subject to rounding errors.
Source: CIA, Handbook of Economic Statistics, 1983, table 44.

(CIA) attempt to isolate the contribution of 'productivity', which has declined since 1970.

Factor 'productivity', however, may have been measured incorrectly and cannot in any case be attributed just to technological change. It also embraces technical efficiency and wrong allocative choices in static terms (see chapter 3 above). Nevertheless, the Soviet authorities have been very concerned since 1970 about the 'extensive' nature of Soviet economic growth and the low (perhaps negative) contribution of factor productivity, or 'intensive' growth (see chapter 8). Their 'intensification' programme has placed a heavy emphasis on the need for better R & D and the first section of this chapter outlined attempted reforms of R & D. To this extent, poor R & D has probably contributed significantly to the collapse of the 'productivity' growth residual in table 7.2. (It is, however, explained in chapter 8 that a similar collapse also occurred in the West.) Bergson (1983, p. 50) reckoned that between 1950 and 1970, technological progress could explain between 53.5 per cent and 79.3 per cent of Soviet variations in total factor productivity.

Case Studies and Soviet Innovation

The case-study approach is always partial and unsatisfactory, but it is unavoidable in R & D, where industries must be studied in depth and broader information is absent. Many studies of Soviet R & D are available. There is only space here for a short review, which takes advantage of Berliner's (1976, pp. 506–9) suggestion that Soviet R & D is applied to first-priority, mission-oriented production, then second-priority sectors of chemicals, electronics and engineering, etc., followed by low-priority sectors, which are primarily in the area of consumer goods. Qualifications must be entered when priorities have shifted. Other summaries may be consulted in Bergson (1983), Amann (1982), Brada (1981) and Hanson (1981, pp. 30–80).

Berliner distinguishes mission-oriented research as being concerned with engineering tasks governed by technical parameters and not social values. There is no question that Soviet R & D has been outstanding in the defence industries and in space research, and it emphatically cannot be concluded that centralised R & D is systemically incapable of producing an excellent innovation record in particular areas. Success in space and defence has been achieved, however, at the cost of wide income differentials in the industry, of perhaps less Party control over the activities of the military complex than of other industries, and certainly of stretching the administrative resources of the central authorities. Priority programmes have been attempted for agriculture, energy conservation, railways to the East, and oil and gas pipelines to the West. With centralised R & D, however, it will prove very difficult to sustain more than a few privileged areas of high priority, where researchers are highly motivated, but the client (e.g. the Ministry of Defence) monitors their activities closely. It follows that with centralised R & D and general resource allocation, the burden of Soviet defence efforts is greater than mere shares of GNP expended would suggest. Nevertheless the OECD (1985, p. 40) identified many areas of Soviet technological excellence besides space and defence. These included welding equipment, cooling technologies for blast furnaces, electromagnetic casting of copper, and surgical instruments.

At the opposite end of the spectrum of priorities, the technological level in many traditional, low-priority industries has been poor. This category would include most services, distribution, transport and communications (with the exception of public passenger transport), food, retailing and clothing. Indeed, the low-priority category could arguably be extended to cover most consumer goods (Berliner, 1976, p. 509) and services. Technologies in these industries are fairly primitive. In the most extreme case of the retailing industry, even casual visitors to the Soviet Union can still observe the wide application of the abacus (i.e. wooden beads) instead of electric cash registers.

Between the atypical extremes of very low-priority and very high-priority industries falls the bulk of Soviet output and employment in second-priority, science-based industries like chemicals, motor vehicles and computers, as well as high-priority industries like iron, steel and machine-tools that are not research-intensive, where the USSR has been able to scale up established technologies (see OECD, 1985, pp. 39–40). The R & D achievements of this sector can be summarised as generally lagging behind Western levels, with lags lengthening as one moves through the R & D process from basic research down to the industrial installation of new technologies. Allowances must be made for the initial backwardness of Soviet industry, but centralised Soviet R & D has largely been conducted without the wide integration of applied research and production despite reforms, and this phenomenon has been the major concern of the reformers. Seen in the light of the discussion above, the problem for Soviet industrial enterprises and research institutes is one of soft budgets and distance from buyers with weak bargaining power (Kornai). Suppliers are dominant, and Freeman (1974, p. 167) noted that one-sided innovations are unlikely to succeed. Alternative inputs and alternative suppliers of existing inputs in the USSR are rare, and this denies the Soviets a rich source of innovation, on Western experience. Instead, an industrial enterprise must depend largely on innovations developed in its sponsoring ministry. In relation to energy, Campbell (1980, p. 249) concludes that: 'what constitutes the real weakness in the R & D process . . . is its general clumsiness in its movement back and forth along the R &

D spectrum – it makes commitments too soon, generates too few technological alternatives at each stage, finds it difficult to move backward to correct the consequences of miscalculations once commitments are made'.

Some representative evidence is shown in Table 7.3, which emphasises that although Soviet industry has generally made a slow start, the major problem has been the length of the time-lag from the first installation of a new technology to its accounting for a specified proportion of output. This evidence is reinforced by Hanson's (1981) survey of the experiences of Western suppliers of fertiliser technology to the Soviet Union. Hanson (1981, p. 190) surveyed 32 contracts and discovered that the mean lag between the first enquiry and the handing over of fertiliser plant was almost seven years, more than double the average lag experienced when selling to Western buyers. New fertiliser plant was operated capably in the Soviet Union, but the diffusion of new Western technologies throughout the Soviet fertiliser industry was found to be relatively slow. Multinational enterprises like Shell are notorious centralisers, too, but Stock Market survival demands that research be decentralised into the product divisions.

Hanson's general conclusion echoes the Kornai position: 'In a capitalist economy the lure of profits, the threat of business failure and the pressures of competition (generally imperfect and often oligopolistic competition but still competition of some sort) together with the far greater decision-making autonomy of the individual business unit, make the whole setting of innovation quite different'(1981, p. 61). Reforms of Soviet R & D have been attempted, but incentives and contract R & D have been insufficient to give researchers autonomy over their specialist decisions (and responsibility for them) on a Western scale. Science-based research associations have been designed to co-ordinate research with the needs of industry, but official claims that (Amann 1982, p. 32) reductions in the lead times of 25–30 per cent have been achieved for research projects should be treated with caution. Campbell (1980, p. 246) reports that R & D in some associations is now *more* centralised, as enterprises pass on to the institutes minor development tasks that they previously fulfilled themselves.

This brief review would seem to confirm the 'conventional wisdom' (Hanson, 1981, p. 74) that, apart from some patchy successes, Soviet performance in the field of innovation has been relatively weak. There is plenty of evidence to suggest that the Soviet leadership is well aware of this conclusion but choose to do little about it for two reasons. First, effective decentralising reforms would involve costs in the form of wider income differentials, possible class conflict and, to be cynical, a change in the political status quo. Second, a poor R & D performance can be remedied to some extent by importing innovations from the West, or by imitating

Table 7.3 Introduction and diffusion of new technology

New technology	*Date of first installation*	*Date of first USSR installation*	*Years from first installation to specified % of output*		
			First	*USSR*	*Slowest*
			(Years to 20% of steel output)		
Oxygen steel	1954 (USA)	1956	5 (UK/Ja)	16	16 (USSR)
			(Years to 5% of steel output)		
Continuous steel casting	1954 (FRG)	1955	7 (USA)	17	17 (USSR)
			(Years to 33% of chemical fibre)		
Synthetic fibres	1938 (USA)	1948	21 (USA/Ja)	25	25 (USSR)
			(Years to 15% of plastics)		
Polyolefins	1937 (UK)	1953 (estimate)	9 (Ja)	17	21 (FRG)
			(Years to 10% of lines 100kv+)		
HVAC transmission lines	1954 (USA)	1956	7 (UK)	14	18+ (FRG)
			(Years to 2% of electric power)		
Nuclear power	1954 (USSR)	1954	6 (UK)	21	21 (USSR)
			(Years to 1% of machine tools)		
Numerically-controlled machine tools	1952 (USA) (prototype)	1958	12 (UK)	13	15+ (FRG)

Countries in survey were USSR, USA, Japan (Ja), UK, Federal Republic of Germany (FRG).
Source: Davies, 1977, pp. 55–7.

them. Although technology imports require hard currency, this particular economic problem may be easier to handle than other intractable problems involving, say, hidden inflation or a slowdown in economic growth.

The most realistic stance for the Soviet authorities would be to admit that central planning is relatively ineffective in promoting innovation, but to point out, first, that product innovations may be less necessary in a socialist system supposedly concerned with basic needs rather than frivolous consumption; and second, that there are other social and economic factors besides innovation which deserve prior attention. They would hope, then, to perform better in areas discussed in other chapters of this book.

CHAPTER EIGHT

ECONOMIC GROWTH

The rate of growth of the economy is of particular concern to the central authorities of the Soviet Union. It would not be unfair to represent it as *the* component of economic efficiency that dominates their thinking. Certainly, the need for rapid economic growth lies behind their choice of an economic strategy based on the development of heavy industry and high levels of investment. Fast economic growth alone can generate the high material living standards that can realise their dream of the satisfaction of all basic human needs and the achievement of 'pure communism'.

As with material living standards themselves (which are examined in the next chapter), there is insufficient space in this book to philosophise on the desirability of rapid economic growth. It is assumed that conventional measures of national income (under Western or Soviet conventions) are such that one can conclude that more national income is a 'good' thing. (Of course, Soviet net material product is a far less comprehensive measure than Western gross national product, which includes administration and the production of 'non-material' services as well as NMP's material goods.) We must disregard problems involving 'externalities', the production of 'regrettable' items like defence, and aspects of the 'quality of life' that are not captured by national-income measures.

This chapter follows the structure already used in most of the others. In this case, economic growth is analysed in terms of the claims of the central authorities in the Soviet Union, the Kornai perspective, and the empirical evidence available on Soviet performance. Before this structure is adopted, however, it is necessary that readers should broadly understand the terminology of 'Growth Accounting', a technique for measuring the different sources of economic growth.

Figure 8.1 Sources of economic growth: growth accounting.

(A) <u>Increases in the quantity of inputs</u> Labour force (see chapter 5) Capital stock (see chapter 6) Land, resources, etc.	Extensive growth
(B) <u>Increases in the quality of inputs</u> (or increases in output per unit of input) Increases in static efficiency (allocative and productive efficiency, chapter 3) Increases in dynamic efficiency (Chapter 7)	Intensive growth (also known as the 'residual' or as 'total factor productivity')

GROWTH ACCOUNTING

Growth accounting is summarised in figure 8.1. Just like a university, a football team or an industrial enterprise, an entire economic system can develop as a result of (A) acquiring *additional* resources (teachers, players, or other workers and machines) and/or (B) improving the productivity of *existing* resources. It is a question of increasing (A) the quantity ('extensive growth') and/or (B) the quality of inputs ('intensive growth').

This distinction is useful, and since the mid-1960s Soviet politicians and economists have openly and repeatedly discussed the need for 'intensification', or more (B) intensive growth. Measurement of the two sources of growth is, however, more controversial. This involves using an economic model of an entire economy as if it were a giant factory turning out one composite product from inputs of homogeneous labour, capital and other factors. In practice, fairly simple models have proved adequate, and Whitesell (1985) provides recent confirmation of the acceptability of the fairly elementary Cobb–Douglas production function for this purpose. One property of this two-factor (labour and capital) model has been emphasised in more detail by one of the authors (see Buck, 1982, pp. 149–54):

$$\dot{Y} = a\dot{l} + (1-a)\dot{k} + \text{a residual}$$

(The growth of national income)	=	(The growth of labour times labour's share of national income)	+	(The growth of capital times capital's share of national income)

Non-economists should understand the gist of this formula without worrying about its derivation. The first two expressions on the right-hand side of the formula together add up to (A) the 'extensive growth' component in figure 8.1, while the 'residual' of growth unexplained by extensive growth is a measure of (B) 'intensive growth' or total factor productivity. This residual will increase if static efficiency in allocation and production (chapter 3) increases or if there is technological progress (chapter 7).

In an imaginary economy, if national income growth ($\dot{Y}$) in one period was 20 per cent, the labour force ($\dot{l}$) grew by 8 per cent, the capital stock ($\dot{k}$) by 10 per cent and labour enjoyed 75 per cent ($a = 0.75$) of national income, then the formula would tell us that:

$$\begin{aligned} 20 &= (0.75) \times (8) + (0.25) \times (10) + \text{a residual} \\ 20 &= 6 + 2.5 + \text{a residual} \end{aligned}$$

so the residual is estimated as a balancing factor of 11.5 per cent, which equals intensive growth. Extensive growth is the sum of:

$$\begin{aligned} a\dot{l} + (1\text{-}a)\dot{k} &= 6\% + 2.5\% \\ &= 8.5\% \end{aligned}$$

Controversy surrounds growth accounting, *not* because the usefulness of the terms intensive and extensive growth is doubted, nor because economists question the appropriateness of the Cobb–Douglas model (although much more complex alternatives have been proposed). Critics of growth accounting generally focus on its *measurement* problems. In an economy like the Soviet Union with prices for labour and (especially) capital that are considered 'artificial' in Western terms, it is very difficult to estimate (a) and hence ($1 - a$) realistically. More fundamentally, however, it is extremely difficult to measure the *quantity* of labour (l) and capital growth (k), when additions to the labour and capital stocks will embody new training, technology and hence *quality* improvements. Again, economists have proposed ingenious and complex solutions to disentangle quantity from quality, but at the end of the day we have to content ourselves with official statistics on the quantity of labour and capital inputs, and trust that quality corrections have been carried out in a reasonable fashion. With these concepts and their limitations in mind, the usual chapter structure can be developed.

SOVIET ECONOMIC GROWTH – THE OFFICIAL VIEW

The central authorities in the Soviet Union would claim that their centrally planned economy is capable of faster and more stable economic growth than alternative systems, and they would extend this claim to both 'extensive' and 'intensive' sources. It is possible to keep discussion of these claims brief, as they have been considered already in earlier chapters.

Central planning, especially in the early years of its application, is claimed to be extremely effective in (A) mobilising resources in the form of increases in the labour force and capital stock (see figure 8.1). The mobilisation of *labour* reserves was discussed in chapter 5. Centrally planned economies can divert jobs to areas where excess supply is expected, so reserves of unemployed labour can be absorbed. Policies to raise the labour participation of persons of working age can be effective, particularly in relation to females.

In addition to labour growth, central planning is held to possess a great ability to accumulate *capital* (see chapter 6). Investments can be planned and do not have to pass rigorous tests of profitability, as in the West. Of course, high investment implies low consumption, but Robinson Crusoe was able to consume more fish in the long run when he sacrificed a day's fish-spearing to make a net. In the long run, successful investments achieve higher levels of consumption, too, through more 'roundabout' methods of production.

Central planners would also claim that their economic system has a capacity to grow faster as a result of (B) intensive growth (see figure 8.1). The central co-ordination of resource allocation (see the first section of chapter 3), ought to secure more output from given inputs, and the advantages of centrally planned innovation (chapter 7) imply intensive growth through technological progress.

Finally, central planning can claim with some authority that economic growth rates should be more *stable* than under capitalism, where investment has to pass profitability tests that are crucially dependent upon business expectations. At the onset of a recession, the 'animal spirits' of capitalist entrepreneurs become pessimistic about the profitability of future sales. Investment falls and effective demand with it, so recession becomes a self-fulfilling prophecy. Centrally planned investment should be immune to the whims of individual decision-makers. Investment programmes are planned for five-year periods and sometimes longer, and centrally planned economies are allegedly subject to less uncertainty (see chapter 6). As usual, however, these claims must be confronted by the criticisms of central planning suggested by Kornai's perspective.

SOVIET ECONOMIC GROWTH – THE KORNAI VIEW

If this study is correct in attributing relatively soft budgets to the Soviet economy, then each component of the official view on economic growth discussed above must attract a Kornai-type criticism. Again, this section says little that has not been discussed already in earlier chapters, so it can be brief.

Kornai would probably not dispute (A) the proposition that central planning is capable of generating high rates of growth from extensive sources. Rather, he would probably stress that soft budgets achieve economic growth rates that are initially *too* fast. Labour and capital are consumed by enterprises relatively unconstrained by budgets. Over-employment and over-investment lead initially to rapid extensive growth, but inevitably run up against physical *resource* constraints.

Over-employment was discussed in the second section of chapter 5 in relation to the insatiable demands of soft budget enterprises for all inputs in their attempts to meet taut gross-output targets. This over-demand is likely to be more significant for labour than other inputs in Soviet industry because of the persistent links between bonus payments and the size of the wages fund. Any over-demand for labour can lead to irreversible 'feather bedding' in employment and subsequent low productivity. If labour is required to man new machines and factories (labour and capital are complementary), the over-demand for labour can, in addition, feed off over-investment.

Over-investment is central to Kornai's view of the centrally planned economy (see chapter 6). Investments financed out of ministry budgets and not enterprise profits are almost a 'free' good for enterprises, and make gross output targets more easily attainable, unless targets are raised on account of the new machines. Furthermore, insatiable investment 'hunger' can generate investment rhythms that are unique to central planning. Of course capitalist investment and growth rates can be extremely unstable, but even under central planning ambitious investment projects taken on board early in a five-year plan may remain uncompleted, and realised investment may fall towards the end of the five-year period. The consequence of over-investment is low capital productivity, and long-term increases in material living standards may not live up to the expectations which were entertained when current consumption was sacrificed for investment.

Low labour and capital productivity through soft budgets and rapid extensive growth provide the link to (B) intensive growth. A Kornai perspective suggests that fast economic growth of an extensive kind leads to over-employment, over-investment, diminishing returns, and low productivity of labour and capital. In addition, it was shown in chapter 7 how soft budgets retard technological progress, since enterprises and ministries no longer need to innovate to ensure survival. On the contrary, there are good reasons why soft budgets may encourage conservative attitudes to innovation.

In this way, Kornai would anticipate slow intensive growth as a result of static productivity and dynamic technological factors for a centrally planned economy with relatively soft budget constraints. In the next section this prediction is exposed to the empirical evidence on economic growth that is available from the Soviet Union.

ACTUAL SOVIET ECONOMIC GROWTH

Judgements on any country's economic growth rate must be subjective. Growth rates in the end always fall with the level of economic development, so it is easy to demonstrate the rapidity of a nation's economic growth by comparing it with a sample of relatively mature economies. In the Soviet Union's case, faster growth can be 'proven' more easily if industrial production, real GNP or real GNP per capita is substituted for GNP, money GNP or GNP per person economically active as the indicator of economic growth. With careful selection of variables, time-periods and countries, it would be easy to put forward a case that fitted the official or Kornai views. Reality is not so simple, however.

Table 8.1 gives the reader some idea of the complexity of rates of growth of real GNP per capita, as calculated by the CIA. (The choice of variable favours the Soviet Union, but not as much as *industrial* production would have done.) On the face of it, the Soviet Union's rate of growth is quite different from those of the rest of Eastern Europe, is rather higher than that of the United States (with the exception of 1976–9), and is apparently more stable, with a small negative entry for 1979 alone. It must be remembered, however, that Soviet inflation may be underestimated by the CIA (see chapter 4). Wiles (1982a, p. 144) proposes a price deflator of 3 per cent per annum since 1975, which is about twice the rate applied by the CIA.

The official view on Soviet growth can be further supported by a selective use of evidence. Soviet growth rates are boosted by the adoption of a Soviet definition of national income (net material product), which is limited to material goods (see table 8.2). Even without this device, however, CIA analyses of real GNP growth and its sources provide more support for the official view (see table 8.3). Here (rows 7), the US overall growth rate was faster only in 1981, although it must be pointed out that in 1983 (beyond this table's scope) US real GNP growth was 4.8 per cent, which is unlikely to have been matched by the USSR. The official view is similarly supported by the consistently high levels of extensive growth shown by table 8.3 (rows 3) for the USSR compared with the USA. Labour growth in the USA only once exceeds that of the USSR (1976–80, by 0.1 per cent, see rows 1) and rates of capital growth (shown by rows 2) are massively larger in the Soviet Union, as predicted by the official view, and

Table 8.1 Real gross national product per capita growth

	Average annual rate of growth								
	1961–5	*1966–70*	*1971–5*	*1976–7*	*1978*	*1979*	*1980*	*1981*	*1982*
OECD									
United States	3.2	1.9	1.4	4.0	3.6	1.2	−1.4	1.3	−2.7
Australia	2.7	3.6	1.6	2.9	1.5	3.0	0.3	2.5	0.5
Canada	3.7	3.1	3.6	2.8	3.0	2.3	−0.6	2.7	−6.6
Japan	10.1	10.0	3.1	4.2	4.1	4.2	3.6	2.5	1.8
Sweden	4.5	3.3	2.3	−0.8	1.0	4.0	1.7	−0.8	0.5
Switzerland	3.3	3.4	0.4	1.1	0.2	2.3	4.2	1.6	−2.3
European Community	3.7	3.7	2.2	3.6	3.1	3.1	0.9	−0.6	−0.3
Belgium	4.4	4.6	3.2	3.1	2.9	2.3	2.9	−1.8	−0.7
France	4.8	4.1	3.2	3.7	3.4	2.9	0.7	−0.3	1.0
Italy	4.2	5.3	1.6	3.3	2.2	4.5	3.7	0.4	2.4
Netherlands	3.5	4.2	2.2	3.1	2.0	1.4	0.1	−1.8	−1.7
United Kingdom	2.5	2.0	1.9	2.5	3.7	1.5	−2.1	−2.0	0.5
West Germany	3.6	3.9	1.8	4.6	3.2	4.0	1.6	negl.	−1.2

Table 8.1 continued

	Average annual rate of growth								
	1961–5	*1966–70*	*1971–5*	*1976–7*	*1978*	*1979*	*1980*	*1981*	*1982*
Communist countries									
USSR and Eastern Europe									
USSR	3.5	4.2	2.7	3.1	2.5	−0.4	0.9	1.4	1.2
Eastern Europe	3.2	3.1	4.1	2.3	2.2	0.5	−0.7	−1.4	−0.6
Bulgaria	5.5	4.4	4.1	0.5	2.1	3.7	−3.6	2.6	2.6
Czechoslovakia	1.8	3.2	2.7	2.2	1.0	0.3	1.6	−1.1	0.1
East Germany	3.1	3.1	3.7	2.8	1.8	2.9	2.3	2.4	0.5
Hungary	3.5	2.7	2.9	2.7	2.2	negl.	0.8	0.3	1.8
Poland	3.4	3.3	5.5	1.2	2.5	−2.4	−3.3	−6.3	−4.8
Romania	4.7	3.6	5.7	5.6	3.8	2.8	−2.3	−0.2	2.2
Other									
China	n.a.	5.5	3.3	1.4	11.1	5.8	4.0	1.6	5.8
North Korea	6.6	2.6	7.1	−4.6	4.4	0.5	0.3	−0.3	3.5
Yugoslavia	5.8	4.8	4.9	4.9	6.0	6.1	1.7	0.8	−0.4

Source: CIA, *Handbook of Economic Statistics*, 1983, p. 35.

Table 8.2 Economic growth in the USSR: Soviet official net material product and CIA gross national product (average annual percentage rates)

	NMP produced	*NMP used*	*GNP*
1950–60	10.3		5.7
1960–70	7.1	6.5	5.1
1970–5	5.7	5.1	3.7
1975–80	4.3	3.9	2.7
1980–4		3.2	2.6

NMP produced differs from NMP used in that the latter takes into account foreign trade and also losses in the distribution system.
Source: Bergson, 1985, p. 12.

have been sustained over a long period. Again, contrary to the Kornai view, labour productivity's contribution (rows 4, table 8.3) to intensive growth has always been higher in the USSR, again with 1981 as the exception. Finally, table 8.3 (rows 7) also shows that Soviet real GNP growth has been within a range from 2.0 per cent to 5.3 per cent: always positive and significantly more stable than US variations from −2.9 per cent to +2.8 per cent.

It can be seen that even a cursory review of the evidence provides much support for the official view, which could go on to question why the USA shows such a collapse of the residual (intensive growth, see row 6 for the USA in table 8.3) after 1970, when capitalism is supposed to generate high levels of static efficiency in production and of technological progress. It should be noted, however, that in 1983 (beyond the scope of table 8.3) the US residual recovered to contribute 2.8 per cent to real GNP growth. In addition, comparisons with the USA are unfair to the West in the sense that the USA had the worst 'productivity slowdown' in the 1970s by a wide margin (see Baumol and McLennan, 1985). Comparisons with other developed Western economies would provide more support for Kornai.

Some support for the Kornai view can still be derived from these US figures, however. Soviet economic growth has been heavily reliant on extensive sources. Capital productivity has been massively negative for each period (row 5 of table 8.3) and intensive growth (total factor productivity, row 6) has been usually negative and lower than US levels, with the exception of 1982. This is not typical of other CMEA economies, however (see Pryor, 1985, p. 89), where intensive growth has been faster. Whitesell (1985, p. 241) attributes some of this difference to the relative physical size of the Soviet Union and the difficulties this creates for

Table 8.3 Extensive and intensive growth of gross national product: (a) USSR; (b) USA

(a) USSR

	1966–70		*1971–5*		*1976–80*		*1981*		*1982*	
1. Quantity of labour	2.0		1.7		1.3		1.0		1.1	
2. Quantity of capital	7.4		8.0		6.9		6.7		6.1	
3. Total extensive growth		4.1		4.2		3.6		3.2		3.1
4. Productivity of labour	3.2		2.0		1.3		1.2		0.9	
5. Productivity of capital	−2.0		−4.0		−4.0		−4.2		−3.8	
6. Total intensive growth		1.1		−0.5		−0.8		−1.0		−1.1
7. Total GNP growth		5.3		3.7		2.7		2.2		2.0

Additions do not always tally because of rounding errors and the omission of 'land' from the CIA data.
Source: CIA, *Handbook of Economic Statistics*, 1983, p. 66.

Table 8.3 continued

(b) USA

	1966–70		*1971–5*		*1976–80*		*1981*		*1982*	
1. Quantity of labour	0.8		0.2		1.4		0.7		−3.1	
2. Quantity of capital	2.3		1.5		1.5		4.6		2.7	
3. Total extensive growth		1.5		0.7		1.4		2.0		−1.2
4. Productivity of labour	2.0		0.8		0.4		1.9		0.2	
5. Productivity of capital	0		−0.6		0.3		−1.5		−4.5	
6. Total intensive growth		1.4		0.3		0.4		0.7		−1.5
7. Total GNP growth		2.3		0.9		1.7		2.8		−2.9

Source: Calculated from *US Monthly Labor Review*, US Department of Labor, September 1985, 108(9), table 28. These data are slightly different to the CIA estimates for the USSR as they are restricted to the 'private business sector'.

planning production and innovation. It is significant, however, that when he disaggregates total factor productivity by industry (p. 239) he finds that in the Soviet Union it is higher in low-priority industries such as light industry and food-processing, where budget constraints are relatively hard. Productivity gains have been lowest in Soviet machine-building, metal-working and construction industries, where the level of priority has been high and input demands relatively unconstrained by a lack of finance. This supports Kornai's view. Kornai would certainly question the ability of the Soviet economy to sustain growth rates heavily reliant on extensive sources. The rate of growth of the labour supply is unlikely to exceed 1 per cent per annum for the rest of this century (see Schroeder, 1982a, p. 18), and capital growth can only be sustained at the expense of consumption. There are less obvious constraints on intensive growth, which depends largely on human ingenuity, and slow (negative since 1970) intensive growth in the USSR has been a proper cause for concern for the Soviet authorities since about 1965.

Table 8.4 Official USSR national income (national material product produced) as a percentage of US national income

	USSR as % of US
1950	31
1960	58
1970	more than 65
1980	67
1982	67

Source: Narodnoye khozyaystvo, 1982, p. 56.

A slowdown has undoubtedly occurred in the rate of growth of the Soviet economy. This has been universal since about 1970, but even official Soviet statistics (see table 8.4) now suggest that income growth may have stopped catching up with the US rate, despite the fact that the absolutely larger and more mature US economy should have a slower rate of growth, other things being equal. To this extent, the Kornai view is vindicated, and the outcome would be clearer in per-capita terms or with realistic adjustments for inflation. There is little evidence, however, of less stability in Soviet economic growth. Wiles (1982b) does find some evidence of Soviet investment fluctuations, but these are extremely weak compared with the West.

CONCLUSIONS

Soviet economic growth has been relatively fast and stable compared with that of the relatively mature economy of the USA, but not with other Western nations like Japan. There has been a heavy reliance on extensive sources, as Kornai would predict for an economy with relatively soft budget constraints, and there are physical limits to the USSR's ability to sustain high growth rates through increases in labour and capital inputs. There must be doubts, too, over the USSR's 'intensification' drive in the twelfth five-year plan (1986–90), if it is not accompanied by a significant hardening of the budget constraint in industry.

Overall, however, the central authorities in the Soviet Union can feel happier with their achievements in relation to economic growth than with achievements discussed in other chapters in this book. Growth rates have been sustained at a relatively high level, largely through massive capital inputs. Growth does not guarantee higher living standards if over-investment occurs, however, and chapter 9 reviews progress with Soviet living standards in this context.

CHAPTER NINE

LIVING STANDARDS

This chapter will not follow the pattern set in the others, but will be closely related to all of them. Material living standards constitute the net outcome of all the other aspects of economic efficiency discussed elsewhere. Better allocation and production (Chapter 3), and low levels of inflation (chapter 4) and unemployment (chapter 5) will all lead to higher living standards, as will high levels of investment, at least in the long run (see chapter 6), innovation (chapter 7) and economic growth (chapter 8). A 'fairer' income distribution (chapter 2), in the sense of a more equal one, will lead to a more uniform distribution of living standards. It can be seen therefore that living standards are a 'rag-bag' in economic terms. They represent the net outcome of the interplay of all the economic processes listed above, and the purpose of this chapter is to provide a review of the empirical evidence on actual Soviet living standards.

We do not have the space to philosophise on the desirability of higher material living standards, as conventionally measured. Many expenditures, like police or defence, are 'regrettable', but are still included at cost in national income. 'Goods' such as leisure and home-produced services are excluded, along with 'bads' like smoke pollution. Wiedermann (1984) has constructed alternative 'social indicators' for EEC and CMEA countries, but has excluded the Soviet Union. Indeed, one could question the whole emphasis of this chapter on *material* living standards to the exclusion of more spiritual matters like the 'spirit of socialism' or the 'freedom of the individual', although one would expect these to be reflected in conventional economic indicators to some extent. Certainly the Soviet authorities have always placed a heavy emphasis on the ability of their economic system to 'catch up' with the West in material terms. Khrushchev boasted in 1961 (*Pravda*, 19 October 1961) that by 1981 the USSR would have the highest living standard in the world, and Soviet statistical digests are full of carefully selected economic comparisons between the USA and USSR.

Like Khrushchev, we concentrate here on income as conventionally measured, but refer in passing to other indicators of welfare such as life expectancy, infant mortality and literacy rates. It must be noted throughout that the Soviet measure of net material production (NMP) which is, roughly speaking, the total production of physical goods, is quite different from Western GNP (see the official view of Soviet inflation, described in chapter 4).

There is no need to consider in detail the contrasting views of Kornai and the Soviet authorities on the ability of Soviet central planning to raise material living standards. Since living standards are the product of all the aspects of economic efficiency in chapters 2–8 above, the official and Soviet views can be referred to only in passing. It seems obvious that Kornai would emphasise that the relatively soft budget constraints of Soviet central planning keep down living standards in static terms, as they hinder efficient allocation and production, generate overall excess demand, and lead to over-full levels of employment. In the longer run, Kornai would expect central planning to suffer from over-investment (and the consequent sacrifice of current living standards), slow technological progress, and low rates of economic growth from productivity gains. On the other hand, the official Soviet view would emphasise low levels of unemployment, the mobilisation of reserves of labour and capital, an absence of inflation, and the advantages of centralised innovation under Soviet planning. All these factors could be expected to raise material living standards.

The rest of this chapter tests these opposing views. We consider first living standards in general and then the particular issues of mortality and life expectancy, and the regional distribution of living standards within the USSR.

GENERAL SOVIET LIVING STANDARDS

Comparisons of relative incomes and living standards between countries are notoriously difficult. Countries may stand at different stages of economic development, consumers may enjoy different 'baskets' of goods and services, hidden price inflation or unrealistic exchange rates may obscure the outcome and private incomes may be understated in official statistics. A single experience by one of the authors in a centrally planned economy (Hungary in 1984) may emphasise the importance of these difficulties: he enjoyed a three-mile taxi ride (shared with three others), a ballet performance (including champagne and caviare during the interval) and a taxi back. He still had change from £1.00! It is also significant that in

1983 the World Bank suspended the series of estimates of Soviet GNP that has appeared in its *World Bank Atlas* since 1966, after failing to establish realistic comparisons. With much trepidation therefore, we review general Soviet material living standards, first over time and then in relation to other countries.

Soviet Trends

The use of Soviet official living standard statistics is fraught with difficulty. They cannot be used for comparisons with other countries. Their reliability or accuracy is not questioned here, but the conventions used in their compilation are quite arbitrary. In itself, this is nothing new, since all measures of living standards involve arbitrary rules. Unfortunately, Soviet conventions are quite unusual.

The USSR's Marxist heritage has produced a unique view of *consumption*, for example. Marx's view of 'non-productive' activity has meant that consumption includes only physical goods and 'material' services like freight, distribution and retailing that contribute directly to the consumption of physical goods. Excluded, 'non-productive' services cover (Becker, 1972, p. 72) general administration and the judicial system, defence, scientific organisations, finance and credit, education, health and culture, housing, passenger transport, communications serving households, and personal services like hairdressers, cemeteries and public baths. Most of these items are included in Western measures of consumption, and the growth of personal services is one of the most significant aspects of modern economic development. It follows that the growth of official Soviet consumption over time is probably understated in Western terms.

Similarly, the Soviet measure of *real income* per capita 'clearly measures something other than the deflated summation of money incomes plus benefits minus taxes' (Schroeder, 1972, p. 305). It is not clear whether housing subsidies are included in real incomes and it would appear that although produce from private plots is valued at actual sale prices, the incomes in kind received by collective farmers in payment are valued at much lower state prices. The family budget surveys and price indices on which the real-income series depends have never been explained in detail and it is difficult to argue with Schroeder's conclusion that 'The exact nature of the published indexes of real income remains a puzzle' (1972, p. 305). Again, the deeply conservative attitudes of the Soviet statistical service prevent realistic comparisons that would not always put Soviet performance in an unfavourable light. Nevertheless, it is suggested that so long as direct international comparisons are not made, official statistics on Soviet living standards over time do reveal interesting trends.

The achievements of the Soviet economy in relation to living standards have been real. Even on CIA estimates, the growth of real per capita consumption has been around 3.4 per cent per annum between 1950 and 1980, and real consumption has tripled over these three decades. There has, however, been a significant slowdown in the rate of growth over time according to the CIA, with comparable figures below 2 per cent for 1981 and below 1 per cent in 1982 (see Schroeder, 1982c, p. 368).

Tables 9.1–9.3 confirm different aspects of this general slowdown. Table 9.1 depicts total consumption as measured by the CIA and the Soviet authorities. This slowdown can be explained in terms of poor harvests and the notoriously soft budgets of high-priority producer-goods industries (see chapter 6 above). Under soft budgets, table 9.2 shows the fate of just one (in 1980) of the attempts in a five-year plan to divert resources towards consumption and away from industrial investment. It seems that the tendency to over-invest in industry is unavoidable and gradually reasserts itself over the five-year period.

Table 9.1 Growth of total (personal and social) Soviet consumption (percentage per annum)

Year	Soviet estimates	US estimates
1976–80	4.5	(2.8)
1981	4.0	(2.1)
1982	1.2	(1.5)

Sources: The figures *not* in brackets are official Soviet estimates taken from the United Nations *Economic Survey of Europe in 1983* by the Economic Commission for Europe, New York, 1984, p. 118. It is probable that if the figures were deflated by a reasonable consumer price index (see chapter 4 above) and calculated on a per-capita basis, they would all be negative.
The figures in brackets are estimates of the growth of real consumption from the CIA, *Handbook of Economic Statistics*, 1983.

Table 9.3 shows changes in real income in per-capita terms from official Soviet sources, and emphasises the slowdown and the attempts of the authorities to 'rescue' the situation in five-year and annual plans. Again, the nature of the slowdown is emphasised and the first hint of an absolute decline appears for 1982. It seems likely that adjustments for a more realistic inflation rate (see chapter 4) and for population growth would produce negative values in the 1980s for most elements in tables 9.1–9.3.

It can therefore be concluded from official statistics that the growth of officially measured Soviet consumption and real income has been rapid, but that a significant slowdown has occurred in the 1980s. The Soviet

Table 9.2 Total consumption's share of Soviet national income

Year	*Soviet estimates (%)*
1976–80	74.1
1981	76.4
1982	73.8
1983	73.2[a]
1984	75.0

[a]It is interesting that in the 1983 version of the UN Survey (p. 171), the original estimate for 1983 was exactly 75.0 per cent, the same as the 1985 estimate for 1984 in the table. There might be an element of wishful thinking in these estimates.
Sources: These figures are official Soviet estimates taken from the United Nations *Economic Survey of Europe in 1983*, New York, 1984, p. 171, and from the United Nations *Economic Survey of Europe in 1984–1985*, New York, 1985, p. 144.

Table 9.3 Growth of Soviet real income per capita (percentage per annum)

Real income per capita (%)	*Year*	*Real wage/salary per earner (%)*
3.4	1976–80	3.0
3.3	1981	2.1
0.1	1982	2.8
2.0	1983	2.6
3.0	1984	2.5
3.3	1985 plan	3.0
3.1	1981–5 plan	2.8

It must be remembered that Soviet real income is based on the Soviet measure of net material product (which omits non-material services and administration) and on the official price index.
Source: Taken from the official Soviet figures published in the United Nations *Economic Survey of Europe in 1984–1985*, New York, 1985, p. 177.

statisticians go on to make international comparisons from their figures, but they are bound to be superficial and selective. The bottom half of table 9.4 shows the sort of partial comparisons with the USA that appear in all Soviet statistical digests. The authorities are unlikely to choose items that put the USSR in an unfavourable light, and the USA produces similar, equally prejudiced comparisons (see the top half of table 9.4).

Table 9.4 emphasises that partial comparisons involve bias and that more general reviews of living standards must take into account different patterns of prices and consumption. The last entry in table 9.4 is intended to be frivolous, but underlines the point: tea consumption is traditionally low in the USA, but stood at 3,189 grams per capita in the UK, 1980–2. We must therefore turn to unofficial comparisons of general Soviet living standards for the purpose of international comparison.

Table 9.4 Components of living standards – selected comparisons, USA and USSR

		Year	*USA*	*USSR*
1	Car registrations (per 000)	1982	537	31
2	Telephones in use (per 000)	1982	791	84
3	Cinema attendance (per capita, per annum)	1981	4.6	15.9
4	Books in libraries (000)	1978–80	439	1,824
5	Tea consumption (grams per capita)	1980–2	366	725

Sources: Rows 1–2: CIA, *Handbook of Statistics*, 1983, pp. 20–1.
Rows 3–5: *UN Statistical Yearbook*, 1982, Washington, DC, 1984, pp. 187, 432, 434, 449, 452.

International Comparisons

The first general attempt to compare international living standards was made by the United Nations International Comparisons Project (ICP), but the USSR declined to join the ICP, unlike other CMEA countries. This project was necessary because it is pointless to compare the average US 'basket' of consumption goods at US prices with the USSR basket at USSR prices, converted into dollars at an official exchange rate of, say, 1.5 dollars to the rouble. Such a comparison would give an unrealistic comparison of real consumption levels because (a) the items in the USSR 'basket' would differ from the US items and (b) official rouble exchange rates are kept at unrealistically high levels by the Soviet authorities. In any case, official exchange rates reflect only the prices of goods and services that are traded internationally and omit those items that cannot be traded (e.g. cinema visits), yet may contribute to domestic living standards.

The ICP (see Kravis et al. 1978) was unable to produce a standard 'basket' of identical commodities in all countries who were members of the project, but it did produce a list of heterogeneous, but 'matching' goods and services. The valuation of this list of representative matching items in domestic currencies meant that if the total value of the list for one country in its prices and currency were divided into another, 'purchasing-power parities' (PPPs) could be derived. PPPs would be imaginary exchange rates that could be used to make realistic comparisons of the real value of different expenditures in different countries. In chapter 4, Soviet black-market exchange rates were used as an indicator of PPPs.

The USSR refused to join the ICP, however, yet Schroeder (1983, pp. 311–49) was able unofficially to measure and group Soviet and US expenditures on the ICP format of matching items, as if the USSR were a member of the project. Her results are shown as table 9.5. Although PPPs could not be calculated for a representative basket of goods, Schroeder concluded that 'the results are probably not seriously misleading' (1983, p. 316).

The first two columns of table 9.5 simply show per-capita expenditures on matching items at USSR and US prices and quantities (columns (1) and (2) respectively). Soviet quantities were then revalued at US prices and the ratio of this hypothetical expenditure to actual US expenditure is shown in column (3), as a quantity index with US prices and US quantity = 100. Similarly, column (4) shows the ratio of actual Soviet expenditures divided by hypothetical expenditures of Soviet prices times US quantities. These two columns – (3) and (4) – provide alternative and equally 'correct' quantity indices of per-capita consumption, and column (5) provides another alternative and equally arbitrary average (geometric mean) of columns (3) and (4).

Overall, 1976 real Soviet consumption per capita is calculated as between 27.6 per cent and 42.8 per cent (geometric mean 34.4 per cent) of the US level, and it is possible to demonstrate unambiguously higher levels of consumption (at both US and USSR prices) for the Soviet Union only for alcoholic beverages and public transport. According to Schroeder (1983, p. 318), Soviet per-capita consumption in 1976 (geometric mean) was perhaps half that of France and the Federal Republic of Germany, just over half that of the UK, two-thirds that of Japan, three-quarters that of Italy, and Hungary exceeded the Soviet level by one-fifth. With the exceptions of public transport and alcoholic beverages noted above, the Soviet Union showed relatively low consumption on all goods and services except for education, which probably accounts for high Soviet literacy rates. The low status of personal services is particularly notable – only one-eighth of the Soviet labour force was employed in 'trade and personal services' in 1977 compared with one-third in the USA.

The relative neglect of many public services in the USSR is attributed by Pryor (1985, p. 92) to the priority given to industrial investment. Nowhere is this tendency more apparent than for residential housing in the USSR (and the rest of Eastern Europe). On the face of it, one may puzzle at the low priority given by socialist societies to such a basic need as housing,

Table 9.5 Comparison of USA and USSR consumption per capita, 1976

	Per-capita expenditures		*USSR, quantity of consumption per capita (USA = 100)*		
	USSR (Roubles) (1)	*USA (Dollars) (2)*	*Dollar comparison (3)*	*Rouble comparison (4)*	*Mean rouble–dollar comparison (5)*
Food	382.3	868.5	55.8	42.5	48.7
Alcoholic beverages	138.3	133.0	104.7	135.5	119.1
Other beverages	10.7	53.6	38.1	35.0	36.5
Tobacco	14.8	75.3	18.1	18.1	18.1
Clothing & footwear	199.0	358.1	55.9	39.0	46.7
Gross rent	43.3	787.7	15.2	15.2	15.2
Fuel & power	19.0	210.2	26.3	20.1	23.0
House furnishings, etc.	61.5	372.5	29.7	13.8	20.2
Medical care	45.5	646.6	60.1	17.6	32.5
Private transport	27.3	665.2	4.6	3.3	3.9
Public transport	31.4	45.0	241.9	262.7	252.0
Communications	6.2	103.1	17.5	17.4	17.5
Recreation	61.9	417.0	40.4	21.8	29.7
Education	69.8	472.1	96.7	65.7	79.7
Personal care	37.6	132.0	50.3	28.1	37.6
Misc. services	2.5	243.3	2.8	3.4	3.1
Total consumption	1,152.6	5,583.3	42.8	27.6	34.4

Figures have been rounded, so that columns do not add up exactly to totals.
Source: Taken from Schroeder, 1983, pp. 316–17.

though it must be noted that such housing as is available is greatly subsidised by the state, largely out of enterprise taxes, and the Soviet economy has an enormous back-log of pent-up housing demand to deal with before standards can be raised.

Nevertheless, housing's place in the pecking-order of Soviet economic priorities seems to be sinking, if anything. In 1975, house construction absorbed 14.2 per cent of total Soviet investment, compared with 22.5 per cent in 1960 (Morton, 1980, p. 237). Living space per capita in the USSR was only 9 square metres (10 square metres in Moscow) in the mid-1970s, which amounts to an area of about 9-feet square per person in which to eat, sleep and entertain (see Morton, 1980, p. 235). New Soviet dwellings offered on average 55.4 square metres of total housing space (including kitchen, bathroom, corridors and storage area) in 1983 (United Nations, 1985, p. 151), which corresponds to only about 37 square metres of living space for an average household. This is low by standards in developed countries and the lowest in Eastern Europe, where housing space in new dwellings in 1983 averaged 73.2 square metres (Hungary) and 75.3 square metres (Czechoslovakia) (see United Nations, 1985, p. 151). The total number of new Soviet dwellings constructed fell to 2.08 million per annum in the period 1978–84, compared with a range from 2.11 million to 2.28 million between 1970 and 1977 (United Nations, 1985, p. 230), although this is still over double the US rate. Soviet housing-quality statistics are notable by their absence from official USSR and UN statistical yearbooks.

Non-housing comparisons with the USA of the sort indicated in the bottom half of table 9.4 are more frequent in USSR statistical digests, however. In a sense, these comparisons are unfair to the USSR, since most economists outside that country would agree that the USSR is being compared with a country at a higher level of development. One unofficial study by Bush (1981, 1984) takes into account the fact that US wages and salaries are higher by standardising expenditures not in dollars or roubles, but on the amount of local average work-time that is needed to purchase certain standard items. Bush's results are summarised in table 9.6, or rather table 9.6 shows selected results for 21 everyday items from Bush's survey on behalf of Radio Liberty.

The results in table 9.6 are not inconsistent with an average level of real consumption in Moscow of around one-third of the Washington level in terms of work-equivalent, where take-home pay in 1982 was about 2.5 times the Moscow level at official exchange rates. Table 9.6 also reveals the relative cheapness of Soviet local public transport, housing and health care in terms of work-time, but at the expense of many other items. The most significant result is probably in the first row of table 9.6, where Bush values a standard Moscow 'basket' of food, drink and tobacco in terms of Moscow and Washington average work-time. His methodology is not explained in detail, but he concludes that:

Table 9.6 Work-time equivalents of consumer goods, March 1982

	Washington	*Moscow*	*Munich*	*Paris*	*London*
Standard weekly 'basket' of food, drink & tobacco for a family of 3.5 persons	16.3	46.8	20.4	19.4	22.5
Cosmetics, drugs etc. (in minutes)					
Toilet soap (small bar)	4	20	6	7	5
Toilet rolls (2)	7	32	5	13	10
Aspirin	5	246	64	21	9
Lipstick	30	69	80	76	60
Transport (in minutes)					
Petrol, 10 litres, regular	32	185	61	87	85
Taxi fare, two miles	21	37	35	27	52
Bus fare, two miles	7	3	8	9	11
Train fare, 60 miles	104	258	86	87	119
Small car (months)	5	53	6	8	11
Clothing					
Tee-shirt (in minutes)	19	185	50	53	66
Pair jeans	3	46	7	6	6
Pair men's shoes	8	25	5	7	7
Consumer durables					
Small refrigerator	44	155	42	53	40
Automatic washing machine	47	165	96	56	81
Colour TV	65	701	143	106	132
Housing & services					
Monthly rent, subsidised, unfurnished apartment, 50 m^2	51	12	24	39	28
One month's gas (in minutes)	290	39	125	369	568
One month's water (in minutes)	32	123	37	95	97
Family medical insurance	22	nil	33	nil	nil
Mens' haircut (in minutes)	63	37	60	108	34

Hours of average local work-time needed to buy specified goods, except where stated otherwise.

In the original list of 23 basic goods making up the representative 'basket' in the first row of the above table, in not one case did Moscow have the lowest price in terms of work-time. Compared with Washington alone, Moscow is cheaper for one item only: cod.

Source: Taken from Bush, 1984, pp. 256–85.

The basket of food, beverages and cigarettes is at Soviet levels of consumption (it thus excludes, inter alia, coffee) and is limited to those items priced in the survey. It tends to confirm the pattern of expenditure of Soviet families that have an average of 1.6 wage-earners and that spend over one-half of their disposable income on food, drink and cigarettes. (Bush, 1981, p. 255).

Overall, it seems fair to conclude from unofficial studies that living standards are still fairly low in the Soviet Union compared with other countries, but are distributed in a relatively egalitarian way (see chapter 2). In the subsection on Soviet trends above, it would appear that even official statistics show a slowdown in the growth of consumption after 1979. This is probably largely attributable to the 'investment hunger' identified by Kornai as being a characteristic of soft budget economies, as investment consistently takes a higher share of national income than has been planned, always at consumption's expense.

BIRTH AND DEATH RATES

Children are an important aspect of 'consumption' for parents, but an investment, too, from the state's viewpoint. Policies to raise female participation in the labour force have been so successful that in 1979 the Soviet female activity rate was 83 per cent, (Pietsch, 1986, p. 176), which compares with an average of 44 per cent in developed Western countries (see Pryor, 1985, p. 83). In the long run, however, female labour participation *reduces* the workforce as birth rates fall and the Soviet authorities are now contemplating financial incentives for third and fourth children. (1981 was the 'Year of the Baby' in the USSR, and in 1986 it was reported that paid maternity leave was to be extended from twelve to eighteen months.) This all has implications for the rate of economic growth, and the growth of labour supply is discussed in chapter 8 above. In relation to living standards, however, it is important to note the shortage of effective contraceptive devices in the Soviet Union and the reliance on abortion to avoid unwanted births. The *Cambridge Encyclopaedia* (Brown et al., 1982, p. 380) estimates that about 8 million (official and unofficial) abortions are carried out every year, and a recent article in an official journal (Popov, 1985) disclosed that official abortions alone account for 2.08 terminations for each birth.

Death rates are an even more contentious aspect of Soviet living standards. The Soviet child mortality rate in 1980 was high at 230 per 10,000 live births, compared with 192 in the US and 178 in the UK (Lane, 1985, p. 62), but increases in the 1970s probably reflected more comprehensive registration (Chesnais, 1983, p. 1046). Overall life expectancy is a different matter, however. Although the 1979 Census was largely suppressed and age-specific mortality statistics stopped in 1974, a disturbing trend towards lower life expectancy for males above the age of 20 was already well established before 1974 (see Helgeson, 1982, p. 124). Since then, Chesnais (1983) has been able to estimate general life expectancy in the Soviet Union up to 1980, although this must depend upon the age-structure of the population. He shows (p. 1044) that male life expectancy *fell* by 4.3 years to 61.9 years between 1965 and 1980, and that Soviet women in 1980 survived their men by an average of 11.6 years.

These Soviet trends of lower male life expectancy and an increasing gap between the life expectancy of men and women are unique in the developed world. In the UK, the male/female 'gap' is a fairly typical 3.9 years and male life expectancy has generally increased in the West. Chesnais (1983, p. 1048) points out that whereas a Soviet and Japanese male could expect to live for approximately the same number of years in 1960 (66.2 years in the USSR and 67.7 years in Japan), by 1980 male life expectancy was 61.9 year in the USSR and 73.6 years in Japan.

It is possible that male life expectancy has increased again in the 1980s, but an explanation of increased male mortality in the 1970s is still needed. Chesnais (1983, p. 1047), Helgeson (1982, p. 125) and the United Nations *Economic Survey of Europe* (1985, p. 162) provide similar explanations, although the UN does consider 'the so-called "war-generation effect", which indicates that people especially affected by the last war tend to experience high mortality when they reach late middle or early old age'. Apart from this possibility, the blame is laid on stress-related deaths due to heart disease, cancer, accidents, alcohol abuse, poor diet and possibly gaps in care of the elderly.

In general, a consideration of Soviet birth and death rates implies wider gaps in living standards between the USSR and USA than the real-income and consumption statistics of the previous section suggest.

REGIONAL VARIATIONS IN LIVING STANDARDS

So far for this chapter has been concerned with the general standard of living in the Soviet Union, whereas this section concentrates on the regional distribution of living standards, how that distribution has been modified over time, and how it compares with the regional distribution of a fairly disparate set of variables on which data are available: retail sales, doctors and hospital beds, students in higher education, and industrial capital.

Eighty years ago, the Russian empire was relatively backward. Some 85 per cent of the population was employed in agriculture, but few owned land; most city dwellers lived in appalling conditions; and a substantial non-Russian population, especially in the southern part of the empire, lived in areas recently colonised and dominated by Russian minorities. According to Bater (1979), St Petersburg was the poorest and most squalid capital city in Europe. Although there have been minor changes in the territorial extent of the USSR since 1917, the country coincides broadly with the Russian empire as at 1900. The country can be compared with an imaginary combination of the UK, Canada and Pakistan, so a great deal of diversity is to be expected, including regional disparities in living standards.

In table 9.7, there are very wide *absolute* disparities in the provision of doctors, hospital beds, places for students in higher education, retail sales, and the distribution of 'productive funds' (broadly, industrial capital) among 24 Soviet regions (14 republics plus 10 subdivisions of the fifteenth republic, Russia itself), although regional variations should not be allowed to obscure the very high levels of health and educational provision, on these indicators, in the USSR. For example, with 197 students in higher education per 10,000 in 1981/2 (see table 9.7), the Soviet Union performed far better than Britain (98) or the Federal Republic of Germany (106) (see Lane, 1985, p. 62).

Not only can very wide absolute disparities on each indicator be noted in table 9.7 between, say, central Russia and Tadjikistan in the south, but the *absolute* gaps between rich and poor areas have widened with time. Although different regions are certainly closer together in *relative* terms, this has generally been achieved by giving preference to republics in the west, while Central Asia and Transcaucasia have lagged behind.

This phenomenon of absolute increase and relative reduction in levels of regional disparities in living standards is universal among developed countries (see Fisch, 1984). The Soviet authorities have felt obliged to give priority to national development over regional equity, while of course raising absolute standards all round by a large amount. The last column of table 9.7 confirms that there has been no systematic attempt to raise productive funds more where levels tended to be lowest than in the other regions.

Although the Soviet authorities have not prevented increases in absolute disparities between republics, may they have prevented these disparities from widening even further? The answer is probably, 'yes'. Table 9.8 provides comparisons of the extent to which certain indicators are evenly distributed between areas of the USSR, USA, ten British Commonwealth countries, and Canada and sixteen European and Asian countries that lie along the fringes of the USSR. In this table, the Gini coefficient is used as a measure of the evenness of the regional distribution of a particular variable in relation to the existing distribution of population. Thus an even distribution of doctors that closely matches the distribution of population will give a very low Gini value, whereas the concentration of facilities in a

Table 9.7 Regional variations in selected indicators, USSR

	Retail sales (roubles per capita)		*Doctors (per 100,000)*		*Hospital beds (per 10,000)*		*Students in higher education (per 10,000)*		*Productive funds (roubles per capita increase)*	
	1940	*1981*	*1940*	*1981*	*1940*	*1981*	*1940/1*	*1981/2*	*1981*	*1975–81*
RSFSR	151	1,175	82	415	43	131	43	219	5,310	155
Northwest	251	1,329	134	524	62	132	82	265		
Centre	209	1,415	114	540	50	132	67	314		
Volga-Vyatka	88	986	44	322	34	129	22	168		
Blackearth Centre	71	895	49	304	29	126	31	160		
Volga	89	955	62	358	35	126	31	190		
North Caucasus	114	946	85	376	39	117	36	168		
Ural	126	1,038	58	342	48	136	27	172		
West Siberia	92	1,124	50	382	36	137	27	220		
East Siberia	146	1,108	67	357	42	136	18	206		
Far East	300	1,396	93	440	48	146	17	181		
Western republics										
Estonia	172	1,609	100	424	48	126	45	171	6,000	138
Latvia	146	1,529	132	449	63	138	52	184	5,490	145
Lithuania	83	1,263	67	398	30	121	20	205	4,900	145
Belorussia	80	1,077	57	345	33	126	24	183	4,000	157
Ukraine	110	972	84	378	38	127	47	176	4,060	144
Moldavia	60	929	42	326	25	122	10	131	3,470	158

Table 9.7 continued

	Retail sales (roubles per capita)		Doctors (per 100,000)		Hospital beds (per 10,000)		Students in higher education (per 10,000)		Productive funds (roubles per capita increase)	
	1940	1981	1940	1981	1940	1981	1940/1	1981/2	1981	1975–81
Southern republics										
Georgia	126	910	133	496	36	107	77	171	3,330	145
Armenia	115	906	75	348	30	84	82	185	3,150	162
Azerbaijan	126	647	100	339	38	97	44	172	2,860	149
Turkmenistan	135	737	76	286	42	106	22	125	3,700	167
Uzbekistan	108	688	47	297	30	115	28	172	2,530	168
Tadjikistan	88	609	41	242	29	101	15	138	1,940	150
Kirgizia	86	750	38	300	24	121	19	155	2,690	147
Kazakhstan	92	903	43	327	40	131	16	176	4,740	149
Total USSR	132	1,068	79	385	40	126	41	197	4,570	153

The final column shows increases in roubles of productive funds per inhabitant in 1973 roubles, 1975 = 100.
Source: Figures taken from various issues of *Narodnoye khozyaystvo SSSR/RSFSR*.

few rich areas will produce high Gini coefficients (see chapter 2). (Although Gini coefficients tend to increase with the fineness of regional disaggregation, and the comparison of 24 regions of the USSR with 51 states of the USA seems to favour the former, in practice it was found that other combinations of regions only made slight differences.)

Table 9.8 confirms that all measured Soviet regional inequalities were reduced during the period 1950–80 in *relative* terms, and ended up fairly small by 1980. In relation to doctors and hospitals beds, their distribution within the Soviet Union was substantially more even than in the USA, the British Commonwealth or the seventeen 'border' countries of Asia, Europe and Canada. Access to higher education follows a similar pattern in the USSR and USA, but retail sales (and real incomes) are probably more evenly distributed in the USA. This latter result is likely to depend on the relative prosperity of US agriculture and the prevalence of household production and exchange in Soviet rural areas outside the formal retail network.

Table 9.8 Gini coefficients of the regional dispersion of selected indicators

	Hospital beds	*Doctors*	*Students in higher education*	*Retail sales*
USSR 1960	0.066	0.147	0.215	0.132
USSR 1965	0.057	0.126	0.165	0.119
USSR 1970	0.050	0.117	0.134	0.115
USSR 1975	0.048	0.104	0.117	0.113
USSR 1980	0.047	0.104	0.122	0.116
Europe–Asia–Canada 1980	0.475	0.445		
British Commonwealth 1980	0.491	0.467		
USA 1970		0.159	0.134	0.081
USA 1980	0.093	0.137	0.122	0.066

See text for explanation of Gini coefficients.
The group 'Europe–Asia–Canada' is an attempt to compose a bundle of countries that together have the same level of economic development and physical characteristics as the USSR. This group of seventeen countries comprises: Canada, Japan, GDR, FRG, Finland, Sweden, Poland, Czechoslovakia, Hungary, Romania, Bulgaria, Turkey, Iran, Afghanistan, Pakistan, Bangladesh, Philippines.
The British Commonwealth was taken to be: UK, Canada, Australia, New Zealand, South Africa, Ghana, Tanzania, Pakistan, Burma, Jamaica. Of course South Africa, Pakistan and Burma are ex-British empire, but were included to provide another bundle of comparable nations.
Sources: Figures taken from various issues of *Narodnoye khozyaystvo SSSR/RSFSR*; *Statistical Abstract of the United States*; *United Nations Statistical Yearbook, 1981*.

CONCLUSIONS

Despite a heavy commitment to military spending, the Soviet Union has achieved substantial improvements in living standards since the Second World War, particularly in the areas of health care, education, public transport and the satisfaction of basic human needs. Overt poverty is rare. Wide regional variations in living standards persist as a result of the distribution of natural resources and the degree of urbanisation, but the relative convergence of living standards between regions is proceeding at a pace that is relatively fast by international standards.

The Soviet authorities, however, would express private disappointment with the growth of material living standards since 1970. Heavy industry is now thoroughly adjusted to soft budgets and it has proved impossible to divert resources from investment into consumption. There is every sign of a slowdown in the rate of growth of living standards in the 1970s and 1980s, even below the reduced rates still enjoyed in the West. The slow growth of material living standards has been accompanied by a disappointing reduction in male life expectancy, and the failure to adopt realistic exchange rates for the rouble against hard currencies implicitly prevents Soviet citizens from comparing their material living standards with those in the West.

CHAPTER TEN

HARD OR SOFT BUDGETS

In this last chapter, important implications of the earlier analysis for the future are drawn.

The first section examines the extent to which the description of the Soviet economy as being characterised by relatively soft budgets in industry succeeds in predicting and explaining the Soviet Union's *particular* economic performance. In the second section, the authors consider whether the hard/soft budget approach casts any light on the choice of economic systems in *general* terms. In the third section, special reference is made to Hungary's attempts to harden budget constraints in industry.

THE EXPLANATION OF SOVIET ECONOMIC PERFORMANCE

There are contrasting views on the explanation of the economic performance of actual economic systems. On the one hand, people like Gregory and Stuart would claim that there are 'observed regularities in the socialist development process that can be contrasted with observed regularities in the capitalist development process' (1981, p. 405). On the other hand, the whole of Pryor's (1985) book is devoted to the claim that the notions and labels of traditional theories of capitalist and socialist economic systems are useless in explaining the performance of actual economies. Indeed, he shows that if one compares the economic performance of CMEA countries as a whole with the industrialised West as a whole, the two systems are virtually indistinguishable.

Economic systems have many dimensions. For example, the extent of public ownership, the role of profits, prices and directives, and the amount of centralised control over enterprise behaviour are crucial. This book seizes on only *one* dimension: the extent to which good/bad performance in industry is rewarded/penalised, or the existence of hard/soft budget or administrative constraints. It is claimed that the hardness of constraints *does* yield some understanding of the performance of different economic systems. It captures the essence of different systems, yet does not give a one-dimensional view, as the hardness of constraints depends on so many institutions and mechanisms.

Relatively hard budget constraints may be imposed by competitive forces from markets or by administrative procedures, although Kornai would insist that administration can never replace market competition as a source of hardness. Nevertheless, he does distinguish the hard/soft administration of state subsidies to industry in a recent paper (see Kornai, 1986, p. 22).

The view expressed in chapter 1 was that hard administration is possible. For example, air traffic control systems seem to exhibit hard constraints at most large airports around the world. Controllers may be motivated to provide correct decisions out of professional pride, concern for potential casualties or for press publicity of errors leading to humiliation and dismissal. They are certainly not motivated by competitive market forces, since airlines wishing to land in a particular country have no choice but to pay landing fees. Other examples of hard administrations in the West are cited in chapter 1. We would insist that the distinctive economic performance of the German Democratic Republic (GDR) can best be explained in terms of 'hard' administration, although the proximity of the Federal Republic of Germany (FRG) must concentrate the minds of administrators, who know that the outcomes of their decisions will be closely compared with the West, and the German culture encourages administrative discipline. By the same token, certain priority sectors of the Soviet economy have been shown to have experienced relatively hard budget or administrative constraints.

Overall, however, it is asserted that the Soviet economy is generally characterised by relatively soft constraints, for reasons that have been repeated in each of the preceding chapters. The difference between the Soviet and GDR situation is one of culture, location and, above all, the size and complexity of the Soviet economy. The administration through vertical hierarchies of an economy covering 8,649,500 square miles and nearly 280 million inhabitants in the USSR is of quite a different order to one of 41,800 square miles and only 17 million people, as in the GDR. Given the complexity of the task and the 'bounded rationality' of the human brain, it seems that it is impossible to apply relatively hard constraints through administrative procedures to more than a minority of Soviet industries or areas.

Figure 10.1 A summary of actual Soviet economic performance.

	Static		*Dynamic*	
Micro	Fairness		Investment	
	(X)	(SU)	(✓)	(SU)
	Allocation & production		Innovation	
	(✓)	(US)	(✓)	(US)
Micro	Inflation		Extensive growth	
	(X)	(SU)	(✓)	(SU)
	Unemployment		Intensive growth	
	(✓)	(SU)?	(✓)	(US)

A tick represents a Soviet performance that seems to conform with predictions based on Kornai's notion of the relatively soft budget constraint.
(US) or (SU) implies a superior performance by the United States (US) or Soviet Union (SU) economies, on each component of economic efficiency. See the end of chapter 1 and individual chapters for an explanation of terms. Of course high investment levels and extensive growth could be considered excessive in the Soviet Union, rather than superior. Similarly, Soviet unemployment 'on the job' may be judged 'worse' than US registered external unemployment.

Although the foregoing discussion consists of untestable assertions, we would argue that the identification of the Soviet Union as having the characteristics of a relatively soft budget economy, and of the United States and the rest of the industrialised West as having relatively hard budget regimes, proves to be reasonably successful in terms of predictive accuracy. Six 'ticks' out of eight in figure 10.1 represents a reasonable performance for Kornai's theory, although *if* the analysis of economic systems were a social science, two refutations out of eight tests would lead one to reject the whole theory on Popperian grounds. (A special case could be made out for each of the 'crosses' in figure 10.1: Kornai's theory has been 'stretched' to embrace 'fairness'; and special institutional features, not hard budgets, have caused inflation in the West.) Unfortunately, the luxury of a scientific pose is not available to us and we would argue that Kornai's theory offers better explanations of Soviet economic performance than any other. Of course the degree of budget hardness can never be measured with precision and any predictions can only forecast the direction of performance over time in one economy or in relation to another.

Kornai's work has always appeared hostile to the soft constraints of the centrally planned economy since the publication of his first book on over-centralisation (Kornai, 1959). Certainly, it predicts for the USSR internal unemployment, over-investment, poor resource allocation, slow innovation and an over-reliance on extensive growth which must hit resource limits. We judge these predictions to be sustained by the evidence, but on the other hand 'SU' does appear on five occasions out of eight in figure 10.1, indicating 'superior' performance relative to the US.

It is fashionable to sneer at the claims of Nikita Khrushchev in the third CPSU programme of 1961, when he claimed that Soviet living standards would catch up with those of the USA in twenty years, there would be a five-hour working day, rent-free accommodation for workers and significant progress towards Full Communism. Although it is true that the USSR produces larger quantities than the USA of goods like iron and steel, oil, coal and cement, which were considered strategically important in 1961, it has to be conceded (chapter 9) that living standards are still disappointingly low, and soft budgets are probably to blame. Nevertheless, the letters 'SU' in figure 10.1 do identify relative Soviet achievements over many decades in the areas of fairness, inflation, external unemployment, levels of investment and extensive economic growth, which are substantial by any standards.

If different systems and budget regimes can produce outcomes that are effectively the mirror-image of each other (see figure 10.1), might it not be possible to combine the best of both worlds in a system that performs well on each of the eight components of economic efficiency? Can economic systems 'converge' on an 'optimal' regime?

CONSTRAINTS AND CONVERGENCE

There are at least three kinds of convergence, or the tendency for economic systems to become more alike. There is the convergence on the left predicted by Karl Marx as a result of the inevitable breakdown of capitalism, and there is the convergence on the right predicted by Von Mises and other members of the 'New Austrian' school as a result of the failures of central planners who cannot have a monopoly of the truth in a world of uncertainty. In between these extremes there is the notion of a hybrid or mixed economic system that might combine the best of both capitalism and socialism without the worst.

Tinbergen (1967) had visions of an 'optimal economic order' that would evolve through market forces or by the actions of rational governments, influenced by the technological features of different industries that suit some to market and others to administrative control. For example, Wilczynski (1982) cites decentralising reforms in the Soviet Union and elements of state intervention in the West as convergence and considers that 'Most of the modifications taking place on each side are not conscious imitations, but rather selective adaptations to a variety of economic and technical changes, independent of any system' (p. 223).

In a similar vein, Nove (1983) proposes a mixed socialist economy in which large centralised state corporations occupy 'the "commanding heights" of large scale industry and public utilities plus finance' (p. 202), because these sectors 'operate in very large, closely interrelated units, or have a monopoly position, or both' (p. 201). Other sectors in Nove's system of 'feasible socialism' would include state-owned enterprises with managements responsible to their workforces, co-operatives and private enterprise limited by legal maxima on numbers employed and value of assets, variable by sector. Private enterprise is justified because 'If any activity (not actually a "social bad" in itself) can be fruitfully and profitably undertaken by any individual, this sets up the presumption of its legitimacy' (Nove, 1983m p. 206). Indeed Kornai himself has suggested that 'our job as social scientists is to search out for at least acceptable compromises' (1985, p. 31).

This notion of convergence on a mixed economic system or compromise has attracted criticism, however. Ellman (1980) has pointed out that governments cannot be considered 'rational actors' in relation to economic systems, although Moroshima (1982) does report on a brave attempt at rationality by the Japanese government. Following centuries of isolation from the West and the Meiji Revolution, the government sent out missions to Europe and America:

> These men brought back with them a wealth of new knowledge and information concerning the modern state. The Meiji government compared and examined all this information to judge which country was the most outstanding and the most advanced in each sphere, for example which country was best in terms of its education system, which country for the navy, and which for the army. In each country they investigated the conditions of such things as the police, industry and finance. On the basis of the information relating to these subjects obtained from the missions the government made its decision as to which sphere should be patterned on which country. For example, the education system promulgated in 1872 was patterned on the French system of school districts. The Imperial Japanese Navy was a copy of the Royal Navy, but the army was very greatly influenced by the French army. The telegraph and the railways followed the British example, universities the American. The Meiji Constitution and the Civil Code were of German origin, but the Criminal Code was of French origin.
>
> In this way, the Meiji state was a hotchpotch of Britain, the United States, France and Germany. (Moroshima, 1982, pp. 88–9)

The strongest argument against convergence is however Kornai's notion of the 'supermarket fallacy':

> The tradition of economics has accustomed us to the concept that everything can and must be 'optimised'. It is therefore understandable that the idea arose that an 'optimum economic system' must be designed, combining the best possible 'rules of the game' and the best operating control mechanisms. Those setting this aim envisage something like a visit to a supermarket. On the shelves are to be found the various components of the mechanism, incorporating the advantageous qualities of all systems. On one shelf, there is full employment as it has been realised in Eastern Europe. On another, there is the high degree of workshop organisation and discipline, like in a West German or Swiss factory. On a third shelf is economic growth free of recession, on a fourth, price stability, on a fifth, rapid adjustment of production to demands on the foreign market. The system designer has nothing to do but push along his trolley and collect these 'optimum components', and then compose from them at home the 'optimum system'.
>
> But that is a naive, wishful day-dream. History does not provide such supermarkets in which we can make our choice as we like. Every real economic system constitutes an organic whole. This may contain good and bad features, and more or less in fixed proportions. The choice of system lies only among various 'package deals'. It is not possible to pick out from the different 'packages' the components we like and to leave what we dislike. (Kornai, 1979b, p, 137, quoted in Ellman, 1984, pp. 190–1)

Kornai's observation that one cannot pick out the desirable features of one economic system can, however, be reconciled with his plea for 'acceptable compromises' quoted above. Governments may opt for harder or softer constraints, depending on the circumstances, and this may lead to convergence on a mixed system. The change in the nature of a budget constraint must prove a mixed blessing, however, and it will always bring with it losses on some aspects of efficiency as surely as gains on others. Indeed, gains can only be achieved, if the costs are borne. For example, market competition can only be effective in raising labour productivity, if workers and managers are threatened by unemployment and/or the liquidation of the enterprise. If unemployment pay is introduced to soften the pain of unemployment, it is inevitable that the budget constraint is also softened as the fear of unemployment is reduced. (During the 1980s, the British government has arguably tried to harden the budget constraint in British industry by reducing effective demand and unemployment benefits and by refusing to rescue some bankrupt operations.) The art of government is now seen to be to achieve acceptable compromises and to dispense with the notion of 'optimal economic orders'.

One may doubt the ability of economic systems like that of the USSR to move towards compromises that involve harder budget constraints. The authorities may consider the costs too great for society as a whole, or particular interest groups may resent any loss of power or security that the existing system offers. For example, harder budgets imply less centralised control, with individual managers held responsible for their own decisions, but this means that the central planners cannot centrally co-ordinate resource allocations that are beyond their control. The managers may be anxious to loosen controls from the centre, but 'At the same time, they are grateful if the state yields to pressure and helps them in case of financial failure and they would not like to lose the privilege of this safety' (Kornai, 1983, pp. 249–50).

Even if the *economic* hierarchy is prepared to live with the costs and benefits of harder budgets, the shadow *political* hierarchy of the Communist Party may not be. Harder budget constraints would loosen the ties of co-responsibility for enterprise and industrial performance that bind together managers, ministries and the Party. Central planners would not be able to 'pull rank' on managers to persuade them to take decisions in the interests of central co-ordination (i.e. to cover up for mistakes elsewhere), and managers would be appointed and retain their jobs on merit, not at the whim of the Party hierarchy. Similarly, enterprise managers could not count on informal contacts through the Party's hierarchy to secure supplies.

Central planning for an economy like that of the Soviet Union implies relatively soft constraints, and without reforms it must get used to the pattern of gains and losses in economic efficiency that this implies (see figure 10.1). If it wishes to harden budget constraints, it may be possible to avoid costs in the form of unemployment, given the existing state of chronic over-demand for labour, but 'the apparatus' may obstruct reforms and there may be forces in the economic and political hierarchies that mean 'once a centrally planned economy, always a centrally planned economy'. This obstruction would imply that no convergence is feasible.

Certainly, the fate of successive waves of 'economic reforms' in the Soviet Union supports this view, with reforming vigour being gradually replaced by cynicism and retrenchment. The most serious attempts at economic reform in the CMEA bloc have been in Hungary, where Kornai, at the Budapest Academy of Sciences, has been uniquely placed to provide a commentary (see Kornai, 1983). It is worthwhile, therefore, to consider the fate of Hungarian reforms, even in a book on Soviet economic performance.

HUNGARIAN REFORMS

On the face of it, Hungary should find it much easier than the Soviet Union to harden budget constraints in industry. It is a small country with fewer than 11 million people and it is exceptionally open to foreign trade, which accounts for over 40 per cent of its national income. This openness and the Hungarian culture have always encouraged the Hungarian economy to compete in foreign trade, even during the Stalinist period of central planning after 1945.

Serious economic reforms began in 1968, but achieved little, ostensibly because balance of payments deficits (exacerbated by the slump in import demands from the West in the throes of an oil crisis) made it necessary to introduce controls on both foreign and domestic trade. The reform process resumed after 1979, and this section is concerned with the situation in the 1980s. It is convenient to consider the reforms in the context of Kornai's five features of a perfectly soft budget constraint described at the end of chapter 1.

Enterprises are price-makers under perfectly soft budgets and can pass on any cost increases to consumers in sellers' markets. In Hungary the 275 largest enterprises accounted for 78 per cent of total industrial output in 1980. Thus the opportunity for monopolistic price-making behaviour was great. The reforms have established more realistic exchange rates for the Forint and have exposed domestic producers to some competition from Western imports. Some producers have been able to raise domestic prices only to levels they can prove have been profitable in exports to the West that account for more than 5 per cent of their total output. Foreign trade corporations have lost their monopoly of foreign trade, and individual producers are now permitted to export on their own. In the state industries, 'economic teams' with a maximum of thirty members have been allowed to compete on a private basis for non-standard work and they have been able to undercut 'in-house' prices and outside tenders. Capitalist firms with a maximum of ten employees have also been allowed to compete with state enterprises on peripheral activities, especially in the retail sector. Private operations have effectively legitimised black market activities, which are now subject to taxation.

One should not go overboard on these reforms intended to increase price competition, however. A shortage of hard-currency reserves has persuaded the government to impose controls on industrial and agricultural prices, but of course this is not uncommon in the West. During 1986, price competition from imports was disrupted by a series of administrative devices. In the case of Western home computers, for example, customs officials are now quite bewildered by almost weekly changes in regulations from the bureaucracy. In 1985, the Hungarian Cable Works (MKM) became technically bankrupt and a committee of the National Bank recommended a 5 per cent increase in domestic cable prices, just like old times. Branches of the National Bank are supposed to compete as separate merchant banks in the supply of industrial credit by

1987, but this has been the policy for at least four years, without effect!

Enterprises determine their own tax payments with perfectly soft budgets. Tax payments are now public knowledge in Hungary and companies seeking to raise private bonds (see below) are required to disclose details of their income, turnover and productivity. On the other hand, Kornai (1983, p. 230) reveals that each branch or sub-branch of the economy is still treated differently in relation to taxes, and in practice this has meant that companies who have raised prices and incomes as a result of successful exporting have paid higher rates of tax. In the case of the 'bankrupt' MKM cable works (see above), the National Bânk has recommended a partial respite from taxes for the next five years.

Enterprises enjoy state grants for deficits under perfectly soft budgets. Kornai (1983, p. 233) reports that in 1980 state grants and soft loans were unable to prevent the liquidation of thirteen enterprises, and in 1984 1,300 workers lost their jobs in the IGV Business Machine Works and 1,500 at the Tungsram light-bulb factory. Even at MKM (see above), top management was dismissed and other headquarters staff had a choice of production-line jobs or dismissal. At the same time, however, Kornai (1983, p. 232) shows that subsidies are still being paid to companies with low profits, and staff still enjoy job security, although this may involve retraining and/or relocation. At MKM in 1985, the National Bank provided a short-term loan to cover operating deficits, and in 1986 Hungary's three largest steel companies employing more than 40,000 workers had debts of £333 million written off by the state.

Enterprises enjoy subsidised credit without a serious analysis of the prospects for repayment, and defaults are permitted. Since 1984, Hungarian state enterprises have been allowed to float bonds with variable-interest coupons related to the company's prospects. In some cases, companies have offered bond-holders' privileges – for example, the entitlement to a telephone within three years, in the case of the Szeged Post Office's bonds! It should be emphasised, however, that these bonds involve no equity stake and bond-holders are not expected to interfere with the decisions of enterprises. Apart from these variable-interest bond transactions, which resemble an embryonic Western-style Stock Market, finance is available from the National Bank, which *administers* loans according to the applicant's prospects for hard-currency exports. In 1985, ten of the Bank's twelve directors were Party members.

The state bears all enterprise risks under perfectly soft budgets. The Hungarian reforms have involved the growth of agricultural co-operatives and the floating of new subsidiaries by state companies and private enterprise in the form of small capitalist firms and work-teams in the state factories. None of these ventures is underwritten by the state, and in practice only the best workers have been invited to join small firms and work-teams. The management teams of state firms are now elected by and are answerable to their workforces rather than to the ministry and the Party.

These reforms of 1982 cannot be expected to have worked overnight, but investigations by one of the authors in 1986 suggested that Party secretaries are still being elected to managerial posts as before and work-teams have turned out to be little more than the old weekend overtime work-teams, organised and controlled by existing full-time management in the state firms.

In the summer of 1986, a new Hungarian bankruptcy law was introduced which should involve creditors, the courts and a state Rehabilitation Office. The writing-off of debts in the steel industry referred to above was rushed through before the new law came into effect, however, and it remains to be seen how many other 'exceptions' arise in future. As things stand, Hungarian law allows for liquidations that simply transfer the assets of firms to others seeking the plant or workforce of victims. The loss of Western export sales has caused some recent 'proper' liquidations, however.

No empirical evidence is available on the extent to which the central authorities feel co-responsibility for, and share risks with, enterprises. On the face of it, output directives no longer exist and the single ministry that deals with all Hungarian industry simply listens to the intentions of the enterprises for the next plan period and modifies prices to avoid potential bottlenecks. It is totally impossible to judge whether the informal telephone call from the ministry or the comment from a Party superior influences the enterprise manager more than the old directives, but they certainly still occur. When subsidies are removed or exporting permits price increases, old patterns of profitability still manage to reassert themselves with time (Kornai, 1983, p. 227). Kornai suggests that 'differences in the prestige of economic units, and in their relations to the higher authorities may mean that a "well-in" enterprise soon regains its old position while a "badly-in" enterprise soon loses the new advantages; there may be variations in the extent to which an economic unit can escape restrictions and control' (1983, pp. 227–8).

This short account shows Hungary's struggle to harden budget constraints in industry. Clearly, progress with reforms has been limited, even after over two decades of effort, and in the Soviet Union the obstacles to reform are even more formidable. In any case, it should not be forgotten that harder budget constraints inevitably bring costs as well as benefits. In Hungary, the targets for the 1981–85 plan were not achieved: NMP rose by only 7 per cent over the period compared with the plan of 14–17 per cent. The non-fulfilment of central plans is an inevitable consequence of decentralised decisions, although in this case other influences were at work. Inflation rates of 8 per cent per annum have been publicly conceded, although private estimates circulating in Budapest are much higher. The central authorities have had to cope with a massive balance of payments deficit as a result of imports and foreign travel, and the ultimate consequence of enterprise liquidation must be external unemployment. In the state enterprises, visitors often hear complaints about the effects of private work, work-teams and even agricultural co-operatives on the distribution of income. In Hungary, the authorities are confident that a higher rate of economic growth, the utilisation of idle reserves of labour and the overall level of over-employment will prevent the creation of high unemployment by harder budgets.

CONCLUSIONS

The lesson of this book is that there are no obvious lessons. Different countries choose or evolve economic systems that feature different mixtures of plan and market, centralisation and decentralisation. In the case of the USSR, the use of central plans for such a massive and complex economy seems inevitably to guarantee relatively soft constraints for industry in general. Paradoxically, central planning is arguably least suited to the USSR and most suited to a country with Hungary's culture, size and location. Yet Hungary is struggling to throw off the yoke of central planning.

Relatively soft constraints imply certain characteristics for an economy and Kornai's work has provided a reasonably accurate explanation of modern Soviet economic performance. With more markets and capitalism and less central planning, the USSR would probably have been able to offer its citizens a higher average material standard of living, largely as a result of less consumption being sacrificed at the altar of investment in heavy industry, but also as a result of faster technological progress and less static waste in industry generally. Despite the existence of elite groups, however, it seems clear that a capitalist USSR would be far less egalitarian and would offer far fewer employment opportunities.

Unemployment provides the starkest contrast between the USSR and the West. At a time when countries like Britain are trying to cope with male unemployment in excess of 13.5 per cent, the Soviet Union is desperately trying to live with labour *shortages*. The Moscow evening newspaper *Vechernogo Moskva* of 13 June 1986 noted that a tough new Census system is to be used to winkle out idle labour. The Moscow city council has decreed that all adult residents in Moscow will have to present the local housing department with a certificate from their place of work in an attempt to stimulate the supply of labour at a time when the British government tries to bribe employers through a variety of subsidies to create jobs, or raise the *demand* for labour. In relation to unemployment and most other aspects of economic efficiency, the USSR's economic performance is virtually the mirror-image of that of the West.

Despite the significant achievements of the Soviet economy in relation to *some* aspects of economic efficiency, it is tempting for the central authorities there to look with envy at the contrasting performance by Western economies with their relatively hard budgets in relation to the *other* aspects. Certainly, Hungary and China have to some extent reduced their emphasis on collective agriculture and investment in heavy industry in favour of decentralised decisions based on market forces, but this will lead to a less equal distribution of income and ultimately more unemployment.

It would be nice if there were some optimal economic order, a mixed economic system, that could be demonstrated to achieve maximum economic efficiency on all counts. The existence of such a system could reduce political and economic rivalry and make a substantial contribution to world stability. It does not exist. Instead, the world is left with an economic choice of relatively hard or soft constraints, achieved through markets or administration. The adoption of any one regime for its benefits makes it ultimately impossible to avoid the associated costs, and this conclusion applies to any reforms that tinker with the basic regime.

This book has not been concerned with non-economic issues such as the freedom of the individual and the spirit of socialism, except for a few comments in the Preface. Perhaps the right conclusion would be that different economic systems should recognise their relative strengths and weaknesses with honesty. Such a realisation could make a real contribution to the reduction of international tensions. No actual (as opposed to theoretical) economic system can be justified in boasting unduly about its performance.

REFERENCES

Adam, J (1980), 'The Present Soviet Incentive System', *Soviet Studies*, 32(3), 349–65.

Amann, R (1982), 'Industrial Innovation in the Soviet Union: Methodological Perspectives and Conclusions', in R. Amann and J. Cooper (eds), *Industrial Innovation in the Soviet Union*, Yale University Press, New Haven.

Askansas, B and Laski, K (1985), 'Consumption Levels in Poland and Austria', *Journal of Comparative Economics*, 9(2), 164–77.

Bater, J H (1979), 'The Legacy of Autocracy : Environmental Quality in St Petersburg', in R A French and F E I Hamilton (eds), *The Socialist City*, Wiley, Chichester.

Baumol, W J and McLennan, K (1985), 'US Productivity Performance and Its Implications', in W J Baumol and K McLennan (eds), *Productivity Growth and US Competiveness*, Oxford University Press, New York, pp. 3–28.

Becker, A S (1972), 'National Income Accounting in the USSR, in V G Treml and J P Hardt (eds), *Soviet Economic Statistics*, Duke University Press, North Carolina, pp. 69–119.

Bergson, A (1982), 'Toward a New Growth Model', *ACES Bulletin*, 24(2), 89–92.

Bergson, A (1983), 'Technological Progress', in A Bergson and H S Levine, *The Soviet Economy: Toward the Year 2000*, Allen and Unwin, London.

Bergson, A (1984), 'Income Inequality under Soviet Socialism', *Journal of Economic Literature*, 22(3), 1052–99.

Bergson, A F(1985) 'Gorbachev Calls for Intensive Growth' *Challenge*, 28(5), 11–14.

Berliner, J S (1976), *The Innovation Decision in Soviet Industry*, MIT Press, Cambridge, Massachusetts.

Binyon, M. (1983), *Life in Russia*, Hamish Hamilton, London.

Birman, I (1978), 'From the Achieved Level', *Soviet Studies*, 30(2), 153–72.

Bornstein, M (1978), 'Unemployment in Capitalist Regulated Market Economies and Centrally Planned Economies', *Papers and Proceedings of the American Economics Association*, 68(2), 38–43.

Bornstein, M (1985), 'Improving the Soviet Economic Mechanism', *Soviet Studies*, 37(1), 1–30.

Brada, J C (1974), 'Allocative Efficiency and the System of Economic Management in Some Socialist Countries', *Kyklos*, 27(2), 270–83.

Brada, J C (1981), *Technology Transfer between the US and Countries of the Soviet Bloc*, Istituto di Studi e Documentazione Sull'Este Europeo, Trieste.

Brada, J C and Jackson, M R (1978), 'The Organization of Foreign Trade under Capitalism and Socialism', *Journal of Comparative Economics*, 2(4) 293–319.

Britton, C R and Gay, D E R (1984), Review, *Kyklos*, 37(1), 137–8.

Brown, A et al. (1982), *The Cambridge Encyclopedia of Russia and the Soviet Union*. Cambridge University Press, Cambridge.

Buck, T W (1982), *Comparative Industrial Systems*, Macmillan, London.

Buck, T W (1985), 'The Convergence of Economic Systems and the M-Form', *Journal of Economic Behaviour and Organisation*, 6(2), 123–37.

Bush, K (1981, 1984), 'Retail Prices in Moscow and Four Western Cities in March 1979', L Schapiro and J Godson (eds), *The Socialist Worker*, Macmillan, London.

Campbell, R W (1958), 'Inventory-Output Ratios, a Comparison of Soviet and American', *American Economic Review*, 48(4), 549–65.

Campbell, R W (1967), *Soviet Economic Power*, Macmillan, London.

Campbell, R W (1974), *Soviet-Type Economies*, Macmillan, London.

Campbell, R W (1980), *Soviet Energy Technologies*, Indiana University Press, Bloomington.

Chapman, J G (1983), 'Earnings Distribution in the USSR, 1968–1976: Comments on the Notes of Nove and McAuley', *Soviet Studies*, 35(3), 410–13.

Chesnais, J-C (1983), 'La Durée de la Vie dans les Pays Industrialisés', *La Recherche*, 14(147), 1040–48.

Cohn, S H (1982), 'Sources of Low Productivity in Soviet Capital Investment', in *Soviet Economy in the 1980s : Problems and Prospects, Part I*, Joint Economic Committee of the Congress of the US, Government Printing Office, Washington DC.

Cole, J P (1983), *Geography of World Affairs*, Butterworths, London.

Cole, J P (1984), *Geography of the Soviet Union*, Butterworths, London.

Cole, J P (1985), 'The Geography of Soviet Foreign Trade: Statistics and Commentary', *Soviet Geography*, 26(5), 315–82.

Committee of Vice-Chancellors and Principals (1985), *Report of the Steering Committee for Efficiency Studies in Universities*, London.

Converse, R (1982), 'An Index of Industrial Production in the USSR', in *USSR: Measures of Economic Growth and Development, 1950–80*, Joint Economic Committee of the Congress of the US, Government Printing Office, Washington DC.

Culbertson, W P Jr, and Amacher, R C (1978), 'Inflation in the Planned Economies: Some Estimates for Eastern Europe', *Southern Economic Journal*, 45(2), 380–93.

Danilin, V I, Materov, I S, Rosefielde, S and Knox Lovell, C A (1985), 'Measuring Enterprise Efficiency in the Soviet Union', *Economica*, 52(206), 225–33.

Davies, R W (1977), 'The Technological Level of Soviet Industry: an Overview', in R Amann, J Cooper and R W Davies (eds), *The Technological Level of Soviet Industry*, Yale University Press, New Haven.

Davies, R W (1986), 'The Ending of Mass Unemployment in the USSR', chapter in D Lane (ed.), *Labour and Employment in the USSR*, Harvester Press, Brighton.

De Alessi, L (1983), 'Property Rights, Transactions, Costs and X-Efficiency', *American Economic Review*, 73(1), 64–81.

Desai, P and Martin, R (1983), 'Efficiency Loss from Resource Misallocation in Soviet Industry', *Quarterly Journal of Economics*, 98(2), 441–55.

Dirksen, E (1981), 'The Control of Inflation? Errors in the Interpretation of CPE Data', *Economica*, 48(191), 305–8.

Drewnowski, J (1982), 'The Anatomy of Failure in Soviet-type Systems', in J Drewnowski, *Crisis in the East European Economy* Croom Helm, London.

Durgin, F (1984), Review of Goldman, *USSR in Crisis: The Failure of an Economic System, ACES Bulletin*, 26(2–3), 99–110.

Durgin, F A Jr (1983), 'More on the New Model of Soviet Growth', *ACES Bulletin*, 25(1), 35–46.

Dyker, D A (1985), *The Future of the Soviet Economic Planning System*, Croom Helm, London.

Ellman, M (1979), 'Full Employment – Lessons from State Socialism', *De Economist*, 127(4), 489–511.

Ellman, M (1980), 'Against Convergence', *Cambridge Journal of Economics*, 4(3), 199–210.

Ellman, M (1981), 'Agricultural Productivity Under Socialism', *World Development*, 9(9/10), 979–89.

Ellman, M (1982), 'A Roundtable Discussion : Outlook for the Socialist Economies', *Marxism Today*, 22–28, February.

Ellman, M (1984), *Collectivisation, Convergence and Capitalism*, Academic Press, London.

Feldbrugge, F J M (1984), 'Government and Shadow Economy in the Soviet Union', *Soviet Studies*, 36(4), 528–43.

Fisch, O (1984), 'Regional Income Inequality and Economic Development', *Regional Science and Urban Economics*, 14(1), 89–111.

Freeman, C (1974), *The Economics of Industrial Innovation*, Penguin, Harmondsworth.

Friedman, M (1984), *Market or Plan?*, Centre for Research into Communist Countries, London.

Gardner, R and Strauss, J (1981), 'Repressed Inflation in the Soviet Union – a Temporary Equilibrium Approach', *European Economic Review*, 16(3), 387–404.

Gidwitz, B (1982), 'Labor Unrest in the Soviet Union', *Problems of Communism*, 31(6) 25–42.

Goldman, M I (1983), *USSR in Crisis: The Failure of an Economic System*, W W Norton, New York.

Gorlov, V N and Baburin, V L (1985), 'The New Soviet Industrial Corporations and Research-based Industrial Corporations as an Economic-Geographic Study Object', *Soviet Geography*, 26(3), 177–83.

Gregory, P R and Stuart, R C (1981), *Soviet Economic Structure and Performance*, Harper and Row, New York.

Grossman, G (1982), 'A Note on Soviet Inflation', in *Soviet Economy in the 1980s: Problems and Prospects. Part I*, Joint Economic Committee of Congress, Government Printing Office, Washington DC, pp. 267–86.

Gutmann, P M (1985), 'The Subterranean Economy, Redux', in W Gaertner, and A Wenig (eds), *Economics of the Shadow Economy*, Springer-Verlag, Berlin.

Hall, J B (1983), Review, *Journal of Economic Issues*, 17(4), 1162–66.

Hanson, P (1981), *Trade and Technology in Soviet-Western Relations*, Macmillan, London.

Hanson, P (1983), 'Success Indicators Revisited: the July 1979 Soviet Decree on Planning and Management', *Soviet Studies*, 35(1), 1–13.

Hanson, P (1984a), 'The CIA, THE TsSU and the Real Growth of Soviet Investment', *Soviet Studies*, 36(4), 571–81.

Hanson, P (1984b), 'The Serendipitous Soviet Achievement of Full Employment.

Labour Shortage and Labour Hoarding in the Soviet Economy', paper presented to the Conference on Employment and Labour Policy in the USSR, University of Birmingham, June 1984.

Hanson, P (1986), 'The Serendipitous Soviet Achievement of Full Employment', in D Lane (ed.), *Labour and Employment in the USSR*, Harvester Press, Brighton.

Haraszti, M (1977), *A Worker in a Worker's State: Piece-rates in Hungary*, Penguin, Harmondsworth.

Harrison, M (1986), 'Lessons of Soviet Planning of Full Employment', in D Lane (ed.), *Labour and Employment in the USSR*, Harvester Press, Brighton.

Havlik, P (1985), 'A Comparison of Purchasing Power Parities and Consumption Levels in Austria and Czechoslovakia', *Journal of Comparative Economics*, 9(2), 178–90.

Helgeson, A (1982), 'Demographic Policy', 118–145 in A Brown and M Kaser (eds), *Soviet Policy for the 1980s*, Macmillan, London.

Helgeson, A (1986), 'Geographical Mobility – Its Implications for Employment', in D Lane (ed.), *Labour and Employment in the USSR*, Harvester Press, Brighton.

Hough, J F, (1969), *The Soviet Prefects: The Local Party Organs in Industrial Decision–Making',* Harvard University Press, Cambridge, Massachusetts.

Howard, D (1976), 'A Note on Hidden Inflation in the Soviet Union', *Soviet Studies*, 28(4), 599–608.

Jackson, P M (1982), *The Political Economy of Bureaucracy*, Philip Allan, Oxford.

Jefferson, M (1983), 'Economic Uncertainty and Business Decision Making', in J Wiseman (ed.), *Beyond Positive Economics*, Macmillan, London, pp. 122–59.

Kamien, M O and Schwarts, N L (1982), *Market Structure and Innovation*, Cambridge University Press, Cambridge.

Kapitány Z, Kornai J and Szabó J (1984), 'Reproduction of Shortage on the Hungarian Car Market', *Soviet Studies*, 36(2), 236–56.

Kornai, J (1959), *Overcentralisation in Economic Administration*, Oxford University Press, Oxford.

Kornai, J (1976), 'Pressure and Suction on the Market', in J Thornton (ed.), *Economic Analysis of Soviet-Type Systems*, Cambridge University Press, Cambridge.

Kornai, J (1979a), 'Resource-Constrained Versus Demand-Constrained Systems', *Econometrica*, 47(4), 801–19.

Kornai, J (1979b), *The Dilemma of a Socialist Economy: The Hungarian Experience*, The Economic and Social Research Institute, Durbin.

Kornai, J (1980), *The Economics of Shortage*, Volumes A and B, North-Holland, Amsterdam.

Kornai, J (1982), *Growth, Shortage and Efficiency*, Blackwell, Oxford.

Kornai, J (1983), 'Comments on the Present State and the Prospects of the Hungarian Reform', *Journal of Comparative Economics*, 7(3), 225–52.

Kornai, J (1985), 'Hungary's Reform : Halfway to the Market', *Challenge*, May/June, 22–31.

Kornai, J (1986), 'The Soft Budget Constraint', *Kyklos*, 39(1), 3–30.

Kravis, I B et al. (1978), *A System of International Comparisons of Gross Product and Purchasing Power*, John Hopkins University Press, London.

Kushnirsky, F I (1984), 'Inflation Soviet Style', *Problems of Communism*, 33(1), 48–53.

Lane, D (1985), *Soviet Economy and Society*, Blackwell, Oxford.

Leggett, R E (1981), 'Measuring Inflation in the Soviet Machinebuilding Sector, 1960–1973', *Journal of Comparative Economics*, 5(2), 169–84.

Leibenstein, H (1981), 'Microeconomics and X-Efficiency Theory', in D Bell, and I Kristol (eds), *The Crisis of Economic Theory*, Basic Books, New York.

Lenin, V I (1968), *Selected Works*, Lawrence and Wishart, London.

Levine, H S (1982), 'Possible Causes of the Deterioration of Soviet Productivity Growth in the Period 1976–80' in *Soviet Economy in the 1980s: Problems and Prospects*, Joint Economic Comittee of the US Congress, Government Printing Office, Washington DC.

Macariello, J A (1984), *Management Control Systems*, Prentice-Hall, Englewood Cliffs, New Jersey.

McAuley, A (1979), *Economic Welfare in the Soviet Union*, University of Wisconsin Press, Madison.

Malle, S (1986), 'Heterogeneity of the Soviet Labour Market as a Limit to a More Efficient Utilisation of Manpower', in D Lane (ed.), *Labour and Employment in the USSR*, Harvester Press, Brighton.

Marrese, M and Mitchell, J L (1984), 'Kornai's Resource-Constrained Economy : a Survey and an Appraisal', *Journal of Comparative Economics*, 8(1), 74–84.

Martens, J A (1983), 'Soviet Patents and Inventors' Certificates', in *Soviet Economy in the 1980s : Problems and Prospects, Part I*, Joint Economic Committee of Congress, Government Printing Office, Washington DC.

Matthews, M (1978), *Privilege in the Soviet Union*, George Allen and Unwin, London.

Meshkov, N N (1983), 'Co-operation in the Training of Students between Higher Education Institutions and Industry', *Quarterly Bulletin of the European Centre for Higher Education*, 8(4), 32–6.

Miller, J B (1984), 'The Big Nail and Other Stories: Product Quality Control in the Soviet Union', *ACES Bulletin*, 26(1), 43–57.

Miller, J H (1982), 'The Communist Party: Trends and Problems', in *Soviet Policy for the 1980s*, A Brown and M Kaser (eds), Macmillan, London.

Miller, R F (1985), 'The Role of the Communist Party in Soviet Research and Development', *Soviet Studies*, 37(1), 31–59.

Moroshima, M (1982), *Why Has Japan 'Succeeded'?* Cambridge University Press, Cambridge.

Morrison, C (1984), 'Income Distribution in East European and Western Countries', *Journal of Comparative Economics*, 8(2), 121–38.

Morton, H W (1980), 'Who Gets What, When and How? Housing in the Soviet Union', *Soviet Studies*, 32(2), 235–59.

Murrell, P (1981), 'An Evaluation of the Success of the Hungarian Economic Reform : an Analysis Using International-Trade Data', *Journal of Comparative Economics*, 5(4), 352–66.

Nove, A (1979), 'Inflation in Communist Countries', in D F Heathfield (ed.), *Perspectives on Inflation*, Longman, London.

Nove, A (1982), *The Soviet Economic System*, George Allen and Unwin, London.

Nove, A (1983), *The Economics of Feasible Socialism*, George Allen and Unwin, London.

Nove, A and Nuti, D M (1972), *Socialist Economics*, Penguin, Harmondsworth.

Ofer, G (1973), *The Service Sector in Soviet Economic Growth*, Harvard University Press, Cambridge, Massachusetts.

Ofer, G and Pickersgill, J (1980), 'Soviet Household Saving: a Cross-Section Study of Emigrant Families', *Quarterly Journal of Economics*, 95(1), 121–44.

Organisation for Economic Co-operation and Development (1985), *East-West Technology Transfer*, Paris.

Parker, J E S (1974), *The Economics of Innovation*, Longman, London.

Parrott, B (1983), *Politics and Technology in the Soviet Union*, MIT Press, Cambridge, Massachusetts.

Pick, F (1978), *Currency Yearbook, 1976–77*, Pick Publishing, New York.

Pietsch, A-J, (1986), 'Shortage of Labour and Motivation Problems of Soviet Workers', in D Lane (ed.), *Labour and Employment in the USSR*, Harvester Press, Brighton.

Popov, B A A (1985), 'The Control of the Family's Reproductive Function and its Determining Factors', *Soviet Health*, no 7, 36–39. Article translated in *Current Digest of the Soviet Press*, 37(39), 10.

Portes, R (1977), 'The Control of Inflation: Lessons from East European Experience', *Economica*, 44(174), 109–29.

Portes, R and Winter, D (1980), 'Disequilibrium Estimates for Consumption Goods in Centrally Planned Economies', *Journal of Economic Studies*, 47(1), 137–59.

Pravda (1982), Y Andropov's Address to the Plenary Session of the CPSU, translated in *Current Digest of the Soviet Press*, 34(47), 5.

Pravda (1983), 'Will the Net Output Index Ever Work?', 17 March p 2. Translation appears in *Current Digest of the Soviet Press*, 35(11), 9.

Pravda, (1986), M Gorbachev's Address to the CPSU Congress, 26 February 86', translated in *Current Digest of the Soviet Press*, 23(8), 12.

Pryor, F L (1985), *A Guidebook to the Comparative Study of Economic Systems*, Prentice-Hall, Englewood Cliffs, New Jersey.

Rosefielde, S (1983), 'Comment: Disguised Inflation in Soviet Industry', *Journal of Comparative Economics*, 7(1), 71–6.

Rumer, B (1984), 'Structural Imbalance in the Soviet Economy', *Problems of Communism*, July-August, 24–32.

Rutland, P (1984), 'The Shchekino Method and the Struggle to raise Labour Productivity in Soviet Industry', *Soviet Studies*, 36(3), 345–65.

Rutland, P (1986), 'Productivity Campaigns in the Soviet Unon', in D Lane (ed.), *Labour and Employment in the USSR*, Harvester Press, Brighton.

Schroeder, G E (1972), 'An Appraisal of Soviet Wage and Income Statistics', in V G Treml and J P Hardt (eds), *Soviet Economic Statistics*, Duke University Press, North Carolina, pp. 287–314.

Schroeder, G E (1982a), 'Soviet Economic 'Reform' Decrees: More Steps on the Treadmill', in *Soviet Economy in the 1980s: Problems and Prospects, Part I*, Joint Economic Committee of the Congress of the US, Government Printing Office, Washington DC.

Schroeder, G E (1982b), 'Managing Labour Shortages in the Soviet Union', in J Adam (ed.), *Employment Policies in the Soviet Union and Eastern Europe*, Macmillan, London.

Schroeder, G E (1982c), 'Soviet Living Standards – Performance and Prospects', in *Soviet Economy in the 1980s: Problems and Prospects, Part I*, Joint Economic Committee of the Congress of the US, Government Printing Office, Washington DC.

Schroeder, G E (1983), 'Consumption', in A Bergson, and H S Levine (eds), *The Soviet Economy: Toward the year 2000*, George Allen and Unwin, London, pp. 311–349.

Schroeder, G E and Severin, B S (1976), 'Soviet Consumption and Income Policies in Perspective', in *Soviet Economy in a New Perspective*, Joint Economic Committee, US Government Printing Office, Washington DC, pp. 620–660.

Schwartz, H (1965), *The Soviet Economy since Stalin*, Gollancz, London.

Selyunin, V (1983), 'Paradoxes of the New Index', *Current Digest of the Soviet Press*, 35(11), 10.

Siemaszko, Z A (1982), 'Control Instrumentation for Industrial Processes' in R Amann and J Cooper (eds), *Industrial Innovation in the Soviet Union*, Yale University Press, New Haven.

Spechler, M C (1983), 'Soviet Policy Towards Technological Change Since 1975', in *Soviet Economy in the 1980s: Problems and Prospects. Part I*, Joint Economic Committee of Congress of the US, Government Printing Office, Washington DC.

Stein, J B (1981), 'Soviet Energy: Current Problems and Future Options', *Energy Policy*, 9(4), 301–15.

Steiner, J (1978), 'Inflation in Soviet Industry and Machine-building and Metalworking 1960–1975', Military-Economic Analysis Center, Government Printing Office, Washington DC.

Stuart, R C (1984), 'Wheat Yields in Socialist and Capitalist Countries: a Statistical Comparison', *ACES Bulletin*, 26(1), 77–85.

Szelenyi, I (1983), *Urban Inequalities under State Socialism*, Oxford University Press, Oxford.

Tarrant, J R (1984), 'The Significance of Variability in Soviet Cereal Production', *Transactions of the Institute of British Geography*, 9(4), 387–400.

Tinbergen, J (1967), 'Some Suggestions on a Modern Theory of the Optimum Regime', in C H Feinstein (ed.), *Socialism and Economic Growth: Essays Presented to Maurice Dobb*, Cambridge University Press, Cambridge.

Treml, V (1982), *Alcohol in the USSR : a Statistical Study*, Duke University Press, Durham, North Carolina.

United Nations (1985), *Economic Survey of Europe in 1984–1985*, Economic Commission for Europe, New York.

Wagener, H-J (1982), 'The Economics of Socialism as Economics of Shortage. A Critical Review', *De Economist*, 130(4), 514–35.

Whitesell, R S (1985), 'The Influence of Central Planning on the Economic Slowdown in the Soviet Union and Eastern Europe: a Comparative Production Function Analysis', *Economica*, 52(206), 235–44.

Wiedermann, P (1984), 'Comparing the Process of Socio-Economic Development in Market and Non-Market Economies: the EEC and CMEA', *Cambridge Journal of Economics*, 8(3), 311–30.

Wilczynski, J (1973). *Profit, Risk and Incentives Under Socialist Economic Planning*, Macmillan, London.

Wilczynski, J (1982), *The Economics of Socialism*, George Allen and Unwin, London.

Wiles, P (1972), 'Soviet Unemployment on US Definitions', *Soviet Studies*, 23(4), 619–28.

Wiles, P (1982a), 'The Worsening of Soviet Economic Performance', in J Drewnowski (ed.), *Crisis in the East European Economy*, Croom Helm, London.

Wiles, P (1982b), 'Are There Any Communist Economic Cycles?' *ACES Bulletin*, 24(2), 1–19.

Wiles, P (1984), 'Wage and Income Policies', in L Schapiro and J Godson (eds), *The Soviet Worker*, Macmillan, London.

Williamson, O E (1981), 'The Modern Corporation: Origins, Evolution, Attributes', *Journal of Economic Literature*, 19(4), 1537–68.

AUTHOR INDEX

Adam J, 18
Amann R, 121, 122, 133, 135
Askansas B and Laski K, 92

Bater JH, 163
Baumol WJ and McLennan K, 146
Becker AS, 153
Bergson A, 35, 41, 42, 44, 45, 46, 47, 48, 50, 113, 120, 127, 133, 146
Berliner JS, 97, 121, 122, 124, 125, 133, 134
Binyon M, 60, 97
Birman I, 17
Bornstein M, 13, 15, 61, 108, 109
Brada JC, 70, 133
Brada JC and Jackson MR, 64
Britton CR and Gay DER, 26
Brown A *et al.*, 48, 81, 93, 120, 121, 161
Buck TW, 23, 60, 139
Bush K, 159

Campbell RW, 58, 59, 134, 135
Chapman JG, 42
Chesnais J-C, 161, 162
Cohn SH, 59, 116
Cole JP, 49, 62, 70, 72, 74
Committee of Vice-Chancellors and Principals, 5
Converse R, 91
Culbertson WP Jr and Amacher RC, 89, 90

Danilin VI *et al.*, 58
Davies RW, 100, 136
De Alessi L, 52
Desai P and Martin R, 58
Dirksen E, 88
Drewnowski J, 24
Durgin F, 92
Durgin FA Jr, 114
Dyker DA, 109, 110, 111, 116

Ellman M, 35, 43, 47, 72, 74, 100, 101, 112, 131, 172, 173

Feldbrugge FJM, 23, 43
Fisch O, 163
Freeman C, 130, 134
Friedman M, 74

Gardner R and Strauss J, 92, 94
Gidwitz B, 101
Goldman MI, 92, 116
Gorlov VN and Baburin VL, 123
Gregory PR and Stuart RC, 22, 45, 48, 49, 88, 93, 109, 169
Grossman G, 92
Gutmann PM, 44

Hall JB, 26
Hanson P, 20, 21, 59, 61, 88, 91, 101, 104, 114, 116, 133, 135
Haraszti M, 103
Harrison M, 48, 102

Havlik P, 92
Helgeson A, 97, 162
Hough JF, 97
Howard D, 88

Jackson PM, 4, 5
Jefferson M, 7, 16

Kamien MO and Schwarts NL, 130
Kapitány Z, *et al.*, 91
Kornai J, 24–32, 38–9, 47, 55–8, 63–4, 72, 82–4, 87, 92, 93, 98–100, 107–12, 127–30, 141–3, 152, 169–78
Kravis IB, 156
Kushnirsky FI, 87

Lane D, 161, 163
Leggett RE, 90
Leibenstein H, 52
Lenin VI, 7
Levine HS, 61

Macariello JA, 4
McAuley A, 40, 47
Malle S, 101, 102
Marrese M and Mitchell JC, 26
Martens JA, 125
Matthews M, 35, 44, 45
Meshkov, NN, 124
Miller JB, 23, 56
Miller JH, 45
Miller RF, 121
Moroshima M, 172
Morrison C, 40, 44, 45, 46, 48
Morton HW, 47, 87, 159
Murrell P, 70

Nove A, 8, 26, 116, 172
Nove A and Nuti DM, 36

Ofer G, 58
Ofer G and Pickersgill J, 92
Organisation for Economic Co-operation and Development (OECD), 134

Parker JES, 119
Parrott B, 120, 121
Pick F, 90
Pietsch A-J, 48, 83, 100, 161
Popov BAA, 161
Portes R, 81, 86, 93
Portes R and Winter D, 92
Pravda, 21, 115, 123
Pryor FL, 37, 41, 58, 78, 112, 117, 146, 157, 161, 168

Rosefielde S, 90
Rumer B, 72
Rutland P, 102, 103

Schroeder GE, 20, 21, 50, 101, 149, 153, 157
Schroeder GE and Severin BS, 93
Schwartz H, 1
Selyunin V, 20
Siemaszko ZA, 129
Spechler MC, 122
Stein JB, 18, 126
Steiner J, 90
Stuart RC, 75
Szelenyi I, 47

Tarrant JR, 75, 76
Tinbergen J, 5, 171
Treml V, 43

United Nations, 159

Wagener H-J, 26
Whitesell RS, 139, 146
Wiedermann P, 151
Wilczynski J, 18, 172
Wiles P, 24, 95, 96, 100, 143, 149
Williamson OE, 3, 5

SUBJECT INDEX

agriculture, 34, 49, 71–7, 131;
  see also farms
associations, 9, 13, 23, 122

balances,
  material, 12, 13, 17;
  labour, 96
birth-rates, 161
black markets, 22, 60, 84, 89–90, 175
bonus schemes, 18–22, 122, 125, 129
budgets, 4, 15, 16, 17;
  zero-base, 4, 16;
  hard, *see* constraints;
  soft, *see* constraints
buyers' markets, *see* pressure economy

collective farm market (CFM), 88;
  see also farms, collective
Communist Party of the Soviet Union (CPSU), 10, 44, 97, 98, 121, 124, 126, 127, 129, 133
constraints, vii;
  administrative, 24–26;
  budget, 25–9;
  hard, 6, 25–7, 38, 56, 169–79;
  soft, 10, 20, 24–6, 28–9, 38, 55, 57, 83, 108, 127, 134, 169–79
counter-planning, 21

decentralisation, 2, 15, 18–23

economic reform, 18–23, 84, 122–4, 174, 179
extensive growth, 30, 31, 115, 133, 139–50

farms,
  collective, 11, 34, 35, 49, 71, 88;
  state, 11, 34, 71
foreign trade, 61–71, 131–2
From the Achieved Level (FTAL), *see* planning

gross output, 16, 18–21, 24, 28, 55, 56, 57, 83, 98, 108, 111, 127, 142
growth accounting, 132–3, 138–40

hard budgets, *see* constraints
hidden inflation, 86, 87–91, 93, 94, 152
hierarchies, 3, 5, 7, 8, 24, 29, 55, 56
horizontal links, 2, 22, 23, 124
housing, 35, 43, 47, 87, 158, 159

income distribution, 30–50;
  and women, 48, 49;
  and peasants, 49
incrementalism, 4, 5, 16
information, *see* planning and information
intensive growth, 30, 31, 122, 129, 133, 139–50

labour,
balances, *see* balances;
mobility of, 11, 39, 43, 95–7;
over-employment of, 98;
policies, 102–4;
productivity, 59, 101;
turnover, 100
Lenin, 1, 2, 7, 36

markets, 2, 5, 6, 7, 14, 16
Marx, viii, 1, 27, 36, 106, 107, 109, 153, 171
M-form (multidivisional form), 5, 23, 55
mortality rates, 161, 162

Net Material Product (NMP), 79, 139, 143, 146, 149, 152, 155
nomenklatura, 10, 97
NOT movement, *see* work study

Party, *see* Communist Party of the Soviet Union
perquisities, 34, 35, 39–44, 47, 57, 98
planning, central, 3–23;
From the Achieved Level (FTAL), 16, 17, 19, 21;
information and, 14–23;
taut, 17, 18

pressure economy, 25, 38, 84, 129
prices, Soviet, 14, 15, 19, 46, 57, 59, 91, 105, 140
private incomes, 34, 35, 39–45, 57
profits, 6, 19, 20, 111, 141
purchasing-power priorities (PPP's), 157

'ratchet' effect, 19, 84
reforms *see* economic reform
regional variations, 162–6
repressed inflation, 86, 91–3

sellers' markets, *see* suction economy
shortage economy, *see* suction economy
soft budgets, *see* constraints
Stalin, 1, 2, 28, 29, 36, 40, 76, 77, 96, 100, 109, 114, 128, 175
suction economy, 25, 29, 56, 82–4, 97–100, 127

taut plans, *see* planning

valve-judgements, viii, 33, 41, 104
vertical links, 3

women, *see* income distribution
work study, (NOT movement), 55,103